MONEY AND POWER
IN EUROPE

SUNY series in Global Politics
James N. Rosenau, Editor

MONEY AND POWER
IN EUROPE

THE POLITICAL ECONOMY
OF
EUROPEAN
MONETARY COOPERATION

MATTHIAS KAELBERER

STATE UNIVERSITY OF NEW YORK PRESS

332.494
K11m

Published by
State University of New York Press, Albany

© 2001 State University of New York

Printed in the United States of America

For information, address State University of New York Press,
90 State Street, Suite 700, Albany, NY 12207

Production by Diane Ganeles
Marketing by Anne M. Valentine

Library of Congress Cataloging-in-Publication Data

Kaelberer, Matthias, 1959–
      Money and power in Europe : the political economy of European
monetary cooperation
      / Matthias Kaelberer.
            p.   cm. — (SUNY series in global politics)
      Includes bibliographical references and index.
      ISBN 0-7914-4995-5 (alk. paper) — ISBN 0-7914-4996-3 (pbk. :
alk. paper)
      1. Monetary policy—European Union countries. 2. Money—
European Union countries. 3. European Monetary System
(Organization). 4. European Union countries—Economic policy.
I. Title. II. Series.

HG925.K34 2001
332.4'94—dc21

                                                            00-061924

10 9 8 7 6 5 4 3 2 1

To Michelle

Contents

Tables

Acknowledgments

I am grateful to many individuals and organizations for their assistance in writing this book. I would like to thank Joanne Gowa for her encouragement and guidance. Without her ability to be both critical and supportive at the same time, I would not have thought as thoroughly about the arguments I make in this book. Robert Gilpin suggested the topic, and his teaching and his own work stimulated my interests in international political economy. Peter Kenen saved me from many mistakes in dealing with the economic background for this book. His own work in this area often served as the starting and focal point for my investigations. I am grateful to Kathleen McNamara not only for the detailed readings of drafts, but also for inspiring my thinking through her own work on this topic.

Over the years, various aspects of this book were presented in the form of papers at conferences of the American Political Science Association, the International Studies Association, the European Community Studies Association, and others. I would like to thank the various panel and audience members for their comments, but in particular those on whom I could rely for stimulating discussions of European monetary cooperation during those conferences and other occasions: David Andrews, William Bernard, Dorothee Heisenberg, C. Randall Henning, Karl Kaltenthaler, Peter Loedel, and Jim Walsh. We often disagreed over methods, arguments, and conclusions, but their thinking on the same issues consistently forced me to specify and refine my own views. This book has benefitted from their comments and my reading of their own work much more than I can possibly express in footnotes. In addition, I am very grateful to Tom Banchoff, David Cameron, Walter Carlsnaes, Peter Dombrowski, Patrick James, Arie Kacowicz, Steven Lobell, Richard Mansbach, Andrei Markovits, Jim McCormick, Wayne Sandholtz, Todd Sandler, Dietlind Stolle, Horst Ungerer, and John Woolley for all their comments and help in carrying out this project.

The support of various institutions has also been important in writing this book. I am indebted to the John D. and Catherine T. MacArthur Foundation, the Andrew W. Mellon Foundation, Princeton University's Center for International Studies, the Council on Regional Studies at Princeton, the American Political Science Association's Small Research Grant Fund, and the University of Northern Iowa for research funding. I would also like to thank the various individuals associated with the European Union, the German Bundesbank, and other institutions for answering questions and for providing material. I am grateful to Sage Publications for granting permission to reuse some material from my article "Hegemony, Dominance, or Leadership? Exploring Germany's Role in European Monetary Cooperation," published in the *European Journal of International Relations* 3(1), 1997: 35–60, in chapters 2 and 3 of this book. Michael Rinella, Allison Lee, Diane Ganeles, and Anne Valentine of State University of New York Press diligently guided the manuscript through the process. I would like to thank Jim Rosenau for his interest in having the book published in the Global Politics series and the numerous reviewers of SUNY Press for their very helpful comments.

Above all, however, I am deeply indebted to my family. Rachel and Samuel were very patient when Dad needed time to work on this project or when conversations with friends deteriorated into ramblings about some arcane monetary issues. Michelle has been untiring in reading one draft after the other of this project. It has repeatedly amazed me how she could possibly keep her composure in explaining to me that one cannot use the phrase *balance-of-payments adjustment mechanisms* more than once in a sentence. I do not know whether I would have ever finished this book without her help, encouragement, and support.

1

Introduction

How do states reach agreement on a specific issue? Why do they select certain rules and ignore or dismiss other potential rules? In a universe of infinite possibilities, governments theoretically have endless choices. This book seeks to explain the formation of rules for monetary cooperation in the European Union (EU). In doing so, it starts from a seemingly simple insight: States use power to shape the outcomes of international bargaining. Those governments with stronger leverage over the items on the agenda are more successful in getting what they want than those in a weaker bargaining position. The core thesis of this book is that the *relative bargaining power of both weak and strong currency countries has shaped an enduring pattern of negotiations* over the rules of exchange rate cooperation in Europe. Strong currency countries exercise structural power in international monetary relations.

This is by no means a trivial argument. Rather, there is an urgent conceptual need to revisit the question of bargaining power. For one thing, the prevailing literature on European monetary cooperation has pushed the issue of bargaining power aside. It has highlighted such aspects as sectoral and partisan interests, policy ideas, domestic and international institutional structures, and spill-over and regime dynamics. While attention to these issues yields valuable insights, an emphasis on bargaining power provides conceptual order among disparate observations that other approaches cannot synthesize successfully. The politics of European monetary cooperation has followed a remarkably *constant pattern of bargaining*. We can identify *regularities* in the negotiations among EU member states over the rules of monetary cooperation. Indeed, there exists a significant degree of continuity in the bargaining interaction between EU member states in this area since the early 1960s.

The other reason that makes it necessary to address bargaining power is the elusiveness of the concept itself. What do we actually mean when we say that states bring leverage to the bargaining table? This book argues that two closely related factors explain the pattern of monetary bargaining in Europe, namely, the *relative balance-of-payments* position of the EU member states and the role of *leadership* in the context of monetary bargaining.

Differential balance-of-payments positions are the primary indicator for the distribution of monetary power because they distribute bargaining leverage unevenly between weak and strong currency countries. Strong currency countries tend to have lower inflation, are predisposed to experience upward pressure on their currency and are likely to accumulate balance-of-payments surpluses. The most important advantage for *strong* currency countries is the *absence of a reserve constraint*. This situation gives strong currency countries greater freedom of choice among their macroeconomic adjustment options. The costs of their unilateral options tend to be lower than those of weak currency countries. As a result, they have consistently been able to shape the rules of exchange rate cooperation in their favor. Thus, the focus on balance-of-payments positions allows us to draw attention to the pattern of distributional conflict between strong and weak currency countries. Differences in balance-of-payments positions impose powerful constraints on the bargaining process, and they limit the realm of possible bargaining solutions.

The second major explanatory aspect is the role of *leadership* played by Germany, the principal strong currency country in the EU. Although the literature on European monetary cooperation generally acknowledges the central role of Germany, the issue has so far been treated merely casually as "a matter of fact" and not as an analytical issue itself worthy of systematic inquiry. Leadership is a necessary component for the successful negotiation and implementation of rules for monetary cooperation. However, German leadership has not followed the conventional assumptions of hegemonic stability theory. Instead, I describe Germany's position in European monetary politics as *policy based* rather than resource based. The analysis emphasizes Germany's role as the *standard setter* for monetary cooperation in Europe. Rules for macroeconomic standard setting have come on German terms—or else they had no chance for implementation. Nevertheless, German policymakers have made a number of compromises at critical junctures in the bargaining process. While these were concessions at the periphery of the agreement and not in its substantive core, they were nevertheless important for resolving bargaining impasses.

Overall, these two theoretical claims offer a comprehensive interpretation of the patterns in European monetary politics. In addition to its analytical perspective, this book also fills a significant substantive gap in the literature by tracing the long-run pattern of European monetary politics. It is the first book to analyze the history of European monetary cooperation in its entirety from the early 1960s to the implementation of the Maastricht Treaty in the 1990s. The prevailing literature concentrates mostly on the European Monetary System (EMS)—in operation since 1979—and the 1991 Maastricht Treaty, paying only limited attention to prior attempts at monetary cooperation. This investigation, however, analyzes all the major attempts at closer exchange rate cooperation within the EU from the early 1960s to the 1990s: the Action Programme of 1962, the Werner Report of 1970/71, the Snake between 1971 and 1979, the European Monetary System and the attempt to form a monetary union (EMU) associated with the Maastricht Treaty. This long-term perspective uncovers the persistent patterns of European exchange rate cooperation.

Before addressing these constitutive elements in the remainder of this introduction, we must first elaborate the larger question at hand.

The Puzzle of European Monetary Cooperation

On 24 October 1962 the Commission of the European Communities issued its *Action Programme for the Second Stage,* which proposed stabilizing exchange rates within the Community and fixing them permanently in a monetary union. At the time, the Commission hoped to realize a monetary union no later than 1970. Since then, there have been a number of similar attempts in the history of the European Union.[1] The Werner Report of 1970/71 and the Maastricht Treaty of 1991 both anticipated a full monetary union among the EU member states. The Snake, which operated between 1972 and 1979, and the EMS between 1979 and 1999, aspired to stabilize exchange rates among the members of the EU.

The degree of success in achieving these goals has varied substantially. Neither the Action Programme nor the Werner Report established a currency union. The Snake survived merely as a limited "deutsche mark zone" for Germany and its small neighbors. Only the EMS achieved a significant degree of success for a longer period of time—and for many observers it even exceeded the early expectations. In 1992/93, however, the once flourishing EMS hit an unprecedented crisis, from which it never fully recovered. Speculative attacks against EMS currencies in financial markets, the withdrawal of Great Britain and Italy from the EMS in September 1992, and the decision to suspend narrow bands for exchange rates in August 1993 constituted the most visible signs of turmoil in the EMS. The road toward monetary union along the design of the Maastricht Treaty was also torturous, and its outcome remained doubtful for a long time. On 1 January 1999, however, eleven EU member states finally launched the common currency "Euro."

This brief description of various attempts at monetary cooperation indicates a significant fluctuation in outcomes of European monetary cooperation. Indeed, these visible ups and downs have been the starting point for much of previous scholarly work in this area. The prevailing literature tends to ask questions such as: Why did the EU member states create the Snake, the EMS or EMU? Why was the EMS more successful than the Snake? Have interests in monetary cooperation changed over time, and what explains these changes? What explains the move toward the goal of monetary union in the Maastricht Treaty?

Scholars have devoted attention to the role of domestic factors in the process of preference formation to answer these types of questions. Aspects emphasized within this literature are economic sectors (Frieden 1991), partisan orientation (Oatley 1997), the role of interest groups (Hefeker 1996), policy ideas (McNamara 1998) and the interactions of domestic institutional and societal structure, in particular the issue of central bank independence (Goodman 1992; Heisenberg 1999; Henning 1994; Kaltenthaler 1997, 1998; Kennedy 1991; Loedel 1999; Oatley 1997). Another important strand of the literature stresses the interconnection of international institutions and state interests and such processes as issue linkage, spill-over and regime dynamics in the process of interest articulation and policy formation (Cameron 1993; Dyson 1994; Sandholtz 1993a; Woolley 1992). In addition, attention has been paid to the influence of a changing international environment, in particular increasing capital mobility, on state interests and policies (Andrews 1994; McNamara 1998).

All of these studies point to important aspects of European monetary politics. Most significantly, they address issues of preference formation and policy implementation. However, this focus tends to neglect another very important characteristic of this policy area, namely, the role of bargaining power as a central explanatory variable for European monetary relations. This argument does not deny that interests and policies are a relevant part of this story. For example, it is important to understand why EU member states were suddenly more interested in establishing a regime for exchange rate stability in the *late* 1970s, than they were in the *early* 1970s. Similarly, the emergence of EMU on the European agenda in the late 1980s and early 1990s also reflects changing interests. However, these interests are not the systematic and analytical focal point of my investigation. Rather, I seek to understand another aspect of these episodes. This book directs attention to a common background feature of all episodes of monetary cooperation, namely, the consistency with which strong and weak currency countries engage in certain types of bargaining exchanges. In this sense, the analysis presented in this book complements rather than substitutes for other explanations of European monetary cooperation.

For example, with respect to the EMS, some of the crucial questions this book raises are the following: Why did EMS rules in real substantive terms look very similar to the rules that guided the Snake previously? Why did EU member states squabble over almost identical items as they did during the Snake negotiations? Or with respect to the EMU project: Why do most of the substantive rules for EMU reflect German preferences, even if EMU was largely driven by French demands for a more symmetrical monetary arrangement in Europe? These questions point to a much more deeply ingrained pattern of bargaining in European monetary affairs than is visible in the contemporary literature on this subject. The ultimate purpose of this book is to reveal the long-running logic in European monetary politics.

Domestic politics models have significant problems explaining this pattern and continuity. An emphasis on partisan politics, for example, identifies the monetary interests of policymakers on the basis of party-constituency relations (Oatley 1997). However, such a model cannot explain the continuity of European monetary politics. The partisan makeup of governments in Europe has changed over time; the pattern of rule making, however, has been consistent.[2] Similarly, the ideas that provide conceptual guidance to the macroeconomic policies implemented by European decision makers may have changed over time (McNamara 1998), but they do not help us shed light on the continuity of the rule-making process in the EU. Weak currency countries continued to bargain for similar goals even after changes in their macroeconomic thinking, and the outcomes of negotiations reflected similar bargaining exchanges.

Models of domestic institutional structures have similar problems. Certainly, an emphasis on the independence of Germany's central bank, the Bundesbank, is vital for the explanation of interest articulation in Germany (Heisenberg 1999) as is the interaction between the politically independent Bundesbank with other societal and political players (Kaltenthaler 1998). Moreover, the observer of the domestic political level may even reach the conclusion that German policymaking with regard to international monetary cooperation is characterized by inconsistency and discontinuity because power can shift among various domestic players or because they exercise influence during different stages of the policymaking process (Kaltenthaler 1998). On this level of analysis, squabbles between central bankers and government officials, for example, may indeed be important.

However, if viewed from a systemic level, Germany's bargaining position has been quite consistent. It has continually acted as the strong currency country and forced others to make the crucial bargaining concessions. From this vantage point, it is the *stability* of the rule-making process, rather than instability and change, that stands out as the most remarkable feature of monetary cooperation. There is something beyond domestic political changes that gives consistency to European monetary politics. On this level of analysis, the structural conflict between strong and weak currency countries overshadows any domestic disagreements. Ultimately, states' relative balance-of-payments positions shape the patterns of international negotiations and set the range of choices for participants in negotiations.

Instead of the conventional focus on interests or policies, bargaining over the *rules for exchange rate stabiliza-*

tion among the members of the EU is the center of attention for the present investigation.[3] This definition includes *systems of pegged but adjustable* exchange rates—as in the Snake and EMS—or systems of *permanently fixed* exchange rates—as envisioned in the EMU projects of the Action Programme, the Werner Report, and the Maastricht Treaty. Both arrangements are examples of cooperation to stabilize exchange rates. In a monetary union, exchange rates are stable as long as the union exists; within a pegged exchange rate regime, they are stable within specified fluctuation bands and between realignments.

The emphasis on rules has a number of analytical advantages. Rules establish explicit rights and obligations for the participants. They are usually subject to clearly observable bargaining and are often specified in written documents. In the case of monetary cooperation, rules define the procedures for exchange rate changes, access to financial support, or specific regulations for the pursuit of domestic economic policies. As I will demonstrate in subsequent chapters, policymakers had multiple options available to design rules for these issues at various stages of European monetary negotiations. Thus, the task here is to trace the negotiations of the EU member states over the rules of exchange rate cooperation and to explain *why they chose the rules they did and why they dismissed others.*

The attention given to rules in this investigation is an important qualification because one can, of course, achieve exchange rate stability simply based on policy decisions without rule-based cooperation. The exchange rate between Austria and Germany, for example, had been stable for many years prior to Austria's entrance into the EMS in 1995. This pre-EMS exchange rate stability, however, resulted from the unilateral pegging of the schilling to the deutsche mark. Unilateral policy options do not require mutually agreed upon rules between the partners. In other words, pre-1995 Austrian-German monetary relations— notwithstanding their harmonious nature—do not satisfy the definitional criteria used here. They miss the crucial component of rules—a situation that obviously changed once Austria became a member of the EMS.

The example of Austria illustrates once more the emphasis on explaining the nature of monetary *rules* in Europe, rather than monetary *policies* or *interests*. As a matter of monetary *policy*, the Austrian government's decision to peg the schilling to the deutsche mark may be as significant as the attempts of EMS member states to keep their currencies pegged to the deutsche mark. For reasons I will not investigate further, the EU member states have consistently preferred a rule-based system over other methods of exchange rate stabilization. Thus, the emphasis on rules is a useful operationalization for this study.

Argument and Analysis

The starting point for this book is the claim that the conflict between strong and weak currency countries shapes the pattern of European monetary cooperation. Chapter 2 defines the terms *weak* and *strong currency countries* and describes the differences in the adjustment logic between the two types of currency countries. The main criteria for distinguishing between strong and weak currency countries are the level of inflation, the external strength of a national currency, and the existence of actual current account surpluses or deficits. On the basis of these criteria, Germany emerges as the strong currency leader in Europe over the past few decades. Although others—notably France—have caught up with Germany on many indicators in recent years, none of them matches Germany's long-run historical record. Not surprisingly, the relative balance-of-payments position of countries also provides an accurate explanation for the coalition patterns in European monetary politics. Despite the growing number of countries in the hard core of European monetary relations, from a long-run perspective, the fairly tight and enduring alliance of the stronger currency countries

(Germany, the Netherlands, Denmark, and Belgium) appears to be a straightforward consequence of their relative balance-of-payments position.

A country's status as a *strong* or *weak* currency country has significant implications for its bargaining position within European monetary negotiations. Balance-of-payments positions indicate power relationships in the sense that they distribute asymmetrical burdens of adjustment and bargaining leverage. Most important, a weak currency country's leverage in negotiations is limited by its reserve constraint. As chapter 2 will explain, weak currency countries are able to finance their balance-of-payments deficits only as long as they have access to strong currency reserves—either their own central bank's reserves or those provided by bilateral or multilateral international agreements. Strong currency countries by contrast can choose more freely among their options of internal adjustment, external adjustment, and financing. This greater latitude of choice for strong currency countries translates into a significant bargaining advantage, since their unilateral options are often less costly than those of weak currency countries. In other words, strong currency countries have a credible "exit threat." Moreover, weak currency countries have no corresponding "threat of exclusion," since the participation of strong currency countries is necessary to give credibility to the newly formed regime. These conditions provide strong currency countries with bargaining power, which has allowed them to determine the "bottom line" of the negotiation outcome.

The primary result of this asymmetry in bargaining leverage within European monetary politics has been that Germany and its allies have been able to protect their domestic policy preferences. In terms of the concrete rules for exchange rate cooperation, this has consistently meant that strong currency countries rejected compromise on issues of domestic adjustment. By contrast, rules for external adjustment and financing have been negotiable in European monetary cooperation as long as they did not conflict with Germany's domestic interests. Indeed, in the two cases of pegged exchange rate systems under investigation here—the Snake and the EMS—the EU member states concentrated bargaining on these types of issues and left internal adjustment unregulated. In negotiations over a full-fledged monetary union, however, bargaining emphasis shifts toward domestic adjustment, since participants renounce the use of exchange rate changes, and the common currency makes the financing of disequilibria automatic. Thus, the realm for bargaining compromises on rules for monetary unification narrows severely. During the Maastricht negotiations, Germany refused to compromise its vision for domestic macroeconomic priorities. The only compromises Germany would make in the context of the EMU negotiations were limited to side payments.

These considerations are also the base for my second major analytical claim. Chapter 3 analyzes the role of *leadership* in the process of monetary rule-making. I argue that Germany has assumed a leadership role in the European monetary bargaining process over the past forty years. Most important, Germany has served as the *standard setter* for monetary cooperation. It has used its position as a strong currency country to exercise structural power in the bargaining process. However, in contrast to the assumptions of traditional hegemonic stability theories, Germany's leadership role is not so much resource based as *policy based.* Its particular role rests much more on its long-running low inflation credibility than on tangible resources. In exchange for playing the role of a standard setter, German policy makers occasionally have been willing to make bargaining concessions on other issues in the negotiations that did not directly affect core standard-setting questions. These compromises were sometimes crucial in avoiding bargaining deadlock and in allowing for the successful conclusion of monetary negotiations. During the EMS negotiations, German policymakers gave in on questions of external adjustment and financing and the Maastricht process saw a number of German side payments.

This conceptualization of bargaining exchanges in European monetary negotiations solves a pervasive ambiguity that has characterized the literature on European monetary cooperation. Some observers point to the over-whelming and almost dictatorial influence of Germany on the rules of monetary cooperation (e.g., Marsh 1992), whereas others have been surprised by the tendency of the German government to make important bargaining conces-sions at crucial junctures during monetary negotiations (e.g., Bini-Smaghi, Padoa-Schioppa, and Papadia 1994; Gros and Thygesen 1992; Italianer 1993; Ludlow 1982; Sandholtz 1993b). There is a systematic answer to this puz-zling contrast: German policymakers are tenacious on domestic macroeconomic objectives but more flexible on external adjustment, financing, and side payments since compromises on these issues often do not impinge on domestic economic priorities. Indeed, the analytical sepa-ration between these issues makes it possible to present a more comprehensive account of the monetary bargaining interaction in Europe.

The case studies in the later part of this book pick up these analytical elements of balance-of-payments position and German standard setting and investigate how they have shaped the bargaining over monetary rules in each of these episodes. This long-term historical and comparative analysis also opens the perspective toward an alternative conceptualization of European monetary cooperation. By addressing the often neglected earlier attempts at mone-tary cooperation and integration, this book focuses on the historical trajectory of European monetary cooperation and uncovers the deeply ingrained pattern that has character-ized bargaining over the rules of European exchange rate cooperation.

The case studies reveal a remarkable degree of conti-nuity in European monetary bargaining over the past three decades. Many of the themes that characterized the early attempts at exchange rate cooperation repeatedly recurred in later episodes. For example, chapter 4 demonstrates that the substance at stake in the conflict between the so-called "economists" and "monetarists"—conventionally associated with the debate over the Werner Report and Snake—emerged in the deliberations over the Action Programme during the early 1960s and has since marked every major attempt at monetary integration. While the "economists" insisted on the convergence of economic conditions prior to monetary unification, "monetarists" proposed early monetary union as a means to forge convergence through permanently fixed exchange rates. The causes for the continuous reappearance of this conflict were not philosophical differences among the EU governments over the means of establishing a monetary union, but rather manifest distributional concerns. The case studies illustrate that the debate between "monetarists" and "economists" reflects an intrinsic conflict between strong and weak currency countries over who should have to bear the costs of exchange rate cooperation.

The other major focus of the comparative case studies concerns the central role of Germany in European monetary cooperation. From the early 1960s on, Germany has consistently rejected compromising its own domestic economic priorities—in particular low inflation. Instead, German decision makers have insisted that agreement over the rules of domestic macroeconomic adjustment can only come on German terms. No other European player has at any point during these decades commanded enough leverage to force Germany to compromise its standard.

The case study chapters follow a chronological order. Chapter 4 analyzes monetary politics within the EU during the 1960s. It explains the bargaining interaction during the earliest attempt at monetary cooperation in the EU: the Commission's *Action Programme for the Second Stage* of 1962. Overall, this is certainly the weakest case of the five analyzed in this book. While the chapter explains that the Western Europeans had incentives to pursue closer exchange rate cooperation, the functioning Bretton Woods System took away some of the urgency that accompanied later attempts at exchange rate cooperation. Thus, the interest of the member states in pursuing exchange rate cooperation was much lower than in the 1970s and 80s. Nevertheless, the case of the Action Programme already contains some of the elements that became characteristic of European monetary politics during later decades. Most important, the chapter reveals the formation of the "economist" position on European monetary integration in the domestic German discussion of the Action Programme. Germany's policymakers were unwilling to sacrifice their domestic economic priorities. This meant that monetary integration could not happen without the prior convergence of other EU members to the German standard.

Chapter 5 explains EU bargaining over the 1970/71 *Werner Report* and the *Snake* between 1971 and 1979. The success of these attempts at monetary cooperation was minimal. The Werner Report did not lead to the establishment of the proposed economic and monetary union, and the Snake functioned for the most part merely as a limited deutsche mark zone for Germany and its smaller neighbors (also often termed the "mini-Snake"). Nevertheless, an analysis of these episodes reveals important insights. Bargaining over rules of monetary cooperation followed a clear alignment of weak against strong currency countries. And within the mini-Snake, Germany emerged as standard setter, anticipating a feature that ultimately also characterized the much larger and more successful EMS a decade later. Nevertheless, the breakdown of the Bretton Woods system produced circumstances in which Germany could not gain sufficient legitimacy for its position in the Snake. Moreover, German incentives to make concessions on external adjustment and financing were relatively low.

Chapter 6 explains bargaining over the rules governing the *European Monetary System* (EMS). While the most obvious feature of the EMS compared to the Snake may be the contrast between the relative success of monetary cooperation in the 1980s to the relative failure of the Snake during the 1970s, the analysis of this chapter actually emphasizes the pervasive pattern of continuity in bargaining interaction between the two periods.[4] Again, balance-of-payments considerations informed the bargaining position of the various EU member states. Ultimately, very little had changed between the visions of weak and strong currency countries for the rules of European monetary cooperation between the Snake and EMS negotiations. While strong and weak currency countries clashed over the distribution of economic adjustment costs, Germany successfully resisted efforts to restrict its own domestic macroeconomic preferences. As a result, Germany served as the standard setter for the EMS. In exchange, German policymakers were willing to make various concessions on external adjustments and financing mechanisms and to extend side payments if these were necessary to avoid deadlock. These assumptions also allow for a unique explanation of the difficulties engulfing the EMS in the early 1990s. According to the perspective developed here, the EMS crisis resulted from a relative loss in the legitimacy of Germany's position. The costs of reunification meant that Germany started to export greater externalities than its major partners in the EMS in the form of high inflation and high interest rates.

The EU's most recent attempt to create a full economic and monetary union (EMU) in the *Maastricht Treaty* is the focus of chapter 7. It traces the origins of this attempt to the rising difficulties of maintaining an asymmetric monetary system such as the EMS under the conditions of increasing policy convergence—an issue that in itself points to the shaping force of balance-of-payments considerations. Despite the attempt to create a more symmetrical system, the chapter points out that the EMU process still followed the same pattern as earlier attempts at monetary cooperation. Germany still insisted on its role as the standard setter for the rules of monetary union. It served as the principal architect for the common monetary institutions and pushed through the adoption of convergence criteria in the Maastricht Treaty. Its room for concessions was limited to side payments—most important, the acceptance of a definitive timetable for moving toward the common currency (the "automaticity clause").

Conclusion

This book argues that the monetary power of strong and weak currency countries has shaped a distinct pattern of bargaining among the members of the European Union over the rules of monetary cooperation. Relative balance-of-payments positions affect the opportunities and constraints states experience in constructing rules for exchange rate cooperation. Given their greater flexibility in adjustment options, strong currency countries have pushed through their visions for rules of internal macroeconomic adjustment and have been willing to compromise only on external adjustment, financing, or side payments. As the principal strong currency country, Germany has played a leadership role in this process, primarily by setting the macroeconomic standard, and secondarily by overcoming bargaining impasses through various concessions.

The analysis in this book directs attention to the broader picture of European monetary cooperation. The goal is to understand the long-running *pattern* of monetary bargaining in Europe. The argument developed here allows the investigation to detect *regularities*. As such, the book provides an *interpretative framework,* and its main purpose is to create conceptual clarity among otherwise disparate observations. It achieves this by depicting a logic of monetary bargaining in Europe that has proven fairly enduring over time.

2

The Structural Logic of European Exchange Rate Cooperation

The conflict between strong and weak currency countries represents the major shaping force of European monetary bargaining. This is due to the fact that monetary cooperation involves a straightforward distributional question: Who should bear the burden of macroeconomic adjustment to establish exchange rate stability? Most important, how do member countries determine the systemwide inflation level of the monetary regime? This book's claim is that governments use their structural power to answer these questions. The first section of this chapter defines the terms *weak* and *strong currency countries* and analyzes the balance-of-payments positions of the EU member countries. It emphasizes Germany's role as the primary strong currency country in the EU and explains the broad coalitional patterns that evolved over time among strong and weak currency countries in European monetary politics. The second section explains the logic of macroeconomic adjustment for weak and strong currency countries. Because they do not face a reserve constraint, strong currency countries have much greater freedom to choose their preferred adjustment option than weak currency countries.

The third section explains how this asymmetry in adjustment options shapes the logic of bargaining over the rules of monetary cooperation. Strong currency countries are often in a superior bargaining position and, therefore, tend to yield stronger leverage over bargaining outcomes.

The bargaining strength of strong currency countries rests on two basic conditions. First of all, strong currency countries have a credible *exit threat* since their unilateral policy options are less costly than those of weak currency countries. Thus, they have a lower incentive to achieve cooperation through their own concessions. Second, weak currency countries lack a *threat of exclusion* against strong currency countries, since successful monetary cooperation is virtually inconceivable without the participation of strong currency countries. These two conditions imbue strong currency countries with powerful leverage: rules for monetary cooperation would either come largely on their terms, or they would not come at all.

The last section explains how this bargaining asymmetry has driven the choice of adjustment rules in European monetary cooperation. Being in a position to choose adjustment options under much fewer constraints, strong currency countries in the EU have consistently rejected monetary rules that would restrict their domestic macroeconomic adjustment options. Given this obstinacy of strong currency countries, questions of external adjustment, financing, and side payments had to become the only feasible area for bargaining compromises between weak and strong currency countries.

Definition and Significance of a Country's Balance of Payments Position

What features characterize a country's balance-of-payments position? This book defines a country's balance-of-payments position as consisting of three interrelated elements: *level of inflation, strength of a currency's exchange rate, and actual payments balance. Low inflation* serves as the most prominent—and for the case of European monetary cooperation, most consequential—definitional characteristic of a *strong* currency country. Low inflation is also correlated to the relative strength of a currency in financial markets and payments surpluses. Con-

Table 2.1
Strong and Weak Currency Countries in the EU

	Depreciation against DM, 1972–1992	Accumulated inflation differential against DM, 1972–1992 (CPI)	Accumulated current account balances, 1972–1992 (in billion U.S.$)
Germany	0	0	248.3
Netherlands	11.5	18.9	83.5
Belgium*	47.6	42.0	21.6
Denmark	78.4	77.4	−24.1
France	114.6	80.8	−41.9
Ireland	186.8	133.9	−12.9
United Kingdom	209.7	124.9	−106.7
Spain	254.5	169.0	−88.9
Italy	406.3	167.2	−103.5
Portugal	965.4	289.9	−14.5
Greece	1,329.2	288.3	−34.4

Calculated on the basis of data in Deutsche Bundesbank, "Entwicklung des Außenwertes der D-Mark: Pressenotiz der Deutschen Bundesbank." Frankfurt am Main. Dezember 30, 1992. In *BAP* 1, January 4, 1993: 18; International Monetary Fund, *International Financial Statistics*, various years; and International Monetary Fund, *International Financial Statistics Yearbook*, 1993.

*Depreciation value is for the Belgian-Luxembourg franc; inflation and current account data are for Belgium only.

versely, *higher* inflation represents the main attribute of *weak* currency countries. Relatively higher inflation also puts downward pressure on the value of the currency and helps to create balance-of-payments deficits.

Gathering data for the three definitional characteristics mentioned above, table 2.1 depicts the balance-of-payments positions of the EU member states. It summarizes the links among currency depreciation, inflation differentials, and current account balances for EU member states from 1972 to 1992.[1] Clearly, the EU member states exhibited sharp differences in their respective balance-of-payments positions. Presenting accumulated data from two decades, the table is merely a static summary. It cannot illustrate the changes that have occurred in this period. Some of these changes will be addressed shortly. Nevertheless, since this book emphasizes long-run patterns of

European exchange rate cooperation, the data collected in table 2.1 provide a useful first cut for analyzing the balance-of-payments position of the EU member states that existed prior to the adoption of the euro in 1999.

From table 2.1 Germany clearly emerges as the principal strong currency country in the EU for the period under investigation here. It was the low inflation leader within the EU, the deutsche mark was the EU's strongest currency, and the German economy produced the largest current account surpluses. The Netherlands enjoyed virtually the same balance-of-payments position as Germany. Thus, it comes as no surprise that the Dutch were consistently Germany's closest ally on all issues of European monetary cooperation. Like the Germans, the Dutch have rejected the efforts of weak currency countries to compromise on the macroeconomic standard that the strong currency countries have set in European monetary politics. Belgium and Denmark were in a slightly weaker position than the Netherlands. However, after their disinflationary successes during the 1970s and early 1980s, both countries shared monetary conditions very similar to those of the Germans and the Dutch.[2] In general, they supported German positions on questions of European monetary cooperation, but their support was less firm and less enthusiastic than the Dutch.

These four countries formed the hard core of European monetary cooperation at least into the second half of the 1980s. During the later part of the 1980s, however, it became increasingly obvious that other EU member states were starting to catch up with this hard core. Inflation rates and ultimately interest rates converged toward German levels. Moreover, German unification resulted in higher inflation, higher budget deficits, and current account deficits, which in the medium term also meant a relative weakening of Germany's position. Not only did convergence erode some of the initial differences in countries' balance-of-payments positions, it was also the major precondition for the move toward monetary union in the 1990s. Without the improvement in particular of the

French balance-of-payments position, German policymakers would have never taken the push for EMU seriously.

Nevertheless, the long-term differences in balance-of-payments positions were the basis for a country's bargaining leverage well into the negotiations over the Maastricht rules. Traditional distributional concerns of weak and strong currency countries continued to shape the rules of European monetary cooperation into the early 1990s. And the Maastricht process itself followed a pattern similar to earlier monetary negotiations in the EU. This argument allows for an intriguing interpretation of the Maastricht Treaty: strong currency countries adjusted to the narrowing gap between strong and weak currency countries by installing their preferred monetary constitution for the rest of Europe. In this sense, the Maastricht Treaty appears to be both an admission of narrowing gaps in countries' balance-of-payments positions *and* of the continued bargaining leverage of strong currency countries.

In the long-term historical perspective, however, all other large EU member states (France, Italy, Great Britain, and Spain) were weak currency countries compared to Germany. Overall, France was the strongest among the weak currency countries in the EU. Its balance-of-payments position was significantly weaker than Germany's for most of the period under investigation here. While inflation rates converged to German levels toward the late 1980s and French franc-deutsche mark exchange rate stability became the center of French monetary policy after 1983, France remained a much weaker monetary player than Germany well into the 1990s. As the 1992/93 EMS crisis clearly underscored, French adjustment options were still confined by the domestic macroeconomic policies Germany pursued. In the summer of 1993, all rescue efforts failed to lift the French franc from its ERM floor, despite a year-long explicit verbal and financial support policy from Germany and despite the fact that the real monetary and fiscal conditions in France were in much better shape than those in Germany. Thus, while German monetary power no longer rested on a real policy advantage, its long-run low

inflation record gave Germany a significant credibility edge
in financial markets.

While weak compared to Germany, the French position
was considerably stronger than Italy's and Great Britain's.
Consequently, French governments were favorably posi-
tioned to become the primary advocate for weak currency
country concerns during European monetary negotiations.
Most importantly, this involved attempts to compromise
the German macroeconomic standard. In particular, France
advocated adopting a more symmetrical intervention
system for the EMS and favored quick monetary unification under rules strongly at odds with German preferences.

France's balance-of-payments position was critical for
the prospects of broader European monetary cooperation. As
the operation of the Snake during the 1970s demonstrated,
Germany, the Netherlands, Belgium, and Denmark faced
fairly few obstacles to cooperation among themselves.
However, because of its implications for the distribution of
adjustment pressures, French participation in the EMS was
essential to allow both Italy and Ireland (and then later,
Great Britain, Spain, and Portugal) to join the arrangement.
Without French participation, the EMS would probably have
been viable only among the strong currency countries.
Simultaneously, however, French governments also sought
to avoid joining a European scheme for exchange rate cooperation if France would be its weakest member. The fact that
Italy and Ireland had committed themselves to the EMS
alleviated French concerns about participating in the EMS.
Similarly, French officials pushed strongly for the participation of Italy or Spain in the common currency during the
implementation of the Maastricht Treaty.

The Logic of Macroeconomic Adjustment

Strictly speaking, balance-of-payments disequilibria
create adjustment pressures for both weak and strong currency countries. In the face of a balance-of-payments crisis,
the government of a weak currency country may decide to

let the exchange rate adjust through devaluation or depreciation, it may adopt monetary and/or fiscal austerity measures or it may decide to finance the payments imbalance for a while—to name the most common policy options. A strong currency country faces exactly the opposite choices. It can adjust to a disequilibrium through appreciation or revaluation of its currency, through expansionary domestic economic policies or through financing its surplus by intervening on behalf of a weaker currency and accumulating currency reserves.

Despite the fact, however, that both sides face adjustment pressure, the structural logic of adjustment is asymmetric. The primary reason for this asymmetry is the fact that a strong currency country is less constrained in choosing among its adjustment options. It could, if it wanted to, voluntarily reflate its economy through expansionary fiscal and/or monetary measures. Of course, Germany never considered this alternative seriously, but if the German monetary authorities had chosen to reflate at any point in time, no one could have prevented them from doing so. As a matter of fact, there are many instances when almost everyone else would have applauded such a course of action—most visibly in the late 1970s and the early 1990s.

A strong currency country could also freely choose to finance its surplus through the accumulation of currency reserves. The most important advantage a strong currency country has over a weak currency country in this respect is that it can finance its payments disequilibrium without facing the danger of exhausting its currency reserves. A strong currency country does not face a reserve constraint. The inherent limit to this option in particular in the eyes of Germany's Bundesbank, of course, has been its potential inflationary impact. In other words, while a strong currency country does not face a reserve constraint, it may face a self-imposed intervention constraint. However, this fact only underscores the asymmetry between strong and weak currency countries: the "intervention constraint" reflects a voluntary choice; the reserve constraint is externally imposed by the structural logic of monetary relations.

Despite these self-imposed limitations, however, financing a balance-of-payments surplus has been by far the preferable option over outright domestic reflation in the eyes of Germany's macroeconomic policymakers. Most important, the Bundesbank retained the option to sterilize interventions and, therefore, to contain the import of inflation.[3] Similarly, the Bundesbank also preserved its option to stop interventions at any time to limit the danger of imported inflation. Interestingly, the intervention rules have received much more attention in the prevailing literature than the sterilization issue to explain EMS asymmetry. However, for the EMS to develop into a truly symmetric regime, it would have been equally important also to limit the ability of strong currency countries to sterilize their interventions (i.e., to prevent them from negating the impact of interventions on real economic conditions).

Finally, as its third option, a strong currency country can choose to let its currency adjust upward. German policymakers have clearly preferred this option over adjustments in domestic policy. The late Bretton Woods period and the various realignments in the Snake and EMS provide many examples of this. However, German policymakers have also continuously worried about the potential costs of revaluations, namely a loss in export competitiveness. In particular during the late 1970s, German policymakers perceived the danger of a "virtuous cycle" of low inflation and further revaluation in which the deutsche mark appreciated beyond inflation differentials, a situation that significantly strengthened German incentives to stabilize exchange rates and establish the EMS. The tradeoffs in adjustment costs meant that German policymakers were confronted with the need to balance rigidity (i.e., absence of exchange rate changes to obtain exchange rate stability) and flexibility (i.e., legitimacy of exchange rate changes to allow for orderly adjustment) of an exchange rate system— an issue that visibly shaped the rules for the EMS.

As opposed to strong currency countries, the currency reserves of a weak currency country are limited. If a weak currency country chooses to finance its disequilibrium, it can do so only as long as its reserves last. In other words, a weak currency country faces a reserve constraint. This situation obviously restricts the ability of a government to use the financing option in times of crisis. The asymmetry in adjustment is further enhanced by the fact that weak currency countries become dependent on the corresponding good will of strong currency countries to continue to intervene in financial markets or the willingness of multilateral institutions to extend financing aid. Strong currency countries can finance their surplus as long as they deem appropriate, and they can stop their interventions at their own volition. Weak currency countries have little leverage to influence these decisions.

As a result of its reserve constraint, a weak currency country faces the choice between external adjustment (depreciation or devaluation) or domestic adjustment (disinflation and austerity measures) much more severely than a strong currency country. While these two options sound equally plausible on paper, in reality there exists another fundamental asymmetry between them. Overall, it is extremely difficult for a weak currency country to avoid domestic adjustments. To counteract financial outflows and to reestablish confidence in private financial markets, a weak currency country is pushed toward adopting higher interest rates and other austerity measures. Moreover, the potential danger of setting in motion a vicious cycle of depreciation and inflation and the politicization of devaluation decisions further constrains the external adjustment options for weak currency countries. Thus, while strong currency countries may choose domestic adjustment on their own volition, domestic policy changes are often unavoidable for weak currency countries in the face of balance-of-payments problems. Whereas weak currency countries have hardly any chance to avoid disinflation, a strong currency country is much more likely to elude reflation. Internal adjustment is more or less voluntary for strong currency countries, while it may be inevitable for

weak currency countries. In other words, the policy options
of weak currency countries are much more confined than
those of strong currency countries.

The different adjustment options explained above
shape the logic of European monetary bargaining. A
country's status as a "strong" or "weak" currency country
has significant implications for its bargaining position and
leverage. While weak currency countries seek generous
conditions for the rules of financing and would like to shift
domestic adjustment obligations to strong currency countries, their leverage to achieve these goals is severely constrained. In other words, balance-of-payments positions
create *power* relationships. Unless it can bring in leverage
from somewhere else through issue linkage, a weak currency country has hardly any chance to force a strong currency country to adjust domestically. Ultimately, a weak
currency country faces greater adjustment pressures
within the international political economy but has fewer
bargaining threats available to change conditions within
its international environment. Before I specify this bargaining logic, I will address briefly two supplementary and
intervening considerations, namely, the influence of economic size and capital mobility.

Size

While the above discussion addressed certain power
imbalances between states, surprisingly it did not pay
attention to such traditional power indicators as economic
"size" or "control over resources." There are essentially two
arguments for this neglect. First of all, a country's balance-
of-payments position is a significant measure of monetary
power, no matter what other power resources are at a particular government's disposal. As I will demonstate shortly,
size is not completely irrelevant in determining a government's leverage in international monetary negotiations.
However, the ability of states to influence the rules of monetary cooperation is clearly confined by their respective
balance-of-payments positions. Second, the EU offers a

unique opportunity to study the impact of relative balance-of-payments positions on monetary bargaining in a fairly favorable environment. In terms of pure size, France, Germany, Italy and Great Britain are relatively closely matched, at least compared to the global monetary system with its significant size asymmetry between the United States and other players.

The United States certainly serves as the prime example for the influence of traditional power indicators on monetary bargaining. This is particularly noteworthy since the United States developed more or less into a weak currency country during the 1960s compared, for example, to Germany. Nevertheless, traditional resources allowed the United States to create monetary bargaining leverage through issue linkage. First of all, as a large economy, the United States was less vulnerable to external shocks and experienced less severe external adjustment pressures than smaller countries (Keohane and Nye 1977). Larger countries can sustain balance-of-payments problems more easily. Moreover, during the Bretton Woods years, the United States was in position to use its security guarantee as a form of leverage to elicit favorable responses from strong currency countries—in particular Germany's restraint on dollar-gold conversions (Bergsten 1975: 329; Block 1977: 171–74; Strange 1976: 270–75). Similarly, the size of its internal market allows the United States to use threats of protectionism in international macroeconomic negotiations (Webb 1991). Also, the sheer magnitude of the U.S. economy and the continued role of the dollar as an international reserve currency and vehicle for transactions still lets the U.S. government exercise greater pressures on other economies than would otherwise be possible for a weak currency country. The willingness of foreigners to hold dollars reduces the costs of borrowing from abroad. All of these factors present an opportunity to the United States occasionally to use the dollar exchange rate as a tool to force adjustment on other countries—the "dollar weapon" (Henning 1994: 253–308).

However, the U.S. example also points to the inherent limits of traditional power indicators for the explanation of monetary cooperation. This is, for example, visible in United States-German macroeconomic relations. Despite their security dependence and smaller economic size, German policymakers could translate their strong currency country status into sufficient leverage to resist U.S. demands for domestic adjustment through reflation on many occasions since the early 1960s. As the principal strong currency country in this relationship, Germany was able to choose its more preferred policy options of financing (including temporary capital controls) and external adjustment (revaluation and floating). In other words, American attempts to influence German domestic macroeconomic policies do not have an impressive track record. Moreover, capital mobility and U.S. dependence on capital inflows have more and more constrained the ability of U.S. governments to use the dollar weapon in recent years. The fact that the United States can borrow at low costs from abroad implies an obvious counterthreat: competitive depreciation of the dollar is politically limited by the potential of capital outflows and the subsequent need for the United States to raise interest rates.

Within European monetary politics there exist no comparable asymmetries to the role of the United States on the global level. Rather, traditional power indicators would suggest a fairly balanced distribution of power among the bigger EU member states France, Germany, Great Britain, and Italy. Indeed, a coalition of weak currency countries should have easily swayed the distribution of power heavily in their favor. Based on pure "size," a coalition of France, Italy, Great Britain, and later Spain should have had the upper hand in a power struggle with a coalition of Germany and its small country allies. The core insight here is that the distribution of power in terms of size yields inaccurate predictions about outcomes in monetary negotiations. This situation enhances the validity of the argument advanced in this book. It is difficult to attribute any real asymmetrical bargaining outcomes to differences in size or control over traditional power resources. Causes other than size would have to explain imbalanced outcomes.

France respresents a partial—albeit very limited—
exception to the above arguments. French policymakers
have been able on a few occasions to translate France's
political importance into leverage in the context of monetary politics. Most significant, its status as one of the four
allied powers in Germany allowed France to bargain for an
acceleration of the EMU process by exchanging its approval
of German reunification for German acceptance of a concrete timetable within the Maastricht negotiations (Baun
1996; Methfessel 1996). It is noteworthy, however, that
even this bargaining exchange did not involve German concessions on domestic adjustment issues, but merely on the
timetable. Concrete bargaining over the rules of EMU
remained as asymmetric as in previous episodes. In this
sense the timetable represents one of the typical concessions of strong currency countries, namely, a side payment.

Capital Mobility

Like size, increasing capital mobility could potentially
be an important variable in the adjustment process. As
asserted by Robert Mundell (1968: 233–71), governments
cannot hope to achieve simultaneously the three objectives
of (1) national policy independence, (2) capital mobility, and
(3) stable exchange rates, a logic now often referred to as
"Holy Trinity" (or sometimes also as "unholy trinity").
Indeed, capital mobility has received a special explanatory
status in many recent analyses of international monetary
relations (e.g., Andrews 1994; McNamara 1998; Pauly
1997; Webb 1991, 1995). After the adoption of the Single
European Act in 1986, the capital mobility argument
increasingly became an intellectual rationale to warn about
future instability of the EMS and the need to complement
the single market with a single currency (e.g., Padoa-
Schioppa 1994).

Clearly, the degree of capital mobility forms an important background variable for the discussion of monetary
bargaining. However, capital mobility does not change the
fundamental logic of adjustment pressures. If anything, it

may actually strengthen the underlying asymmetries. Even under limited capital mobility, governments were not in position to defend an exchange rate forever (Obstfeld 1993: 216). The role that capital mobility plays in this process is that of *acceleration*. Rising capital mobility speeds up the problems of adjustment because weak currency countries run out of currency reserves faster, and they are forced to find other means of adjustment more quickly.

A comparison of the exchange rate crises in the late 1960s and the 1992 ERM crisis illustrates this point. France and Germany debated the realignment of their currencies in 1968 and 1969 in a very public fashion. In Germany, the question of a DM revaluation even became a hotly debated topic in the national election campaign of 1969. In 1992, however, capital flows forced much quicker decisions than in the 1960s. Great Britain and Italy did not have much time to debate the merits of a devaluation. Both governments ran out of options within weeks (if not days). Moreover, Italy had to withdraw from the ERM despite a devaluation of the lira only three days earlier—indicating that external adjustment options become even more constrained under higher capital mobility. In other words, pegged exchange rate regimes are more difficult to maintain the higher the degree of capital mobility (Eichengreen 1994).

Notwithstanding these impressive changes induced by capital mobility, the causal relationships established by Mundell's "Holy Trinity" have different explanatory strength. A more direct causal link exists between policy independence and exchange rate stability. If macroeconomic conditions and policies diverge among countries, exchange rates cannot be expected to remain stable. Capital mobility, however, is not a direct cause but serves as a framing condition. While capital mobility arguably accelerates the dynamics of macroeconomic inconsistencies, the *degree* of capital mobility is not of *causal* significance in this relationship. As mentioned above, even under low levels of capital mobility, it is impossible for governments to maintain a stable exchange rate in the long run if macro-economic conditions diverge. While lower degrees of capital mobility and the imposition of capital controls allow governments to postpone adjustment—or to create breathing room until other adjustment measures take effect—they ultimately cannot prevent some form of real adjustment. Higher capital mobility speeds up the adjustment process but does not change the basic asymmetry in the adjustment options between weak and strong currency countries.

Bargaining Asymmetry between Weak and Strong Currency Countries

The asymmetry in adjustment options identified above has significant implications for the logic of bargaining over the rules of exchange rate cooperation. If the macroecomic policies of participants in an exchange rate regime are not in a "natural" lock step, policymakers must somehow create consistency through deliberate adjustment rules. This necessity has posed an obvious distributional question for European monetary politics—namely, who bears which adjustment costs?

Generally speaking, governments have an obvious incentive to advocate adjustment rules that would allow them to externalize costs and to maintain as much domestic macroeconomic autonomy as possible. While this incentive is common to all participants in monetary negotiations, their ability to achieve these goals is highly uneven. As argued earlier, in the case of weak currency countries, domestic adjustment may frequently be dictated by external constraints. Disinflation is often unavoidable. In contrast, even if strong currency countries also have to adjust to external imbalances, they have a greater latitude of choice among their various options. Reflation remains a voluntary option for them. This greater ability to pursue their own choices presents strong currency countries with the opportunity to exercise greater leverage in the design of the rules governing adjustment.

The connection between adjustment asymmetries and bargaining leverage is based on two presuppositions. First of all, the costs of the unilateral options strong currency countries face in the event of bargaining failure tend to be lower than those for weak currency countries. In other words, the intensity of their preference for successful cooperation is often lower than that of weak currency countries, a situation that strengthens the credibility of strong currency countries' exit threat and, therefore, their bargaining power (Dixit and Nalebuff 1991; Moravcsik 1998). Second, weak currency countries do not have an effective threat of exclusion against strong currency countries, because participation of the strong currency countries is necessary to establish a successful monetary regime. They are essential as sources of financing facilities, for providing the macroeconomic focal point of the system, or for establishing credibility in financial markets.

The logic of the exit threat is based on simple cost/benefit analysis. Strong currency countries often face lower costs from bargaining failure. They have less to lose from the breakdown of negotiations and are, therefore, less compelled to make concessions. Vice versa, governments facing higher costs from bargaining failure have weaker leverage. They tend to be more willing to make concessions in order to achieve their preferred outcomes.

Focusing on the trade-off between a country's reserve constraint and its access to financing facilities helps to illustrate these cost/benefit calculations. Downward pressure on its currency poses adjustment problems for a government both within a negotiated exchange rate regime and under floating exchange rates.[4] While the advantage of floating in such a situation is the absence of a mandatory intervention rule, the government has to bear the full brunt of its reserve constraint. In other words, the core problem for a weak currency country is of a structural nature: it has simply no unilateral tool available to overcome its reserve constraint. However, monetary cooperation at least offers some prospect of relief from the impact of its reserve constraint by agreeing on financing facilities.

The French deliberations during the 1982/83 monetary crisis provide the most dramatic evidence for this contention. Pressure on the French franc following the Mitterrand experiment of expansionary policies and state interventionism triggered a divisive debate within the government about the future of French macroeconomic policy and participation in the EMS (e.g. Hall 1986; Loriaux 1991). Proponents and opponents of continued EMS membership both agreed that macroeconomic adjustment for France would be costly. While maintaining EMS membership at least promised further access to the regime's financing facilities, a floating French franc would have required similar rigid domestic adjustment with access to extended financing only through the IMF (Cameron 1996). Obviously, requesting IMF financing facilities would have been politically embarrassing, given U.S. dominance of that institution, and would have done little to safeguard French domestic priorities because of the IMF's policy of conditionality. Thus, weak currency countries often face a choice between two unappealing options: that of asymmetric monetary cooperation or unfettered market pressures.[5]

A strong currency country may also have interests in stabilizing exchange rates. For example, it may want to limit problems of competitiveness due to its appreciating currency. This motivation played a role among German policymakers to pursue the EMS in 1978/79. However, the implications of this incentive for the monetary bargaining interaction have natural limits. A strong currency country can achieve reflation *unilaterally*, namely, through domestic policy measures (e.g., expansionary macroeconomic policies or unsterilized financing of balance-of-payments surpluses). Thus, even if a strong currency country had an overwhelming interest in achieving exchange rate stability, it could attain this goal largely through its own means. It would not need cooperation to produce the desired effect. In other words, if a strong currency country seeks exchange rate cooperation, the very point of such collaboration would be to unload a significant portion of the costs on weak currency countries. This greater latitude of strong currency countries raises the opportunity costs of agreement for them. With it, the credibility of their exit threat strengthens.

So far we have looked only at strong and weak currency countries in the abstract. Keen observers of the specifically German setting for macroeconomic policymaking may be tempted to construct a more cynical variation on this theme. For example, we could ask if Chancellors Schmidt and Kohl pursued their respective designs for the EMS and EMU in quasi-Machiavellian fashion to undermine the authority of the Bundesbank and to achieve reflation through the "backdoor" of international obligations.[6] While there is undoubtedly some cursory and anecdotal evidence to support this claim, the overall causal connection is fairly weak. Except for a few flippant interview remarks, there is little direct evidence that Schmidt advocated German domestic reflation. In fact, his strong distaste for the Carter administration's macroeconomic policies and his resistance to what he perceived as American bullying tactics to achieve expansionary policies contradict this kind of interpretation. Attempts at fiscal expansion—an area over which the federal government indeed had control—remained timid at best under the Schmidt administration. The stimulus package of 1978 was modest and certainly not proof of a genuine desire for reflation. There is, furthermore, little evidence that Schmidt actively sought to construct a strong domestic alliance favoring reflation and supporting the demands of weak currency countries. Notwithstanding the personal animosity between Schmidt and the Bundesbank's president, Emminger, Schmidt did not visibly resist Emminger's demands for EMS rules. Schmidt's memoirs (1990) also attest to his desire to use the EMS as a device for disinflation in the EU and to his fears over a lack of discipline in the EMS.

Similarly, Kohl's pursuit of EMU does not appear to have many Machiavellian qualities. First of all, EMU became a goal *before* the German government pursued expansionary policies to finance reunification. Thus, the policy conflict between the Bundesbank and the federal government of the early 1990s has little to do with the adoption of the EMU goal. Moreover, it would appear to make little sense to disempower the Bundesbank by constructing an even more independent and possibly more obstinate European Central Bank.[7] In summary, the bargaining asymmetry between weak and strong currency countries is structural. It consists of the inability of weak currency countries to overcome their reserve constraint unilaterally, whereas strong currency countries can achieve external adjustment (i.e., appreciation), internal adjustment (i.e. reflation), and financing through their own means. While all of these options involve costs even for a strong currency country, its main advantage is that it can choose more or less voluntarily *where* to pay the price of adjustment.

The relative opportunity costs of agreement, however, are not the only source of leverage at stake here. If the preferences for cooperation among strong currency countries are so low that weak currency countries deem their demands excessive and too costly, cooperation cannot take place between these two groups of countries. This situation certainly characterized the interaction between strong and weak currency countries during the Snake period. Both sides perceived the costs of their unilateral options as lower than those of cooperation, with the result that the Snake functioned only among the strong currency countries. However, the Snake period provided two important lessons for the bargaining interaction in the EU. First, the continued existence of the Snake underscored that cooperation among the strong currency countries was indeed possible and credible, even if weak currency countries were not part of the regime. Second, the unilateral floating options pursued by France and Italy during this period turned out to be much more costly than anticipated, effectively increasing the urgency for weak currency countries to find some form of agreement during the EMS negotiations.

These examples demonstrate that the strong currency countries' exit threat at stake is supplemented by an insufficient threat of exclusion available to weak currency countries. Strong currency country participation is essential for the credibility of any eventual monetary regime. Cooperation only among weak currency countries was not viable in competition with a floating deutsche mark or deutsche mark bloc. Financial markets would have attached low credibility to the arrangement, and the source of the regime's financing mechanisms would have been an open question. For example, during the EMS negotiations, the option for Germany to maintain a mini-Snake with its strong currency neighbors was much more credible than, say, a joint French-Italian exchange rate regime. Similarly, the Maastricht EMU had to include Germany in order not to doom the project from the beginning. Even a German-Dutch mini-EMU had more credibility than, say, a monetary union between France and Italy (which would have defeated the French political intentions in any case).

Thus, the need to secure participation of the principal strong currency country in any eventual exchange rate regime endowed Germany with additional bargaining leverage. German policymakers were in a position to determine the "bottom line" of the EMS and EMU negotiations and to present their partners with a "take-it-or-leave-it" proposition because they could threaten exit and could not be excluded by other participants. This becomes even more revealing in contrasting the German with the British bargaining position. As its bargaining behavior visibly demonstrates, the British government certainly had an "exit threat," both in the EMS and the EMU negotiations. The intensity of British preferences for cooperation was low, a situation that should have improved British bargaining power. If we were to disregard the causal significance of balance-of-payments positions, there would be no obvious explanation why Germany should have been endowed with more leverage than Great Britain. However, the British exit threat clearly did not translate into bargaining power. Some observers would even argue that in the British case exit threats may have been counterproductive to advancing British interests in the negotiations. Ultimately, the problem for the British bargaining position was that both the EMS and the EMU were conceivable without British participation. German participation, however, was paramount in each case. Thus, the low perceived costs *and* the perceived necessity of German participation form the backbone of Germany's leverage. A weak threat of exclusion must accompany an exit threat in order to generate bargaining leverage.

Up to this point, I have treated the structural logic of bargaining asymmetry in a static fashion and isolated from other issue areas. There are, of course, situations in which other factors might offset or counteract the asymmetry explained here. For example, if a strong currency country would have an intense domestic preference to pursue expansionary policies, it would certainly be more amenable to compromises. The crucial causal shift in such a hypothetical scenario, however, would be toward greater *congruence in interests* between weak and strong currency countries, rather than toward a weakening of the strong currency country's bargaining position. It still maintains a credible unilateral option of reflation and would not need cooperation to achieve that goal. In any case, this situation did not exist in European monetary cooperation, given Germany's obstinacy on this point.

A more complicated countervailing scenario concerns the question of political *issue linkage*. If a strong currency country had very intense *political* preferences for monetary cooperation because it seeks goals in other policy areas, its costs of nonagreement would increase, and weak currency countries would gain more room to solicit bargaining concessions.[8] For example, there is obviously a connection between the overall goal of European integration and monetary cooperation. Indeed, later chapters will report evidence that certain aspects of European integration have helped to trigger initiatives in the monetary realm as well. If strong currency countries had significantly more powerful incentives than their weak currency country counterparts to safeguard other aspects of European integration—say the common market—their opportunity costs of nonagreement would rise, and they would more likely make concessions in monetary negotiations. In other words, strong currency countries would be more accommodating to the demands of weak currency countries, in order to achieve other goals.

However, such a scenario rests on the theoretical assumption that issue linkage is more important for the strong currency country than the weak currency country. If issue linkage is roughly similar, these preferences simply offset each other and restore conditions of asymmmetric monetary bargaining power. There is no doubt that European integration—in particular the customs union and the single market—has been an important political goal for Germany. However, similar things can be said of France. Both countries have had political interests in European integration, and there is no evidence that these issue linkage goals would have been significantly stronger for Germany than for France. The same logic applies to the bilateral French-German relationship as well. Both countries have had similarly strong interests in preserving the special strategic ties between them.

Moreover, there is no evidence of any *necessity* for the EU to pursue monetary integration. The customs union, the Common Agricultural Policy (CAP), or the single market project all provided *incentives* to pursue monetary cooperation. However, the various decisions on monetary cooperation have been deliberate political choices and not mechanical consequences of any preexisting logic of European integration. The fact that neither the EMS nor the EMU has encompassed all EU member states further underscores the absence of an automatic link between European integration and monetary cooperation within it. Monetary cooperation was never inevitable, but it allowed European policymakers to make explicit decisions and to exercise their relative bargaining strength to achieve their preferred outcomes.

Bargaining Asymmetry and the Choice of Adjustment Rules

While the previous section identified the differences in bargaining power between strong and weak currency countries, this section takes a more thorough look at the choices and tradeoffs between the various adjustment rules that are at stake for strong and weak currency countries in negotiations over monetary cooperation. Generally speaking, bargaining over the rules of adjustment in monetary cooperation features three relevant areas: domestic or internal adjustment (such as interest rate changes or changes in fiscal policies), external adjustment (most important, exchange rate changes), and the financing of monetary imbalances.[9] Technically speaking, financing is not an adjustment mechanism since it does not provide a durable solution to the underlying imbalances. However, financing is used as a means temporarily to bridge existing imbalances. As such, financing has always played a significant role in monetary negotiations. The bargaining asymmetry explained in the previous sections has visibly shaped the patterns of monetary negotiations over these issues in the EU during the past four decades. Most important, the choice among rules for macroeconomic adjustment options is constrained by the strong currency countries' ability to reject any compromises on domestic (or internal) adjustment. I will address the issue of domestic adjustment first, before I turn to questions of external adjustment, financing, and side payments.

Domestic Adjustment

At the center of the domestic adjustment problem within the EU has been—for all practical purposes—the issue of inflation. The key question in this context is the standard that should serve as the common reference point for the exchange rate system. This situation obviously poses a cooperation problem for states. What would be an acceptable standard for the system, and how can states establish such a standard? Most important, if inflation rates diverge, who should adjust—the high inflation country or the low inflation country?

Part of the problem is that this requirement for domestic consistency is ultimately a relative (or perhaps arbitrary) category. For example, an exchange rate system could remain stable at a common inflation level of, say, 1 percent or 50 percent. Thus, the inflation target of a system reflects deliberate policy decisions, rather than any absolute criteria. Both the Snake and the EMS left the question of consistency—at least in terms of its explicit rules—unregulated. This necessarily led to a situation in which the strongest country (i.e., Germany) would set the standard for the system. In the cases of the Action Programme, the Werner Report, and the Maastricht Treaty, rules for domestic macroeconomic consistency became the most important issue of the negotiations. In the case of the Action Programme and the Werner Report, the EU member states ultimately could find no agreement. The Maastricht Treaty, however, prescribed five convergence criteria for membership in EMU, namely, rules on inflation rates, interest rates, government deficit, government debt, and exchange rate stability.

These convergence criteria, however, are in essence quite arbitrary. Following one line of thinking in the debate over monetary union, one may wonder why convergence criteria are theoretically necessary at all. As the so-called "monetarist" school of thought in European monetary debates has argued, irrevocably fixing exchange rates would automatically lead to convergence around the "average" macroeconomic standard for the group as a whole.[10] Equally, one may point out that the German monetary union (GMU) of 1990 took place without explicit convergence criteria. The difference here is clearly that there was sufficient political will among (West) German policymakers to accept the adjustment costs of GMU—a situation that did not exist for EMU. Instead, one can interpret the Maastricht convergence criteria as an attempt to force some adjustment costs onto non-German participants of EMU.

In addition to this, the consistency requirement is a relative category also because every exchange rate system can tolerate some degree of divergence. A *pegged exchange rate system* allows participants to change exchange rates or to finance disequilibria. The EMS of the early 1980s under-

Table 2.2
Inflation Differentials in the Early Snake
and Early EMS (in percent)

	1971	1972	1973	1979	1980	1981	1982	1983	1984
Germany-France	0.3	0.7	0.3	6.7	7.9	7.1	6.5	6.6	5.0
Germany-Italy	−0.3	0.2	3.8	10.7	15.9	13.2	11.2	11.3	8.4

Data Source: International Monetary Fund, *International Financial Statistics*, October 1993.

scores this point. It survived despite considerable divergences between the most important players. Table 2.2 illustrates the substantial differences in macroeconomic conditions among France, Germany, and Italy in the first five years of the EMS. The survival of the EMS is even more remarkable if one compares the situation to the conditions that existed in the early Snake period. During the early 1970s, inflation levels among these countries deviated much less significantly, although as a lagging indicator, inflation rates tell us little about the actual policies pursued in this period and should therefore not be overinterpreted. Despite this caveat, however, table 2.2 does indicate that the difference in outcomes between the Snake and EMS is remarkable. The survival of the EMS constitutes a considerable political achievement against the odds. The experience of the EMS shows that a pegged exchange rate regime can survive large divergences if the participants remain *politically committed* to it and maintain a consensus over the *legitimacy* of appropriate adjustment mechanisms—in the case of the EMS occasional realignments and the financing of balance-of-payments equilibria.

Similarly, a *currency union* can also survive macroeconomic divergences if the participants have sufficient adjustment mechanisms at their disposal—for example, factor mobility, changes in domestic economic policies, price and wage flexibility or fiscal transfers. Theoretically and practically, large divergences are possible. As mentioned earlier, German Monetary Union (GMU) is an example of an exchange rate regime with significant divergences among its "member states."[11] Arguably, in economic terms,

GMU is a much more divergent entity than EMU. However, GMU could suvive because the partners were politically committed to enduring the costs associated with these divergences.

The conceptual problem in evaluating the requirements for consistency here is that optimum currency area theory does not specify precise thresholds for the formation of a monetary union or a fixed exchange rate system.[12] This situation limits the theory's predictive and prescriptive value. Economists remain uncertain as to whether the EU constitutes an optimum currency area (e.g., Eichengreen 1992b). However, optimum currency area theory would more likely have predicted a monetary union between (West) Germany and the Netherlands than between East and West Germany. Thus, the determination of what constitutes consistency or inconsistency of macroeconomic policies and conditions depends in the end on the political assessment of the participants. The convergence criteria of the Maastricht Treaty for EMU reflect the political character of the consistency requirement. While optimum currency area theory can be read in general terms as an argument in favor of some form of convergence criteria, economists are often hard pressed to justify the economic rationale for the EMU rules set in the Maastricht Treaty (e.g., Eichengreen 1993; Kenen 1995). Instead, it seems more compelling to understand these rules as a result of political necessities, most importantly the need to accommodate Germany's concerns over the costs of EMU (e.g., Padoa-Schioppa 1994: 198–200).

All of these considerations result in the same conclusion: If there is no preexisting, quasi-"natural" agreement on an appropriate common standard, the problem of consistency somehow needs to be politically resolved among the negotiating partners of an exchange rate regime. Indeed, domestic adjustment has remained the most important obstacle for European monetary relations due to its distributive implications: should a low inflation country bear the costs of establishing consistency by inflating its domestic economy? Or, vice versa, should the high inflation country adjust through a policy of disinflation? Or can the participants meet somewhere in between? Or, finally, can they devise other strategies to deal with divergence among them—for example, realignments? These questions describe the central conflict among the EU member states over exchange rate cooperation during the past forty years.

So far, Germany has always refused to make significant concessions on its macroeconomic priorities to solve these questions. Both in the Snake and the EMS, German macroeconomic policies effectively served as the reference point for the exchange rate system. Despite their explicit efforts, weak currency countries did not succeed in negotiating policy rules that would force domestic adjustment upon the strong currency countries. The Maastricht rules for EMU membership, institutional design, and the pursuit of macroeconomic policies also largely follow German preferences.

These examples demonstrate that the patterns of bargaining also depend on the *type* of exchange rate regime being negotiated. *Pegged* exchange rate systems in general are often flexible enough to exist without explicit rules for domestic adjustment. The negotiations over the rules for the Bretton Woods regime, for example, featured significant differences between Great Britain and the United States over the appropriate rules for domestic adjustment as exhibited in the Keynes and White plans for the postwar monetary order (e.g., Gardner 1956). Ultimately, the Bretton Woods System recognized the need for domestic macroeconomic flexibility and did not stipulate explicit rules for internal adjustment.[13] The same pattern characterized the negotiations over the Snake and the European Monetary System. Recognizing the fact that no consensual agreement existed on an appropriate standard, neither one of these systems established any explicit rules for domestic policy adjustment. Instead, rules for external adjustment and financing have been the primary features of pegged exchange rate regimes.[14]

In contrast, currency unions do not require rules for external adjustment or financing. This puts the issue of internal adjustment into a different light. Indeed, the

Maastricht Treaty contains explicit rules for domestic policy objectives for the potential members of EMU. In other words, monetary unions do not allow member states to shift disagreements over internal adjustment to negotiations over external adjustment and financing. In the end, rules for domestic adjustment had to become part of the Maastricht negotiations in order to satisfy German concerns over a potential inflationary bias in the monetary union.

External Adjustment

Exchange rate changes are the most important form of external adjustment to restore equilibrium in a country's balance-of-payments. Before explaining the significance of exchange rate changes, however, it is necessary to mention briefly other forms of external adjustment. This refers to trade policies as well as capital controls. Both types of policies allow governments to influence the flow of goods, services, and capital across borders. Deficit countries, for example, are tempted to restrict imports to take pressure off their current account. France and Italy at various times during the 1960s and the 1970s introduced trade restrictions during balance-of-payments crises—mostly in violation of EU rules for the common market. Similarly, capital controls can allow governments to restrict the outflow of capital. Deficit countries have at various times introduced these controls to alleviate balance-of-payments deficits. This happened as late as the 1992 currency crisis, despite the abolition of capital controls under the single market project. For surplus countries, the logic has worked the other way around. Germany has often been asked by deficit countries to implement policies that increase imports—although it has rarely heeded these requests. And it has on occasion, although reluctantly, introduced controls on capital inflows.

As indicated earlier, the significance of these two means of external adjustment has declined within the EU over the past few decades. Although trade restrictions and capital controls may provide temporary relief, they are ultimately inefficient. And, more important, the member states have increasingly lost control over these two policy areas within the EU. Unilateral trade restrictions violate the idea of the customs union, and the single market project prohibits now the use of capital controls. Thus, exchange rate changes were the only means of *external* adjustment left to the EU member states until the creation of EMU removed even this last instrument of external adjustment. Here, exchange rates are permanently fixed. In other words, participants of EMU completely forgo the possibility of external adjustment. Instead, adjustment will take place automatically through capital flows.

A pegged exchange rate system, however, allows for alterations of parities. Thus, participants of a pegged exchange rate system negotiate with each other the particular rules and procedures for exchange rate changes. For example, they have to determine if a country can alter its exchange rate unilaterally or if it needs the cooperation of its partners. Similarly, they must determine the central rates of currencies, as well as their fluctuation margins. In this area, Germany accepted a number of bargaining compromises with weak currency countries during the EMS negotiations.

The absence of agreement on internal adjustment and the ability to shift bargaining to questions of external adjustment indicates that the stability of the EMS as an institution must have rested to some degree on the legitimacy of realignments as a form of adjustment. On the one hand, a revaluation of the deutsche mark was consistently the only formal obligation of real adjustment Germany would be willing to impose on itself. On the other hand, in the absence of German reflation or full disinflation of the weak currency countries, periodic devaluations had to become a legitimate tool of adjustment for the weak currency countries if the EMS as an institution was to survive. Table 2.3 illustrates the striking difference between the Snake and the early EMS in this respect. Although the particular conditions for realignments have always remained

Table 2.3
**Number of Devaluations of the British Pound Sterling,
French Franc, and Italian Lira against the Deutsche
Mark in the Snake and EMS**

Number of devaluations against DM	"Snake," 1972– 1979**	EMS, 1979– 1983	EMS, 1984– 1987	EMS, 1988– 1991
British pound sterling***	0	-	-	0
French franc	2	4	2	0
Italian lira	0	5	3	1*

Notes: * This devaluation on January 8, 1990 is often seen as a more or less technical adjustment for the lira to narrow its fluctuation bands from +/–6% to +/–2.5%.
** All three countries withdrew from the Snake at various times to avoid devaluations.
*** Great Britain participated briefly in the Snake after its entry into the EU; it did not participate in the EMS until 1990.
Source: Hellmann 1979; and Gros and Thygesen 1992: 68.

subject to political controversies and the question as to which realignments were justified or not continued to instigate squabbles among the EMS members, there existed a consensus among them that realignments were an appropriate means of adjustment. Both Italy and France used devaluations vis-à-vis the deutsche mark frequently until 1983 and somewhat less frequently between 1984 and 1987 to adjust for macroeconomic divergences. This consensus on realignments got lost toward the latter part of the 1980s, a fact that aggravated the severity of the EMS crisis in 1992/93.

Financing

As in the case of external adjustment, financing rules can become subject to bargaining only in a pegged exchange rate system and not in a monetary union. To some degree, a monetary union represents the ultimate form of financing. Balance-of-payments disequilibria cease to have any real meaning, in the sense that regional central banks cannot run up against a reserve constraint. Financing facilities are not to be confused with structural aid—an issue that has gotten linked to both pegged exchange rate systems and monetary unions. Financing facilities are an inherent element of the intervention procedures to deal with balance-of-payments disequilibria. The purpose of structural aid is to support the real convergence in the targeted countries. I will address this issue subsequently under the heading of side payments.

The typical financing issues for which countries need to find rules are the following: Under what conditions can governments ask for balance-of-payments assistance? How much assistance will countries be allowed to borrow? Are the financing mechanisms bilateral or multilateral? What are the repayment conditions? These issues are much more conducive to compromise. Indeed, strong currency countries have shown some willingness to make concessions on the amounts, lending periods, and repayment conditions of financing facilities.

The key point here is that these types of compromises on financing facilities do not hurt the domestic policy priorities of strong currency countries. Through sterilization, their central banks are in a position to minimize the impact of their interventions in the system, and they can stop interventions when they become too large. The duration of borrowing periods or the conditions for repayments also have little relevance for their domestic economy. Ultimately, these items are relatively painless to agree on, if strong currency countries are sufficiently motivated to overcome bargaining impasses.

Side Payments and Issue Linkage

As indicated earlier, pegged exchange rate systems allow participants to shift bargaining from the intractable question of internal adjustment to the issues of external adjustment (i.e., exchange rate changes) and financing. A monetary union, however, precludes such a tradeoff between negotiable and nonnegotiable issues. As indicated earlier, in a monetary union the two issues subject to bargaining—namely, rules for external adjustment and financing—simply disappear. Since exchange rates are permanently fixed, partners cannot bargain anymore over the rules for parity changes. And since they are subject to a central bank, there is no longer a need for the participants of a monetary union to quibble over the financing of balance-of-payments disequilibria.

This implies a severe political problem for negotiations over a monetary union. Given Germany's uncompromising position on domestic adjustment issues, only side payments and issues somehow linked to monetary negotiations can become subject to bargaining. One of the issues repeatedly linked to European monetary negotiations was the question of structural aid. While Italy and Ireland were successful on this question already in the EMS negotiations, weak currency countries also attached the creation of the so-called cohesion fund to the Maastricht accord. The Maastricht negotiations also saw a number of other side payments. According to many observers, the most important concession at Maastricht was Germany's acceptance of a definitive timetable for moving to stage three in the EMU process. However, this concession follows the same logic described earlier. Germany's traditional position to declare its own macroeconomic preferences as nonnegotiable did not logically preclude a binding timetable. France and Italy had already accepted Germany's conditions for convergence and central bank independence. In addition to the timetable issue, German policymakers made concessions on a number of more or less symbolic issues at Maastricht. All of these concessions were possible because ultimately none of them hampered Germany's ability to protect its own domestic priorities.

Conclusion

The relative balance-of-payments positions of EU member states are important indicators of the leverage they can bring to the bargaining table. Strong currency countries face no reserve constraint and are, therefore, much less confined in choosing their preferred option for adjustment to balance-of-payments disequilibria. The costs of pursuing their policy options unilaterally tend to be lower than those of weak currency countries. At the same time, their participation in an exchange rate regime is necessary to provide credibility to the regime. Strong currency countries are endowed with a powerful exit threat, while weak currency contries do not have a correspondingly strong threat of exclusion. These conditions are the basis for the leverage of strong currency countries in monetary negotiations. As a result, the German refusal to compromise domestic macroeconomic priorities has introduced a visible pattern for European monetary negotiations. While Germany and its strong currency allies were able to keep internal adjustment issues off the bargaining table in the EMS negotiations, their macroeconomic priorities served as the architectural blueprint for the Maastricht EMU. In exchange, German policymakers were willing to make concessions on questions of external adjustment, financing, and side payments in the EMS. The logic of bargaining over the rules of EMU, however, allowed for concessions only on side payments, such as structural funds or the timetable.

3

———

The Politics of Leadership in Monetary Cooperation

The previous chapter explained the significance of a country's balance-of-payments position for its bargaining leverage in monetary negotiations. At the same time, the chapter revealed that the German role in European monetary politics deserves special attention. Its status as the major strong currency country in the EU has endowed Germany with a pivotal position in this policy arena. As a result of their bargaining leverage, German policymakers have consistently been able to shape the rules of European monetary cooperation significantly. This chapter further specifies the role Germany has played in European monetary cooperation. I argue that the most important part of Germany's role consists of standard setting. German macroeconomic policy priorities have consistently served as the reference point for European exchange rate cooperation—either through a classical nth currency solution in pegged exchange rate systems or as the architectural blueprint for monetary union. A supplementary component of German bargaining behavior has consisted of occasional concessions on issues of external adjustment, financing and side payments. Since German obstinacy on issues of internal adjustment could have easily deadlocked negotiations, these concessions have been crucial to break bargaining impasses both in the EMS and in the Maastricht negotiations.

Despite Germany's important status in European monetary relations, however, its role is only partially comparable to that of the United States under the Bretton Woods regime. The first section of this chapter refutes the claim that Germany has played the role of a hegemon as defined by conventional hegemonic stability theory. Germany does not have the overwhelming resources at its disposal that are usually required in definitions of hegemony. The second section examines the debate among economists over the question of German dominance in European monetary politics. Following the emerging consensus in this debate, I will describe Germany as the most influential country within European monetary politics, but hardly as dominant in the sense of affecting the policies of other member states in a unidirectional fashion. As a highly interdependent country, the policies of its partner countries have an impact on German economic conditions and policies. Thus, neither hegemony nor dominance describes adequately the significance of Germany's role in European monetary politics.

Instead, my argument starts from the observation that Germany's monetary power is not resource based, as in the case of U.S. hegemony after World War II, but rather *policy based.* Its record of low inflation and a strong currency has put Germany into a leadership role for European monetary politics. The primary consequence of Germany's policy-based position is that of *standard setting.* I argue that German bargaining had to produce European monetary rules that would allow Germany to set the macroeconomic focal point for any eventual exchange rate system. In the case of the Snake and the EMS, this came in the form of an nth country solution. Within the Maastricht process, German standard setting consisted of providing the architectural design for EMU—most significant, the adoption of convergence criteria and the rules governing the European Central Bank. This chapter also describes the complementary part of Germany's pattern of interaction in European monetary affairs, namely, its willingness to make concessions at critical junctures in the EMS and EMU negotiations. While these concessions were often crucial to let the negotiations succeed, they did not come in areas that affected standard setting. The chapter then addresses the role and impact of the Bundesbank within this particular German bargaining pattern. There can hardly be any doubt about the significant role the Bundesbank played in shaping Germany's bargaining position in European monetary politics. However, I argue that focusing alone on the role of the Bundesbank would miss important aspects of the patterns of monetary bargaining in Europe.

Hegemonic Stability Theory

Numerous analysts have used the term *hegemony* or related concepts to describe Germany's role within European monetary politics or the EU more generally (e.g., Claassen 1989; Giavazzi and Giovannini 1989; Hueglin 1992; Huffschmid 1998; Lankowski 1993; Markovits and Reich 1991a, 1991b, 1997; Marsh 1992). It usually refers to a predominant German position within the decision-making process of the EU. "Hegemonic stability theory" assumes that the existence of a hegemon mitigates the anarchical character of international relations and facilitates political and economic stability.[1] Such stability is conducive to more cooperation and the implementation of institutional frameworks among states. Conversely, the absence of a hegemon leads to greater instability and less successful cooperation among states. The rationale for this assumption is that a hegemon is in a position to solve the familiar public goods problem in international relations through one of two possible mechanisms: (1) either the hegemon is powerful enough to exact contributions from its partners to the public good, or (2) the hegemon has sufficient resources to provide the public good unilaterally or to assume disproportionate costs for its provision.

The most common conceptual approach identifies a hegemon by a state's material preponderance in a number of capabilities. Stephen Krasner, for example, defines hegemony on the basis of a set of variables that describes the distribution of power in the international system (1976: 332). A hegemon, according to Krasner's operationalization of the term, leads other nations in such indicators as per capita income, GNP, share of world trade, and share of world investment. Although Krasner's definition does not spell it out explicitly, the conventional understanding within the international relations literature now largely assumes that a country's lead has to be sizable at least on some of these indicators. Nevertheless, the exact threshold for a hegemonic position has remained largely unspecified.

Robert Keohane's definition of hegemony also uses preponderance in capabilities as a starting point: "Hegemonic powers must have control over raw materials, control over sources of capital, control over markets, and competitive advantages in the production of highly valued goods" (1984: 32). While this description poses similar measuring problems, the last component is a significant qualification. Hegemons do not simply have advantages in any kind of economic production. Rather they possess a significant edge in the leading economic sectors of their time. In addition to these capability indicators, the term *hegemony* usually implies sufficient military capabilities to defend the vital interests of the hegemon and a degree of political leverage to organize relations among the players within the hegemonic system.

While these are general criteria for hegemony, Charles Kindleberger (1981:247) specifies five tasks of leadership to secure the stability of the international monetary system, namely, to provide (1) a market for distress goods, (2) a steady, if not countercyclical, flow of capital, (3) a rediscount mechanism for providing liquidity when the monetary system is frozen in panic, (4) management of the exchange rate system, and (5) some degree of coordination of domestic monetary policies.[2] In his view, Great Britain met these criteria during the nineteenth century and the United States from the end of World War II into the early 1970s. The absence of such leadership explains the instability of the international monetary order during the interwar period. Thus, Kindleberger (1973:305) concludes, "for the world economy to be stabilized, there has to be a stabilizer, one stabilizer."

The assumptions of hegemonic stability theory have been questioned widely in the literature on international cooperation.[3] They do not require further analysis here. While the argument I develop later in this chapter shares some assumptions with hegemonic stability theory, its emphasis is different. Most important, Germany does not qualify as a "hegemon" in terms of the definitional criteria discussed earlier in this section. No member state of the EU has ever been in a clearly preponderant power position during the last forty years. France, Germany, Great Britain, and Italy were of about equal size prior to German unification. While (West) Germany may have been slightly more affluent than its neighbors and its economy bigger than those of its neighbors, its economic lead has not been very large. Certainly, following Krasner's operationalization of hegemony, Germany is ahead of its EU partners in most of the indicators of overall size, but its lead over the other EU member states remains marginal. The large German trade sector—often used as an indicator of German hegemony (e.g., Markovits and Reich 1997)—can also be read as a particular sign of vulnerability, namely, a significant dependence on its major trading partners.

It is also questionable whether Germany fulfills Keohane's criterion of competitive advantages in the production of highly valued goods. Germany's economic strength exists mostly on the basis of traditional manufacturing industries, rather than in some of the leading sectors of high technology and services. Germany's competitive advantage is without a doubt incomparable to the one Great Britain enjoyed in the mid-nineteenth century or that which characterized the United States in the mid-twentieth century. In addition, Germany's military capabilities and political influence do not qualify for hegemonic status. Observers have noticed a surprising lack of political leadership on the part of Germany, which contrasts with its significant economic weight (e.g., Bulmer 1993). In terms of military power, (West) Germany's security during the cold war relied primarily on American protection. And, as the experience of the Gulf War and the wars in the former

Yugoslavia demonstrate, Germany still leaves most questions of military leadership within the EU to its British and French partners. Overall, a status of political or military hegemony is still at odds with Germany's history in the twentieth century.[4]

Moreover, and most consequential for the question at hand, Germany fulfills at best two, if any, of Kindleberger's five criteria for leadership in monetary relations. Its economy is not large enough to serve as a market for distress goods, it does not serve as a source of countercyclical capital flows, and the provision of liquidity in times of exchange rate crisis contradicts the basic policy principles of the Bundesbank.[5] Germany may, however, at least partially fulfill the remaining two criteria mentioned by Kindleberger, namely, those of managing the exchange rate system and of providing for some degree of policy coordination. While it is difficult to operationalize Kindleberger's criteria, one can say that Germany served as the central actor for maintaining the EMS until 1992, and its domestic standard has effectively served as the "focal point" for the macroeconomic policies of the other EMS members. Overall, however, the German leadership position is—to say the least—ambiguous in the light of Kindleberger's definition.

This analysis indicates that Germany does not fully meet the traditional criteria of hegemony. It does not have a vast preponderance in resources that is conventionally associated with the notion of hegemony. In other words, Germany is not a "natural" hegemon in Europe by virtue of preponderant capabilities. Instead, Germany's position of monetary strength vis-à-vis its large European neighbors derives largely from its balance-of-payments position. In other words, its monetary power is not so much resource based as policy based.

Germany's position within European monetary politics is thus quite distinct from the role played by the United States under Bretton Woods. At the end of World War II, the United States possessed overwhelming resources compared to its partner countries within the global economy. The United States was much more a "natural" hegemon for the global international system than Germany is with respect to Western Europe.[6] In a second major difference, the American currency was explicitly put at the center of the global monetary system by virtue of the dollar-gold exchange standard, whereas the role of the deutsche mark within the EMS developed largely through the logic of adjustment and the mechanism of financial markets. And, what looms as the most significant distinction, the United States was capable of maintaining the dollar at the center of the Bretton Woods system throughout the 1960s, despite its development into a weak currency country with balance-of-payments and inflationary problems. Not incidentally, its superior political and military capabilities were helpful particularly for securing the cooperation of Germany in maintaining dollar convertibility through the 1960s (Bergsten 1975: 329; Block 1977: 171–74; Strange 1976: 270–75). Most likely, Germany would have been unable to maintain its pivotal role in European monetary relations as long as the United States, had it developed into a weak currency country.

The Question of German Economic Dominance

A long-standing debate among a number of economists concerns the issue of German dominance in European monetary politics, and in particular within the EMS.[7] The debate relates to the degree of Germany's influence over its partner countries in Europe. In particular, analysts have addressed the question as to how strongly German interest rate decisions influenced economic conditions and, most important, interest rate policies in other countries and to what extent the EMS served as a disciplining device, forcing other countries to follow Germany's rigid low-inflation policies.[8] As with definitions of hegemony, the specific operationalization of dominance remains ambiguous. How strong would the effects of German monetary policies have to be on other EMS members in order to label Germany as dominant?

Despite this definitional problem, some degree of consensus emerges on a middle ground between complete dominance and full symmetry. Virtually all studies agree that Germany was clearly the most influential country among the EMS members. However, no study finds evidence for complete German dominance, in the sense of unidirectional causality. While German monetary policies exercised significant influence over the other EMS members, the policies of the other countries also affected Germany to some degree. Simply speaking, Germany formulated its monetary policies within an interdependent environment and could not fully insulate itself from economic policies pursued elsewhere. It clearly lacked the ability to dominate European monetary politics fully.

The case for German dominance in establishing the EMS as a disciplining device seems at first sight more persuasive. After all, it was a stated goal of German EMS policies to reduce inflationary pressures in its European environment (Schmidt 1990). Moreover, Germany consistently rejected any form of a bargaining compromise on domestic macroeconomic adjustment, thus forcing the other countries either to converge in their policies or to use external and temporary measures of adjustment. In addition, the actual result of increasing convergence toward lower inflation during the 1980s is consistent with this argument. In this view, the asymmetry of the EMS was an intentional scheme to allow for macroeconomic convergence among its member states.[9]

There are, however, a number of caveats to the argument that the EMS served as an intentional disciplining device.[10] First of all, while German policymakers preferred discipline, they helped to design the EMS as a fairly flexible exchange rate regime. As pointed out in the previous chapter, over the first eight years of the EMS's existence, there prevailed a consensus that realignments constituted an acceptable adjustment mechanism. Increasing convergence during the 1980s facilitated the emergence of a more rigid understanding of the ERM. Second, while Germany insisted forcefully that its own domestic policies were not subject to any bargaining among the EMS participants, it did not necessarily force the others to adopt the same policy priorities. Rather, German policymakers were willing to accommodate the concerns of weak currency countries as long as this did not compromise their own domestic policies. As mentioned earlier, Germany made numerous concessions to weak currency countries on questions of exchange rate changes and rules for financing facilities. Third, convergence to lower inflation was equally pronounced in many non-EMS countries (e.g., de Grauwe 1994). This leads to the conclusion that the convergence during the second half of the 1980s resulted more from domestic policy decisions in the weak currency countries than from a direct influence of the EMS. Convergence could not have been successful if it had been based solely on external pressures. While reference to the "imposed" nature of disinflationary policies may help to dispel domestic costs, the policy itself can succeed only if policymakers establish domestic credibility for their policies (e.g., Burdekin, Westbrook, and Willett 1994; Woolley 1991). Thus, the greater degree of policy consensus during the second half of the 1980s seems much more basic than German dominance for explaining progress toward convergence in the EMS. In other words, it is more compelling to interpret EMS asymmetry as systemic rather than as intentional.

Standard Setting

Chapter 2 argued that one of the basic requirements for successful monetary cooperation is macroeconomic consistency among the members of an exchange rate regime. Theoretically speaking, there are potentially infinite reference points to achieve consistency. However, abstract guidelines for choosing among these reference points do not exist. Optimum currency area theory, for example, does not specify clear thresholds. Ultimately, the coordination problem involved in establishing consistency requires an explicitly *political* solution. I argue in this section that the

solution for the context of European monetary politics can
best be described as standard setting.

The basic logic of standard setting is rather simple.
Ultimately, standard setting rests on the distribution of
power among all participants. The player with the
strongest leverage in the issue area is least likely to be
willing to compromise its own domestic economic standard
and is most likely in a position to impose it as the system's
reference point. At first this does not say anything about
any inherent quality of this standard. The standard often
may not reflect the preferences of other partner states, and
it may easily remain controversial. Nevertheless, standard
setting can be an effective tool to solve an oftentimes
intractable coordination dilemma. It removes a major item
from the bargaining agenda. In other words, standard
setting ultimately reduces policy conflict by virtue of providing an unambiguous focal point for the consistency
objective.[11]

Initially we can interpret the standard-setting logic in
the European context simply as a reflection of Germany's
refusal to accept any other standard than its own. Strong
currency countries that are satisfied with their own macroeconomic performance and that are in a position to achieve
their goals largely through unilateral means have very
little incentive to accept any other standard than their own.
As indicated earlier, surplus countries are in position to
choose their mode of adjustment under much fewer constraints than weak currency countries. Thus, strong currency countries have little inclination to accept any
exchange rate rules that would encroach upon their domestic priorities. They control a credible "exit threat" in monetary negotiations and cannot be easily excluded from a
monetary regime. All else being equal, the strongest actor
will set the standard for the system.[12]

While this description so far depicts a simple interaction among players with different interests, there is a more
systematic way of describing the basic standard-setting
logic. This is the N-1 or redundancy problem. As Robert
Mundell (1968: 195) puts it:

The combined balance-of-payments surpluses of the surplus countries exactly matches the balance-of-payments deficits of all the deficit countries, since the global balance (when asymmetrical treatment of gold or other reserve assets is avoided) is zero. This means that if each country has a distinct instrument to control its balance-of-payments there is an additional degree of freedom. Only n-1 independent balance-of-payments instruments are needed in an n-country world because equilibrium in the balances of n-1 countries implies equilibrium in the balance of the nth country. The redundancy problem is the problem of deciding how to utilize the extra degree of freedom.

Technically speaking, Mundell distinguishes between two elements here: the nth country problem and the redundancy issue. According to the nth country problem, it is impossible for all countries to choose their exchange rate autonomously, since there are only N-1 independent exchange rates in a world of N currencies. In a system of N currencies, one country is unable to choose its exchange rate. Thus, a currency system needs an nth country that remains passive in setting its exchange rate. Its currency would serve as the numeraire and intervention currency of the system. The Bretton Woods system solved this problem explicitly by selecting the dollar as the center currency. Neither the Snake nor the EMS, however, ever selected an official nth country. The formal symmetry of these exchange rate systems precluded such a solution. The ECU served as the official numeraire for the EMS, and the dollar remained the primary intervention currency in the EMS until the late 1980s. In this sense, Germany's pivotal role in European exchange rate cooperation is not that of an "official" nth country.

Instead, Germany emerged as the central country in the Snake and the EMS because of its status as the principal strong currency country among the larger EU member states. Technically speaking, Germany solved the second aspect in Mundell's original formulation of the problem, namely, the redundancy problem. Because there were no explicit rules for standard setting in the Snake and EMS, the strong currency country emerged as the de facto standard setter. Since Germany did not face a reserve constraint, it had more leeway to choose its preferred option of adjustment. Thus, it controlled the one free monetary policy instrument in the Snake and the EMS. The deutsche mark served as the "anchor" or focal point for the system. Since the other countries need to maintain their domestic policies consistent with their exchange rate target, Germany is free to pursue its own domestic objectives. In other words, it sets the macroeconomic standard for the other members of the system. Following common usage, I will use the term *nth country* in subsequent discussions to describe Germany's role in solving the redundancy problem in European monetary cooperation.

The irony of the nth currency solution is that it represents at the same time the selfish interests of the center country and a cooperative solution to the consistency problem in monetary cooperation. A reliable and stable focal point eases the bargaining problems that would exist in the absence of leadership. Thus, the self-interested policies of the center country provide a fixed point in a universe of potentially infinite reference points. Using the term *hegemonic power,* Benjamin Cohen (1977: 221) summarizes this interplay of self-interest and cooperative solution in the following manner:

> The principal right of the hegemonic power is to be formally freed from all balance-of-payments constraints. The rationale for hegemony as an organizing principle is that it thus reduces the risk of policy conflict between states through the willingness of the hegemonic power to play the passive, nth-country role in the adjustment process: with only n-1 countries setting independent external financial targets, the redundancy problem is avoided and consistency in monetary relations can be ensured.

Occasionally, Germany's inability to control fully the exchange rate decisions of its partner countries is seen as a weakness of Germany's position within the EMS (e.g., Smith and Sandholtz 1995; Cameron 1993: 64). In particular, Germany was clearly incapable of securing an early revaluation of the deutsche mark after reunification or a realignment in advance of the September 1992 crisis in the EMS. In each case, other member states rejected German demands for exchange rate changes. This "weakness," however, is the logical consequence of Germany's standard setting role. Leaving aside for a moment the particular realignment rules of the EMS, Germany, as the country controlling the free policy instrument in the system, is supposed to leave exchange rate decisions to its partner countries.

Ironically, one can even argue that the particular EMS rules on exchange rate changes have actually *increased* Germany's leverage over the exchange rate decisions of its partner countries, compared to the pure N-1 logic. Since EMS rules prescribe multilateral negotiations over realignments, Germany participates fully in negotiations over exchange rate decisions. Thus, it has frequently been in position to exert pressure for policy changes in other member states in exchange for a realignment. Under the conditions of an N-1 problem, the rule for multilateral decision making must necessarily increase asymmetry in an exchange rate system because it allows the nth country both to pursue its domestic policies without balance-of-payments constraints *and* to have a say in the pegging decisions of other member states (and ultimately the domestic policy decisions of other countries). In order to avoid an asymmetric solution to the N-1 problem in the EMS, it would have been necessary to multilateralize the coordination of economic policies. Without it, a multilateral procedure only for exchange rate changes had to be counterproductive for the goal of greater symmetry.

Clearly, other EMS members have objected to these asymmetric features of the EMS. From their perspective, Germany's standard-setting role may look more abusive than cooperative. In particular, the EMS crisis of 1992/93 revealed a lack of consensus in this respect. Nevertheless, there are inherent limitations to a complete abuse of the nth country role. For monetary cooperation to be stable, the nth country has to exercise its one degree of freedom in a fashion that other participants perceive as responsible and legitimate (Cohen 1977: 225–33; Gilpin 1987: 73). Responsibility implies that the nth country does not create intolerable externalities for the other members of the system. In other words, a "leader must truly be stabilizing, imparting neither inflationary nor recessionary impulses to the rest of the world" (Cohen 1977: 225). Because the center country provides the macroeconomic focal point for the monetary system, part of the responsibility criterion is that its domestic economic policies have to be stable and reasonably predictable. During the 1980s Germany fulfilled this criterion to a significant degree. While the growth performance under the EMS was not necessarily fully satisfactory for all member states, German monetary policies provided a stable inflation performance around which the other member states could pursue their own policy priorities.

Only responsible policies create the legitimacy that is required for the maintenance of cooperation. As Robert Gilpin (1987: 73) has phrased it, "leadership is based on a general belief in its legitimacy at the same time that it is constrained by the need to maintain it." Standard setting can be successful only as long as the followers deem that standard to be legitimate. Once the standard setter creates externalities unacceptable to its partners, cooperation becomes fragile. Clearly, the freedom from balance-of-payments constraints that characterizes the nth country can backfire. It *can* pursue policies that destabilize the system. In the wake of reunification Germany's standard lost legitimacy as the Bundesbank raised interest rates to fight the inflationary consequences of reunification, thereby aggravating recessions in the other EMS member states. The EMS turmoil of 1992/93 underscores the importance of the legitimacy criterion. With the loss in perceived legitimacy, cooperation in the EMS had become fragile to such a degree that some major countries left the arrangement, and core rules had to be changed.

While the issues surrounding German reunification were certainly dramatic and highly visible, these developments were actually preceded by a more incremental and concealed process of challenging Germany's legimitacy as the leader of the EMS, namely, the increasing macroeconomic convergence during the second half of the 1980s in particular between France and Germany. Since Germany's status was more the result of its monetary policy rather than its preponderance in resources, the narrowing of the gap between French and German monetary policies called into question the legitimacy of the existing asymmetry between the two countries. A durable convergence of German and French macroeconomic preferences would make Germany's standard-setting role politically unsustainable in the long run (Matthes 1988). In other words, macroeconomic convergence provided greater legitimacy for a more symmetric solution to the redundancy problem and served as a major impetus to the pursuit of EMU in the Maastricht Treaty. Thus, in this case it was not the policy of the leader that created legitimacy problems, but rather the very success of the EMS. Policy convergence and continued monetary asymmetry between France and Germany, however, were inconsistent and carried the danger of political instability in the long run. Under these conditions a monetary union that establishes formal symmetry but follows basic German policy priorities was preferable to a politically unstable EMS even from the German perspective.

A *monetary union* obviously does not have a redundancy problem in the technical sense described here. Nevertheless, the basic idea of standard setting does not vanish once states join in a currency union such as EMU. To avoid policy conflict, the members of a monetary union must pursue policies in those areas that they still control (such as fiscal policies or possibly wage and price policies) that are consistent with each other and follow a common standard. To assure long-run stability, such a standard must be jointly established by the member states. Without a credible commitment by each member state to common macroeconomic principles, a monetary union would most likely fall apart—even if the exit costs are higher than for a pegged exchange rate system.

Thus, EMU obviously requires more joint policymaking to establish consistency than the EMS. However, the term *standard setting* still describes two major aspects of Germany's role within the EMU process. Most important, Germany served as a "constitutional architect" for the design of EMU. German insistence on strong convergence criteria and the independent status of the eventual European Central Bank explains these central rules of the Maastricht Treaty for the operation of EMU. While other EU members initially had different preferences, the need to secure a German commitment left them little choice but to accept these demands. Second, some degree of asymmetry in the policymaking process continued in the initial stages of full monetary union and is likely to persist for the short-term future. This outcome was in part quite deliberate because one of the immediate goals of EMU was to transfer the credibility of the Bundesbank to the ECB. European monetary officials attempt to guard against any appearance of differences in opinion between Bundesbank and ECB officials, practically ensuring that Bundesbank officials are informally in a privileged position during the early phase of the ECB's operation. With respect to the fiscal criteria, Germany has a strong role in enforcing the rules of EMU.

However, in the long run, such asymmetry would be detrimental to the enduring stability of the monetary union. Over time, it would have to give way to the joint standard setting of all EMU members. Such joint leadership, however, is difficult to establish. In particular, it may require much stronger coordination of fiscal policies than is at this point anticipated in the Maastricht Treaty. The Maastricht design of centralizing monetary policy at the European level and of keeping responsibility for fiscal policies with the individual member states builds into EMU a potential policy conflict between the ECB and the member states (e.g., Obstfeld 1998).

Since member states would forego any chance of using monetary policy, the incentive to use fiscal policies to satisfy the demands of their constituencies could increase (Harden 1993). Germany's push for a "stability pact" was designed precisely to address this problem and to strengthen the weak fiscal enforcement rules of the Maastricht Treaty. The fact that there does not exist a clear relationship between a European constituency and a European government further exacerbates this issue. Since the governments of the individual member states remain the only legitimate representatives of their constituencies, the European Central Bank can easily become isolated in a legitimacy vacuum with no clearly defined constituency.[13] Under these conditions, further political integration may indeed become an important part for the development of joint leadership within EMU.

Bargaining Concessions

Standard setting solves significant cooperation problems in an environment that has theoretically infinite reference points. Nevertheless, alone it is insufficient to establish cooperation. German insistence on safeguarding its own domestic macroeconomic priorities could have easily produced deadlock in monetary negotiations. It is, thus, necessary to address a second aspect of German bargaining behavior in European monetary negotiations, namely, the willingness of German policymakers to make concessions on issues that did not concern core questions of standard setting. While these concessions may seem insignificant and often merely symbolic compared to the German-centered standard-setting logic, they were nevertheless important to finding a zone of agreement among the EU member states on the EMS and the Maastricht Treaty.

As argued in chapter 2, negotiations over pegged exchange rate systems have a much broader area of potential compromise than negotiations over monetary unions.

In particular, a pegged exchange rate regime allows participants to trade off concessions between rules for internal and external adjustment, as well as financing. This possibility was crucial for obtaining a consensus in the EMS negotiations. In exchange for preserving their own domestic priorities, German policymakers were willing to compromise on issues of exchange rate changes and financing provisions. They agreed to more flexible rules on fluctuation margins, and strong currency countries often permitted realignments that would allow weak currency countries to save face. With respect to the financing rules of the EMS, the Germans gave ground on three particular sets of questions, namely, the length of borrowing periods, the quotas of short- and medium-term financing aid, and the repayment conditions for financing assistance. Despite the fact that none of these concessions hurt the pursuit of German domestic objectives, none of them was trivial from the standpoint of the weak currency countries. They were designed to partially protect their hard currency reserves, to provide greater credibility in financial markets, and to enlarge the breathing space for governments.

These compromises allowed the Europeans to establish some form of common ground for cooperation in the EMS. With respect to EMU, this task was much more difficult. Since a monetary union makes it impossible for players to shift bargaining to issues of external adjustment and financing, the crucial issue becomes the macroeconomic standard that should govern the union. German unwillingness to compromise its domestic priorities for the sake of a monetary union severely restricts its ability to concede on any really meaningful bargaining issues.

This situation differs notably from the agreement on the German Monetary Union (GMU). During the GMU negotiations, West Germany did assume a significant part of the domestic costs, in terms of higher inflation, greater budget deficits, and larger transfer payments to East Germany. Within the European context, however, these kinds of concessions were unlikely. As yet there does not exist a similarly high political priority as German reunification on the European level to facilitate such compromises. Throughout the EMU negotiations, Germany insisted that the rules governing EMU membership and EMU policies should reflect German preferences, from the independent political status of the European Central Bank to the convergence rules. Indeed, this bargaining position corresponds to the attempt of German policymakers to sell EMU domestically as the extension of the German monetary order to the rest of Europe.

Despite these limits on the building of compromise, German concessions on some EMU issues have been crucial for the success of the Maastricht negotiations. Clearly, Germany's participation is the cornerstone of the EMU project. Without German entry into EMU, the project would have had little credibility. The pivotal act of creating successful monetary integration, therefore, was the German decision to commit itself to participation in EMU. This was already visible in the negotiations at Maastricht. Chancellor Kohl's concession to accept a definitive timetable for moving toward a common currency (the so-called automaticity clause) helped to forge a positive bargaining outcome. It also underscored Germany's commitment and gave credibility to the project. In addition it was a necessary signal to interested states that the costs of adjustment to meet the Maastricht convergence criteria would ultimately be rewarded through membership in EMU.

Bundesbank Independence and German Monetary Power

One of the underlying assumptions in this chapter has been that Germany's status as the principal strong currency country in Europe was the primary cause for its ability to exercise leverage over the rules of monetary cooperation. Probably the most important competing claim against this argument is that German monetary power in Europe is not so much due to its balance-of-payments position, but rather to the role and independence of the German central bank, the Bundesbank, as the primary driving force for the patterns of exchange rate cooperation in Europe.[14] I agree fundamentally with the assertion that the Bundesbank is a crucial player in German and European monetary relations. Its role may singlehandedly explain many important aspects of European exchange rate cooperation. However, ultimately the *primary* explanation for Germany's leverage and its ability to shape the rules for monetary cooperation in Europe rests on its balance-of-payments position. The Bundesbank contributes to it but does not cause the pattern of bargaining in European monetary relations. In this section, I will briefly explain how the role of the Bundesbank might help us understand certain phenomena in European monetary politics. Then I will elaborate why Germany's status as a strong currency country is a more fundamental explanation for Germany's role in European monetary bargaining than the role of the Bundesbank.

First, the Bundesbank is clearly a central actor in European monetary politics because its policies have shaped macroeconomic conditions and policies in Germany. Indeed, the Bundesbank may be the most important cause for Germany's strong currency country position to begin with. Without Bundesbank independence and its vigorous inflation-fighting record, Germany may have never achieved its position in Europe's balance-of-payments hierarchy. The validity of this alleged causal connection is not directly at stake in this book. My argument is simply based on the fact that Germany *is* a strong currency country regardless of whether Bundesbank independence or other factors have caused that condition.[15] This book investigates the bargaining implications that result from divergent balance-of-payments positions. For that particular question, Germany's status as a strong currency country is primary, the independence of the Bundesbank secondary.

Another important way in which the Bundesbank shapes European monetary politics is by influencing the bargaining objectives German policymakers seek in European monetary negotiations. In many instances, Bundesbank officials themselves participate directly in the negotiations. For example, the central bank governors of the EU member states comprised the Delors Committee, charged with preparing a proposal for EMU. Similarly, Bundesbank President Pöhl used his position as the chairman of the Committee of Central Bank Governors effectively to advance Bundesbank proposals during the Maastricht process. However, the fact that Bundesbank officials are powerful players in European monetary relations does not so much reflect the fact that they are independent from governmental control. Rather their power in the EU institutional framework rests primarily on the fact that they are representatives of the principal strong currency country in Europe. Simply speaking, the Bundesbank would be far less powerful in international negotiations if it were the representative of a weak currency country, no matter how independent its political status. The importance of Germany's central bank is the result of the fact that the Bundesbank is a strong domestic player within the principal strong currency country in Europe. Within international negotiations, the Bundesbank owes its bargaining power to the fact that it represents a strong currency country and not to its independent political status.

Bundesbank officials may be in an even more powerful role within the domestic German decision-making process itself. When German officials negotiate the terms of monetary cooperation, they are clearly constrained by the ability of the Bundesbank to "veto" potential bargaining concessions. Viewed from the perspective of two-level-game analysis, Bundesbank independence creates "smaller win sets" for the German government in international monetary negotiations (Putnam 1988). Because they face potential "ratification" problems, German government officials have only limited room to compromise. Thus, reference to the domestic role of the Bundesbank allows German policymakers to influence bargaining outcomes heavily in their favor (Heisenberg 1994; Loedel 1994; Wolf and Zangl 1996). The Bundesbank is the crucial "ratifier" of any agreement. One particular variation of the argument even asserts that the special role of the Bundesbank within domestic

German politics is the cause for Germany's nth country role in the EMS—in the sense that the Bundesbank was the European player to commit most credibly to its preferred outcome (Oatley 1997).

Clearly, in this role the Bundesbank contributes to Germany's bargaining advantage. As an important domestic constraint, it helps the government to draw a bottom line and forces other participants to make more meaningful concessions. However, this line of argument also has significant analytical problems and is clearly not the primary explanation for German leverage and the logic of monetary bargaining in Europe. First of all, the two-level games argument has a tendency to overdraw conflicts between the Bundesbank and the federal government. The underlying assumption is often that German government officials would have been more accommodating in European monetary negotiations if it were not for the domestic role of the Bundesbank. The primary examples in this context are Chancellor Helmut Schmidt's early comments on the construction of the EMS, which seem to indicate a greater willingness to accept the demands of weak currency countries for more symmetry in the new regime (e.g., Heisenberg 1999; Kaltenthaler 1997, 1998; Oatley 1997). According to this interpretation, only Bundesbank pressure during the course of the negotiations forced the government to insist on typical patterns of German standard-setting.

While two-level games perspectives provide a useful counterweight to unitary actor assumptions, they also tend to create too dualistic a notion of the domestic policymaking process in Germany. Although this book does not follow this conceptual route any further, it is worthwhile pointing out that German monetary policymaking is often too complex to be divided neatly into clearly identifiable camps. Even the Bundesbank is by no means a homogeneous actor, and neither are the government, political parties, and other relevant actors in this policy arena. There are significant opportunities for cross-cutting alliances between various players. Dualistic conceptions of conflict between Bundesbank and federal government would miss this complex interaction. Moreover, Bundesbank positions on international monetary cooperation have shown signs of change over time (Heisenberg 1999).

Beyond this complexity, however, it is also noteworthy that there has existed a broad anti-inflationary consensus in Germany beyond specific institutional or societal affiliations. The Bundesbank can count on many important societal support groups in its anti-inflationary stance. Also, government and Bundesbank officials, despite their differences over details, have consistently advocated positions that reflect the interests of a strong currency country during crucial international monetary negotiations.[17] This holds true even for the EMS negotiations, where—except for a few early Schmidt statements—the positions of involved governmental officials, such as Schulmann, Matthöfer, or Lambsdorff, did not significantly deviate from official Bundesbank positions. Even if Schmidt would not have had to contend with the Bundesbank, he surely would have faced problems within his own cabinet (not to mention with other domestic political and societal players). The core point of this discussion is that *overall, intra-German differences pale by comparison to the conflict of interest between strong and weak currency countries in the EU.* Emphasis on Bundesbank-government conflicts may yield results to answer certain questions. For the question at hand, however, the contrast between strong and weak currency countries has greater explanatory power than intra-German bargaining.

Two-level game perspectives reveal less about Germany's leverage in European monetary bargaining than an emphasis on Germany's status as a strong currency country. A counterfactual scenario may help to illustrate the point: Would Germany's leverage in European monetary politics be equally strong if it were a weak currency country but would still possess an independent central bank (i.e., maintaining the condition of "smaller win sets")? Presumably, Germany's bargaining position and leverage would be quite different. The contrast to Italy is revealing for answering this question. While the Italian

central bank progressively received greater policy autonomy since the 1970s (Goodman 1992), Italy's leverage in
European monetary politics hardly improved as a result of
this domestic process.

Support for this assertion also comes from the contrast
in French and Italian leverage. French demands for a more
symmetrical monetary system were taken more seriously
during the late 1980s than in earlier periods primarily
because of the improvement in the French balance-of-
payments position and not because of any institutional
change in France. The French central bank remained government-controlled until after the ratification of the Maastricht Treaty, while French leverage to put EMU at least
onto the agenda increased simply due to the success of
French disinflation. Thus, balance-of-payments positions
explain a greater portion of the bargaining logic in European monetary politics than the institutional characteristic
of central bank independence.

Similarly, the Bundesbank is not the primary cause for
Germany's nth country role in the EMS or its role as the
constitutional architect for Maastricht's EMU rules.
Germany assumed these roles essentially because of its
status as a strong currency country. Arguing again coun-
terfactually, as a weak currency country Germany would
not have been in position to serve as the standard setter for
European monetary politics, even with an independent
central bank. Oatley's (1997) assertion that the Bundesbank solved the N-1 problem because it was in position to
commit most credibly to its preferred outcome (and therefore tie the hands of other players) overlooks the more fundamental causal connection at stake here. The argument
begs the question why any one of the other players should
have taken the Bundesbank's "exit threat" seriously. For
example, no matter how credibly the British government
would have committed itself to its own goals, any eventual
British "exit threat" lacked the German leverage. Ultimately, both the EMS and the EMU were conceivable
without British membership. However, Germany's exit

threat was effective because European monetary cooperation was not feasible without participation of its principal
strong currency country.

Conclusion

Germany is neither a hegemon nor does it exercise
dominance in a unidirectional sense in European monetary
affairs. Rather its specific role is best described as leadership through standard setting. It has served both as the
nth country in the Snake and EMS and as the principal
constitutional architect for the Maastricht accord on monetary union. German policymakers have complemented this
standard-setting role with occasional concessions in related
areas that did not affect German domestic macroeconomic
priorities—namely, external adjustment, financing, and
side payments. While the Bundesbank is an integral part of
the German bargaining strategy, it is not the primary
driving force for the pattern of bargaining in European
monetary politics. Rather, its position as the principal
strong currency country in Europe has been the most
important source for Germany's bargaining leverage.

4

The Failure of European Monetary Cooperation during the 1960s: The Case of the Commission's Action Programme

The EU Commission's 1962 *Action Programme for the Second Stage* represents the first major attempt at monetary cooperation and integration within the European Community. This proposal—occasionally also referred to as "Hallstein Initiative" after the then-president of the EU Commission, Walter Hallstein—advocated the stabilization of exchange rates within the Community and fixing them permanently in a monetary union by 1970 at the latest. Overall, the Commission's attempt to create closer monetary cooperation failed. None of the Action Programme's original objectives were implemented. The only measurable result of the Hallstein Initiative was the establishment of the Committee of Central Bank Governors.

This chapter examines the discussions over the proposed rules for eventual monetary cooperation in the Action Programme. The guiding questions are the following: Did the conflict between weak and strong currency countries already shape the discussions of the Action Programme? Did Germany already play a pivotal role in this episode of the 1960s? And, does the experience of the Action Programme shed some light on later monetary developments in the EU from the 1970s to the 1990s?

At first sight, the analysis of European monetary cooperation during the 1960s may seem a relatively unproductive exercise. Clearly, incentives for the EU member states to pursue monetary union were fairly insignificant. The EU Commission was the primary driving force behind the proposals of the Action Programme. The member states themselves showed little support, and the public reaction in Germany to the Action Programme was in part openly hostile. International circumstances did not favor monetary unification either. Except for the 1961 deutsche mark and guilder revaluations, the Bretton Woods regime appeared quite stable until the latter part of the 1960s. The functioning global monetary framework reduced incentives for the Western Europeans to pursue separate monetary cooperation.

Despite these caveats, analyzing the fate of the Action Programme reveals important insights into the politics of monetary cooperation in the EU. The debate on the Action Programme exhibits various elements that recurred in later episodes of European monetary politics. Some of the incentives for monetary cooperation the Commission saw in proposing the Action Programme remained relevant for later attempts and increased over time. The debate over the Action Programme also revealed a pattern of monetary politics strikingly similar to that in later periods. During the early 1960s, the EU member states started to split apart into strong and weak currency countries. Strong currency countries expressed this emerging split by developing a position on monetary integration that a decade later in the context of the Werner Report negotiations would become known as the "economist" viewpoint. As the discussion of the chapter will further demonstrate, already during the 1960s German policymakers insisted that the German macroeconomic standard must serve as the focal point for monetary cooperation in Europe.

Thus, the analysis of the Action Programme in this chapter reveals and underscores the significant degree of continuity that has characterized the quest for European monetary cooperation since the early 1960s. The Action

Programme represents the starting point for the unique pattern of monetary politics in Europe that became even more evident in the decades that followed this episode.

Historical Overview

During the early 1960s, the members of the European Community started debating the agenda for European integration after the completion of the customs union. One of the main steps envisioned in these discussions was closer monetary cooperation among the six EU member states. In addition to various governmental officials and other individuals participating in the debate,[1] the European Parliament produced a major report in favor of monetary cooperation (van Campen Report), and it passed a resolution for a common monetary policy.[2] Most important, however, among all these initiatives was the Commission's Action Programme for the Second Stage (Commission of the European Communities 1962). Unlike the European Parliament, which had only severely limited political influence, the Commission was at least in a position to put the issue of European monetary cooperation onto the agenda of EU Council meetings.[3] While most aspects of the Commission's Action Programme failed in the end, one can attribute the one small step taken to greater monetary cooperation during this period—the establishment of the Committee of Central Bank Governors—directly to the proposals of the Commission.

In advocating closer monetary cooperation, the Commission attempted to fill a perceived gap in the Treaty of Rome (Commission 1962: #130). The "Treaty establishing the European Economic Community" did not set up any specific rules and procedures for monetary cooperation among its member countries (European Communities 1978). It did, however, include a number of articles that addressed balance-of-payments issues in very general terms. Article 104 stated as a broad principle, "Each Member State shall pursue the economic policy needed to ensure the equilibrium of its overall balance-of-payments and to maintain confidence in its currency, while taking care to ensure a high level of employment and a stable level of prices." Furthermore, Article 107 stipulated, "Each Member State shall treat its policy with regard to rates of exchange as a matter of common concern." Moreover, the treaty established the Monetary Committee as an advisory body to the Council and Commission (Art. 105). It consists of two representatives from each of the member states (usually one from the government and one from the central bank) and two officials of the EU Commission (European Communities 1979: 9–11). The treaty also promoted the idea of mutual assistance among the member states in case of balance-of-payments difficulties (Art. 108). However, almost retreating from its modest proposals, the treaty also allowed states to take any measures they deemed appropriate in the case of balance-of-payments emergencies (Art. 109).

Thus, while the Treaty of Rome was very specific about the elimination of trade barriers, its monetary provisions remained vague.[4] Most important, the treaty did not specify particular rights and obligations. Hence, the degree to which the Treaty of Rome could serve as a basis for monetary cooperation among its member states was limited. In the view of the Commission, however, the Common Market could not be fully realized without a common monetary policy. According to this perspective, the Treaty of Rome provided a somewhat insufficient basis for the achievement of the Common Market. The Commission sought to rectify this deficiency in its Action Programme.

The most important trigger mechanism for the Action Programme was the 5 percent revaluation of the German deutsche mark and the Dutch guilder in 1961. These revaluations indicated a number of problems in European integration that could possibly be addressed by tighter monetary cooperation. First and foremost, the 1961 revaluations questioned the long-term stability of exchange rates under the Bretton Woods system, and many policymakers viewed growing exchange rate instability as a possible danger to the two primary achievements of the EU at the time, namely, the customs union and the Common Agricultural Policy. As the Action Programme (#128) succinctly stated: "Any major modification (in exchange rates) would so much upset the trade of countries no longer protected by any customs barrier, and because of the guaranteed Community intervention price for grain and other basic agricultural products, would cause such sudden changes in prices of farm products and therefore in farm incomes also, that the Common Market itself could be imperiled."

Exchange rate movements could conceivably compel member states to reintroduce tariffs or nontariff barriers that had been eliminated within the EU (Giscard d'Estaing 1962). Even Karl Blessing (1964:171), then Bundesbank President, accepted this rationale for European monetary cooperation: "Flexible exchange rates are essentially hostile to integration. If you want integration you must want fixed exchange rates." Blessing argued that flexible exchange rates could potentially endanger the reductions in customs duties obtained within Europe—an achievement that reflected most notably German free trade interests. Similarly, Leonhard Gleske (1964:5), at that time president of the regional central bank in Bremen and a member of the Bundesbank Council, acknowledged: "Without economic and monetary cooperation the danger could arise that one or the other member state would take measures to protect itself against unwelcome consequences of the economic policies of its partners—measures that could call into question the current level of integration." Following this line of argument, monetary cooperation was supposed to secure the trade and investment gains already realized through the customs union.

According to the prevailing view at the time, currency instability could negatively affect the Common Agricultural Policy (CAP) in the sense that any change of parities would result in differential prices of agricultural products and farm incomes among the EU countries.[5] Since the CAP rested on fixed prices for agricultural products, exchange rate changes would produce serious imbalances in agricultural markets between the European countries. A devaluation would unilaterally favor the farmers of that particular country over its competitors, and it would encourage overproduction and facilitate inflation. Conversely, a revaluation would penalize the farmers of the strong currency country. Overall, it was conceivable that exchange rate instability could lead to a renationalization of agricultural policies to protect the various national price and wage levels. The introduction of border taxes after various exchange rate changes in the late 1960s (Kruse 1980: 102) and of the monetary compensatory amounts (MCAs) in 1971 ("Regulation (EEC) No 974/71 of the Council" in: European Communities 1979: 149–52) were indeed steps taken partially to divide the common agricultural market.

The second major problem in European integration revealed by the 1961 revaluation decisions was the lack of common decision-making and macroeconomic coordination in the EU. Despite the provision of the Treaty of Rome for handling exchange rate changes as matters of common concern, Germany and the Netherlands acted unilaterally without prior consultation in EU institutions. Given the intensifying interdependence in the EU, unilateral decision making became increasingly problematic (European Economic Community 1962: 9). From the European Communities' standpoint, the threat of economic spill-over strengthened the case for greater macroeconomic coordination among its members (e.g. European Economic Community 1965: 5–8). A few years later, the Italian balance-of-payments crisis of 1963 and 1964 underscored the same point. It was the first crisis that clearly pointed to severe internal European imbalances. Unlike the 1961 crisis, which manifested itself in capital movements between non-EU and EU countries, the Italian balance-of-payments crisis led to large money flows within the EU itself. Despite the intra-European character of the crisis, there was no common European solution. Instead it required American and IMF intervention. Thus, the crisis underscored the need for greater EU policy coordination. Speculative inflows of Italian lira into Germany ultimately strengthened even German interests in closer European monetary cooperation. In particular, it resulted in German support for the creation of the Committee of Central Bank Governors.

Coordination and common policymaking problems were bound to become even more important with the anticipated enlargement of the EU. During the early 1960s, the EU engaged in serious negotiations with Great Britain over EU membership. In proposing its Action Programme, the Commission sought to provide an effective framework for such an expansion (Dyson 1994: 69). Primarily, the Commission attempted to guard against the loss of momentum that would otherwise occur with British entry into the EU (Camps 1966). Interestingly, however, the Commission's agenda was self-defeating by working at cross-purposes to the member states. For its part, the French government— hesitant, if not hostile to British entry—favored monetary cooperation precisely as a deterrent to British participation in the EU, because it would render British entry more difficult (Tsoukalis 1977: 57). This rationale only further reinforced German doubts about the goal of monetary union. Favoring British entry into the EU German officials viewed it as difficult to integrate Great Britain into a monetary union because of the status of sterling as an international reserve currency and existing British balance-of-payments problems (von Falkenhausen 1963). Consequently, de Gaulle's veto of British entry in January 1963 and the ensuing political crisis in the end prevented progress on both widening and deepening.

The third major problem for European integration indicated by the 1961 revaluations was the vulnerability of intra-European exchange rates to external developments. From a joint European perspective, it was important that the primary imbalances at the basis of these revaluation decisions occurred between these respective countries and the United States (European Economic Community 1962: 9; van Ypersele and Koeune 1984: 35). Thus, the episode revealed openly that the international environment could influence European exchange rate stability even in the absence of major intra-European disequilibria. A potential benefit of European monetary cooperation could have been a unified external monetary role of the EU and greater insulation from global monetary disruptions.[6]

To some degree the U.S.-European divergences of 1961 were merely an expression of more fundamental asymmetry in the Bretton Woods system. The 1 percent margins of national currencies around the central parity of the dollar implied that the European currencies among themselves had bands of 4 percent. Thus, European currency values were, at least in theory, more stable vis-à-vis the dollar than vis-à-vis their EU partners' currencies. In reality, of course, intra-European currency parities did not fluctuate during most of the 1960s as widely as allowed by the terms of the Bretton Woods agreement. However, by establishing the dollar as the center currency of the system, Bretton Woods created an asymmetry that—while useful for the immediate post-World War II era—created an increasing sense of vulnerability for the EU members once they recovered successfully from World War II.

Given the relatively high degree of interdependence within the EU, compared to the EU's external relations, the rules of Bretton Woods created an inappropriate focal point for monetary stability within Europe. EU officials, as well as a number of national policymakers, foresaw the possibility that the dollar orientation of the international monetary system could have destabilizing consequences for intra-European economic relations. In addition to wide fluctuation margins for the European currencies, the Bretton Woods rules also strengthened the role of the U.S. dollar as the primary intervention currency even for maintaining intra-European parities. The smaller fluctuation bands of the dollar implied fewer risks in holding dollar reserves and therefore discouraged reserve use of European currencies. The Commission's proposal to create a European reserve currency attempted to address this asymmetry.

The early 1960s also witnessed the first threats to the stability of the Bretton Woods system, in particular the start of balance-of-payments problems for the United States. The late 1950s and early 1960s mark the period in which the global monetary agenda shifted from the problem of a "dollar shortage" to that of a "dollar glut" (Spero and Hart 1997: 13–16). In particular, from the German perspective, this shift enhanced the dangers of imported inflation and destabilizing capital flows (Emminger 1986). These external developments suggested that the global monetary system could not guarantee stable exchange rates at a time when the Europeans seemingly relied heavily on the Bretton Woods system to maintain intra-European exchange rate stability. While the American problems at the time were not as serious as they would be a decade later, the Monetary Committee became concerned over the consequences of this development for Europe (see e.g., European Economic Community1963: 9–11; European Economic Community 1964: 8–9). The Commission proposed closer European monetary cooperation and the creation of a European reserve currency to strengthen the European voice in international monetary relations (Commission 1962: #129).

While the Action Programme did not spell out the precise goals of monetary cooperation, it did propose a monetary union with a central decision-making institution, modeled on the Federal Reserve (#138). It envisioned a full monetary union as the aim of the third stage of the Common Market (approximately by 1970). The Action Programme acknowledged that monetary integration would also require the coordination of fiscal policies. It even went so far as to propose that the Council would determine the size and the type of financing for member states' budgets (#138).

Interestingly, the Commission did not explicitly demand that foreign currency reserves be pooled, not even in the context of its proposal for a European reserve currency. The Commission also remained vague as to whether the monetary union would require a common European currency or simply permanently fixed exchange rates. However, the general discussion on this issue indicates that the Commission most likely preferred a common European currency (e.g., Vereinsbank in Hamburg 1963; Cohen 1963: 616). In addition to these central points, the Action Programme also suggested coordination of all monetary decisions regarding the following issues during the transition period: money creation, changes in official interest rates, open market operations, and the change of exchange rates (#133).

During the following years, however, the EU made little progress in the direction of these goals. Early on, the Commission limited its proposals in a memorandum that it submitted to the Council of Finance Ministers in June 1963 (Commission of the European Communities 1963). Designed to specify further the proposals of the Action Programme, the memorandum advocated the establishment of institutions in four areas: domestic monetary policy, international monetary policy, exchange rate policies, and general fiscal policies. However, the memorandum did not even mention the more far-reaching goals of a monetary union or of a common European reserve currency. It also omitted the proposals of the Action Programme for coordination of interest rate policies and open market operations.

Nonetheless, even these limited proposals did not receive any serious attention by government officials until the Italian balance-of-payments crisis of 1964 had drastically illustrated the weakness of intra-European monetary cooperation (Balassa 1973; Tsoukalis 1977: 58). Instead of relying on its EU partners, the Italian government asked for and received help from the U.S. and the IMF to finance its balance-of-payments problems. The failure of the EU member states to act on behalf of one of its partners finally triggered greater interest in European monetary cooperation among the EU countries. Yet the actual decisions on monetary cooperation taken by the Council of Ministers on 8 May 1964 realized few of the Commission's proposals. Essentially, the only suggestion that survived fully was the establishment of the Committee of Central Bank Governors (European Communities, 1979: 13–14).

The real political implications of establishing the Committee of Central Bank Governors, however, were very small. Central bank governors had convened regularly before this attempt at institutionalization. The Council decision simply codified the preexisting practice of consultations among EU central bank governors in connection with their regular meetings at the Bank for International Settlements (BIS) in Basle (Kohler and Schlaeger 1971; and Blessing 1964: 166–67). Ironically, the formal establishment of the Committee did not even alter this particular custom: The Committee of Central Bank Governors continued to convene on the occasion of BIS meetings (and, thus, outside of EU territory) until it was dissolved and replaced by the European Monetary Institute (EMI)—the European Central Bank's predecessor—in January 1994.

All other Commission proposals were substantially weakened in the implementation process. The Council did establish a Budgetary Policy Committee and a Medium-Term Policy Committee. The regulations governing these institutions, however, were significantly less forceful than proposed by the Commission.[7] In particular, they did not represent an attempt at any serious coordination of macroeconomic policies. Instead, they became simply fora for consultations, with formal links only to the Commission but not to the national decision-making process within the member states. Moreover, despite the Council decision to consult on questions of international monetary relations, it did not establish any rules for the EU's external monetary relations within the Bretton Woods system.[8] It thus came as no surprise that the EU was unable to present a unified position on the international monetary reform negotiations in the ensuing years. And, more important, EU member states could not settle on a common European reaction to the problems and final breakdown of the Bretton Woods systems a few years later.

The second half of the 1960s was marked by little progress in the area of closer European monetary cooperation. The Monetary Committee became preoccupied with the global monetary reform negotiations, and the Commission and member states got increasingly drawn into an "agricultural mythology" (Tsoukalis 1977: 59–63). With the growing institutionalization of the Common Agricultural

Table 4.1
Chronology of the Action Programme

6/7 March 1961	Revaluation of deutsche mark and guilder by 5%
7 April 1962	van Campen Report on coordination of monetary policies within the EU
24 October 1962	Commission's Action Programme for the Second Stage
19 June 1963	Memorandum of the Commission to the Council on monetary and financial cooperation within the EU
Spring 1964	Italian balance of payments crisis; U.S. assistance for financing
8 May 1964	Council decision on Action Programme: establishment of the Committee of Central Bank Governors

Sources: Gehrmann and Harmsen 1972; Deutsche Bundesbank, *BAP*; Kruse 1980; van Ypersele and Koeune 1984.

Policy, the assumption became pervasive that exchange rate changes had become a thing of the past. Even the Monetary Committee felt that the CAP would almost automatically lead to a fixed exchange rate regime in Europe and that the European monetary situation in the mid-1960s resembled almost a *de facto* monetary union.[10] The assumption became popular that the account unit for the CAP (the "green dollar") had created a quasi single currency in the EU (Theurl 1992). Since parities remained stable until 1968, it took the major balance-of-payments crises of the late 1960s and the exchange rate changes of the French franc and the German mark in 1969 to destroy the myth and to start new initiatives in the direction of European monetary cooperation: the Werner Report and the Snake.

The Monetary Politics of the Action Programme

The most interesting aspect of the Action Programme from the perspective of this book is the fact that the internal discussion within the EU over the Action Programme was already shaped by the emerging conflict between weak and strong currency countries over the distribution of adjustment burden under a common monetary framework. In this sense, the case of the Action Programme negotiations previews elements that would become very important factors in European monetary bargaining over the coming decades. While most conventional interpretations of European monetary cooperation view the 1970s as the starting point for controversies between low- and high-inflation countries in Europe, it is noteworthy that the early 1960s had already witnessed the development of a gap between strong and weak currency countries in Europe. Inflation differentials between the members of the EU—especially between Germany on the one hand and France and Italy on the other hand—were noticeable in the late 1950s and first half of the 1960s (see table 4.2). Moreover, in addition to the 1961 revaluations of deutsche mark and guilder, the 1958 devaluation of the French franc by a large 17.5 percent margin had already indicated that the balance-of-payments positions of EU member states were moving in opposite directions (Kolodziej 1974: 192–210).

The disagreements between strong and weak currency countries also took a form that would later become a durable feature of monetary negotiations. What analysts of the Werner Report negotiations ten years later would identify as the so-called "economist" versus "monetarist" controversy actually had its origins in the discussions surrounding the Action Programme. Strong currency countries advocated an "economist" path to monetary union. According to their view, macroeconomic convergence was a precondition for monetary union. In other words, monetary unification was supposed to be the crowning achievement of economic convergence among the EU member states. Such an arrangement would allow strong currency countries to elude a macroeconomic compromise and effectively to set their own standard as the reference point for any eventual convergence. In other words, if the weak currency countries did not adjust and converge to the macroeconomic priorities of the strong currency countries, monetary union would not take place.

In contrast, the "monetarist" approach advocated early fixing of exchange rates without prior convergence. This idea included as its most important ingredient the provision of sufficient financing mechanisms. According to the

Table 4.2

Inflation Rates of EU Member States, 1958–1968

(Percentage Change of Consumer Price Index)

	1958	1959	1960	1961	1962	1963	1964	1965	1966	1967	1968
Belgium	1.2	1.2	0.4	1.0	1.4	2.2	4.0	4.1	4.3	2.9	2.6
France	15.3	5.7	4.0	2.5	5.1	5.3	3.0	2.7	2.7	2.8	4.5
Germany	2.2	0.9	1.6	2.3	3.1	3.0	2.2	3.3	3.5	1.6	1.7
Italy	2.9	-0.5	2.3	2.0	4.7	7.5	5.9	4.3	2.4	3.7	1.5
Netherlands	1.7	0.9	2.5	-0.7	2.3	3.3	5.8	5.9	5.7	3.4	3.9
United Kingdom	2.8	0.6	1.1	2.7	4.0	2.0	3.2	4.6	3.9	2.7	4.8

Source: International Monetary Fund, *International Financial Statistics*, Washington, various years: world tables.

"monetarist" perspective, a monetary union would force its members automatically to harmonize macroeconomic policies in a more symmetric fashion than under the "economist" viewpoint. Easy access to financing would allow weak currency countries partially to circumvent their reserve constraint and to inflict some adjustment costs on strong currency countries. Through mandatory interventions, low-inflation countries would be forced to reflate their economies. Thus, the common macroeconomic standard that would evolve out of a "monetarist" monetary union would be the average economic perfomance, rather than the strict stance set by the strong currency countries.

German policymakers clearly rejected bridging the emerging gap in inflation performance and balance-of-payments position through compromise. If the other European countries wanted to join Germany in a monetary union, they had to adjust to the German standard of low inflation (e.g., Meyer-Horn 1963; Blessing 1964: 162–79; Butschkau 1963: 7–9). As German policymakers stated, the foremost goal of any attempt at closer monetary cooperation had to be the promotion of disinflation in the partner countries (Krämer 1970: 4–5). EU Commissioner M. Robert Marjolin as well as the Monetary Committee corroborated German perceptions on these issues by pointing to the dangers that price developments in France and Italy had for the other EU members (*Die Welt* September 11, 1963; European Economic Community 1964: 9–10 and 15–18; and European Economic Community 1965: 5–6 and 16–19). Thus the primary rationale for any eventual monetary union from the German perspective had to be the prevention of any inflationary spillover into the strong currency countries. The goal of policy coordination and convergence had to be the reduction of inflation in Germany's partner countries (Wadbrook 1972). German central bankers rejected the notion implicit in monetarist thinking that monetary cooperation could serve as a vehicle to achieve European integration (Blessing 1963: 122–23; Troeger 1963). Rather, monetary union had to be one of the last steps in the process of European integration.[11]

From the German perspective, low inflation was the primary objective among the four macroeconomic goals of price stability, economic growth, full employment, and balance-of-payments equilibrium. Indeed, German authorities insisted that price stability was the basis for achieving any of the other macroeconomic goals (Butschkau 1963: 8). Already during the early 1960s, possible Phillips-curve gains did not play a major role in the thinking of German economic policymakers (Wadbrook 1972: 59–67). This indicated a difference in macroeconomic priorities from their partners in the EU, who were more readily inclined to use expansionary policies to stimulate their economies. Thus, under the prevailing circumstances in Europe, German policymakers saw the Commission's proposal to coordinate interest rate policies as a danger to price stability in Germany. Mere coordination without explicit macroeconomic obligations would most likely put pressures on Germany to reflate. Moreover, Bundesbank officials viewed the suggestions on coordination of interest rate policies and open market operations as technically unfeasible before the institutionalization of a European central bank (Blessing 1963: 124–25).

German monetary officials perceived the inflation differentials between France and Italy, on the one hand, and Germany, on the other hand, as an obstruction to closer European monetary cooperation. For example, Otmar Emminger, then member of the Bundesbank Council and its chief specialist for international monetary questions, noted

> that despite the observable convergence in the assessment of price stability in relation to economic growth and other goals there remain differences in the emphasis among the EU members. This is illustrated by the attitude of some of our partners toward the current inflation, which they accept much more leisurely than Germany. This attitude is unacceptable in the interest of long term stability. (As quoted in Meyer-Horn 1963: 10)

In addition, German policymakers also perceived a *political* logic behind the question of monetary cooperation and integration that resembles strikingly German positions in the Maastricht debate of the 1990s. From the German perspective, closer political integration in Europe had to accompany monetary integration. A monetary union could not function without a supporting European political structure. In Blessing's (1964: 171–72) words:

> A monetary union is conceivable only if the member countries are willing to relinquish their main sovereign rights and unite in a federal state. In other words: a common currency and a federal reserve system are conceivable only if there exist common economic, social and financial policies, even common policies in general, i.e., if there exists a federal state with a common federal government and a common parliament. . . . A European currency and a European central bank can become reality only as the result of an organic process that ends in a federal European state.

In other words, a federal reserve system alone would be unsuccessful in enforcing its policies and securing the necessary coordination of monetary policies if it were faced with divergent interests among the member states. Thus, the German position during the 1960s already exhibits patterns of typical German behavior on European monetary cooperation: the German authorities were unwilling to cooperate on terms that would compromise Germany's domestic macroeconomic standard.

Moreover, from the German perspective, the Action Programme's proposal to create financing mechanisms for the EU was dangerous and unnecessary under the prevailing circumstances (Tsoukalis 1977: 54). While special European funds and rules for financing assistance may have been desirable from the standpoint of European integration, the IMF facilities and the rules of Bretton Woods provided a sufficient basis for the needs of the EU member states. Creating more financing facilities would merely have increased money supply and the danger of inflation. Also, as the example of the Italian balance-of-payments crisis suggested, even the weak currency countries did not view the creation of European financing mechanisms as an urgent necessity.

Germany's Role in European Monetary Cooperation during the 1960s

While the previous section already examined Germany's policy stance on crucial issues raised by the Commission's Action Programme, this last section briefly examines Germany's special role in European monetary politics during the early 1960s. Much of the analysis anticipates discussions in subsequent chapters. The crucial point here is the contrast between the role Germany played in the Action Programme negotiations and those on the EMS and Maastricht EMU in later decades. Ultimately, conditions in the early 1960s did not allow Germany to play the role of a standard setter successfully. In addition, there existed little room for appropriate German concessions toward other European players in the European monetary bargaining setting.

Even during this early stage of European attempts at monetary cooperation, Germany already played an important part in the process. Its war-shattered economy had largely been rebuilt by the end of the 1950s and, most important, Germany consistently recorded one of the lowest inflation rates within Western Europe. As argued earlier, German authorities made clear that this macroeconomic standard was not subject to compromise. The goal of any eventual European monetary cooperation had to be the control of external sources of inflation. Sounding almost like a preview of German interests in the EMS during the 1980s, then-Bundesbank President Karl Blessing (1964: 162) remarked in unmistakable terms that "more integration could mean more beneficial pressure to denounce inflation, that is if there are countries that preserve their monetary discipline and force the others to acquiesce in this discipline."

The problem in achieving this goal, however, was that while Germany saw its own domestic priorities as the only acceptable standard for the system, it was not in a position to impose such a standard on its European neighbors, nor was that standard acceptable to other players. In their own evaluation, German policymakers continued to view themselves as fairly weak players in the international monetary game. This was especially true at a time when the dollar and the pound were still much more relevant reserve currencies. While the deutsche mark had gained strength within the postwar monetary system, expressed most visibly in its 1961 revaluation, its role as an international currency was still very limited. German monetary authorities even insisted that European monetary cooperation could not succeed if both the U.S. dollar and the British pound sterling were excluded (e.g. Blessing 1963: 125–26, 1964: 177).

Despite the first signs of difficulties in the American balance-of-payments position in the late 1950s and early 1960s, German-American monetary conflict remained relatively limited. German policymakers saw a replacement of the dollar as the focal point for exchange rate relations as a fairly low priority. Indeed, German authorities sided mostly with the Americans in the French-U.S. controversies over international monetary issues (Kolodziej 1974: 176–231). They tended to blame capital exports for the difficulties in the U.S. balance-of-payments and not domestic inflation (Emminger 1986). In fact, U.S. domestic performance on price stability was mostly better than Germany's, and German complaints over "imported inflation" largely reflected worries over dollar inflows. Furthermore, German monetary authorities were convinced that the American balance-of-payments situation would eventually come under control. From the German perspective, moreover, the Europeans already cooperated on monetary matters (Blessing 1964). This cooperation did not take place in a special regional European arrangement but within the framework of the global monetary system. As long as the German choice remained that between an intra-European compromise with weak currency countries or the U.S. standard under Bretton Woods, the United States provided the superior focal point. Only in the early 1970s did Germany feel confident enough to sidestep this choice altogether and to pursue its own macroeconomic objectives through floating.

Under the conditions of the early 1960s, the conflict over the appropriate macroeconomic standard was essentially a stalemate. The German authorities were not willing to compromise on any standard other than their own but lacked the ability to impose their priorities on the other EU member states. Simultaneously, weak currency countries had no bargaining leverage to force Germany into concessions on standard-setting issues.

Conclusion

The first attempt at closer monetary cooperation within the EU failed miserably. While the Europeans faced some incentives to pursue monetary integration, they were admittedly small compared to those of later periods. Nevertheless, the analysis of the fate of the Action Programme during the early 1960s reveals the development of a number of important features that would endure for more than three decades. Most consequential in terms of the long-run patterns of European monetary politics was the creation of a gap between weak and strong currency countries in Europe and the development of a distinct German policy position on monetary union that would later be called the "economist" position. Starting in the early 1960s, German insistence on setting its macroeconomic standard in any eventual European monetary arrangement became a constant feature for any future negotiations on monetary cooperation.

5

European Monetary Cooperation during the 1970s: Werner Report and Snake

Compared to the previous decade, monetary issues gained a much more prominent status on the European agenda during the 1970s. Increasing turmoil in the international monetary system and the dynamics of European integration raised incentives for monetary cooperation. EU member states initiated two closely related projects during the early part of this decade, the *Werner Report* of 1970/71 and the *Snake*, which operated between 1972 and 1979. The Werner Report envisioned a complete economic and monetary union (EMU) by the year 1980. The Snake was conceived as the first step toward monetary union and was designed to reduce exchange rate fluctuations among EU member states. Given these objectives, both attempts ended for the most part as failures. The EMU project of the Werner Report did not advance much beyond the first stage, and it did not even come close to achieving its goal of a monetary union by 1980. The Snake clearly did not achieve exchange rate stabilization for the EU as a whole. Nevertheless, the Snake did survive as a limited exchange rate regime for Germany and its small neighbors—sometimes referred to as "deutschemark zone" or "mini-Snake"—until it was dissolved into the EMS in 1979.

The context of the 1970s differs substantially from the environment in which the Commission proposed its Action

Programme in 1962. During the early 1960s, the Bretton Woods system provided a more or less stable framework. That basis became increasingly questionable in the late 1960s. And with the end of the dollar-gold exchange standard in 1971 and the breakdown of the Smithsonian Agreement in 1973, it disappeared completely. The problems of the Bretton Woods system certainly helped to trigger the European monetary initiatives. The Werner Report and the Snake were designed in part to insulate the Europeans from global monetary turmoil. Yet the basic ideas of the Werner Report were conceived when the Bretton Woods system still existed, so the breakdown of the global monetary system ultimately withdrew part of the foundation on which the Werner Report was built.

Despite these real differences, however, bargaining over the rules of monetary cooperation in the Werner Report and Snake followed the same basic logic as the politics of the Action Programme. In many ways, the conflict between strong and weak currency countries over the distribution of adjustment costs became an even more dominating force in shaping the politics of these episodes. Indeed, in retrospect, the 1970s represent the high point of the divisions introduced by divergent balance-of-payments positions into European monetary cooperation. Again, as in the case of the Action Programme, strong currency countries refused to agree on any compromise solution for rules of domestic adjustment. The Werner Report did not find any solution to circumvent this obstinate position of the strong currency countries for the construction of a monetary union. And the Snake could survive only as long as the means of external adjustment and financing provided a sufficient basis for cooperation.

Analysis of the Werner Report and Snake episodes also reveals the strong position of Germany within European monetary cooperation. Germany clearly developed into the nth country position in the Snake. Moreover, the survival of the mini-Snake of Germany and its small neighbors indicated that cooperation among the strong currency countries represented no significant political problem. Limited cooperation could survive even if the other large EU member states France, Italy, and Great Britain watched from the sidelines. This made clear that German participation was absolutely essential to any conceivable European monetary regime. The Snake episodes revealed that Germany had developed *de facto* a "veto power" for rules of monetary cooperation. Its strong currency position endowed Germany with a credible exit threat that allowed German policymakers to imprint their bottom line on the outcomes of monetary negotiations. In this sense, the Werner Report and the Snake show the continuity of bargaining among the EU member states over the rules of monetary cooperation.

Historical Overview

After the relatively quiet period between 1964 and 1968, the members of the European Community again started to debate the question of closer monetary cooperation intensively during the late 1960s.[1] As in the case of the Action Programme, it was once more the Commission of the EU that put the topic of closer monetary cooperation on the agenda. And similar to the role played by the completion of the customs union in the Action Programme, it was the achievement of another major aspect of European integration, the Common Agricultural Policy (CAP), that provided the context for the Commission to discuss the prospects of deeper European integration in the future (Peeters 1982: 5). On 12 February 1969, the Commission issued a memorandum to the Council advocating closer coordination of economic and monetary policies within the EU, the *Barre Report*—Raymond Barre being the Commission's vice president at the time (Commission of the European Communities 1969).

In terms of its rule proposals, the Barre Report advocated working toward a complete elimination of intra-European fluctuation bands (Commission of the European Communities 1969 #4). It also suggested closer coordination of short- and medium-term economic policies in order to achieve convergence among the EU member countries (Commission of the European Communities 1969 #8–23). And it recommended the establishment of a Community mechanism for short-term monetary support and medium-term financial aid (Commission of the European Communities 1969 #25–26).

At The Hague Summit in December 1969, the heads of EU governments expressed their intention to achieve closer cooperation on economic and monetary policies. They officially asked the Council of Finance Ministers to draw up a plan that would lead to the achievement of an economic and monetary union (EMU) (European Communities 1970b). This decision was the basis for the establishment of a committee "to prepare a report containing an analysis of the different suggestions and making it possible to identify the basic issues for a realization by stages of economic and monetary union in the Community" (European Communities 1970c). Within a year this study group, under the chairmanship of Pierre Werner, then the prime minister of Luxembourg, issued its "Report to the Council and the Commission on the realisation by stages of Economic and Monetary Union in the Community," the so-called Werner Report (European Communities 1970a).

Overall, the Werner Report was a fairly vague document, at least in terms of designing specific rules for monetary union. At the core of the Werner Report was the proposal to fix exchange rates irrevocably, to eliminate fluctuation margins, and to establish complete freedom of capital movements within the EU. While the report did not necessarily rule out the maintenance of national currencies (within an irrevocably fixed exchange rate regime), the Werner group clearly preferred a common European currency: "considerations of a psychological and political nature militate in favour of the adoption of a sole currency which would confirm the irreversibility of the venture" (European Communities 1970a: 10). In addition, the Werner Report proposed centralizing a number of policy areas at the Community level: liquidity creation and credit policies, rules and policies for the capital market, regional and structural policies, and consultations between the social partners at the Community level (European Communities 1970a: 12). Most important, however, the goal of EMU, according to the Werner Report, also required centralizing aspects of fiscal policies: "the essential features of the whole of the public budgets, and in particular variations in their volume, the size of balances and the methods of financing or utilizing them, will be decided at the Community level" (European Communities 1970a: 12).

Despite this insistence on centralizing certain policies at the Community level, and despite anticipating the need for a "centre of decision for economic policy" (European Communities 1970a: 12) in the Community, the Werner Report remained very vague about the future institutional framework for monetary policy within the EU. Its strategy continued to be gradualism, and it ignored completely the need for a discrete transfer of power in the area of monetary policy. Similarly, while the Werner Report advocated coordination in various aspects of nonmonetary policies (e.g., fiscal policies, structural and regional policies), it did not address the problem of coordinating the specific goals of monetary policies. Furthermore, rules for moving from one stage to the next did not exist.

Similar to the Action Programme, one important motivation for this new initiative was the idea of safeguarding the customs union and Common Agricultural Policy (Commission of the European Communities 1969 #7; Hendricks 1988; Kruse 1980: 22–25; Pearce 1983). As the late 1960s demonstrated, the customs union was by no means irreversible. To combat its rising balance-of-payments problems in 1968/69, the French government adopted selective import quotas and promoted aid to exporters. These policies violated explicit EU rules on the customs union (Kolodziej 1974: 206–8; and Münchmeyer 1968). In this sense, monetary cooperation and continued free trade within Europe seemed to be linked to each other.

Moreover, the Werner Report contended that monetary union would facilitate gains from a fully integrated market by promoting factor mobility. Evaluating the contemporary state of economic integration in the EU, the Werner Report reasoned that the "extension of the liberation of movements of capital and the realization of the right of establishment and of free rendering of services by banking and financial undertakings have not progressed far enough. The delay has been caused by the absence of sufficient coordination of economic and monetary policies" (European Communities 1970a: 8).

In this respect, the logical sequence in the Werner Report was the opposite of that which drove the Maastricht Treaty process toward EMU roughly twenty years later.[2] According to the Werner Report design, EMU should help to establish a single market. With the Single European Act (SEA) program already in progress by the late 1980s, this nexus reversed itself for the Maastricht accord. Now a monetary union could supplement and safeguard the achievements of the single market project. In other words, the conditions for a successful monetary union clearly improved from the Werner Report to the Maastricht process. Yet history has partially vindicated the argument in the Werner Report. What Werner Report and Snake did not achieve, the EMS accomplished during the 1980s. According to many observers, it is very unlikely that the EU member states would have ever ventured into the SEA program without the achievements of the EMS (Jenkins 1991; Schmidt 1990; Ungerer et al. 1990). Thus, in retrospect, the achievement of at least some modest exchange cooperation during the 1980s appears as a necessary requirement for deeper market integration in the EU.

The exchange rate instability during the last years of the Bretton Woods system, in particular the 1969 French devaluation and German revaluation, threatened the Common Agricultural Policy of the EU. According to some observers, the CAP was on the verge of a complete breakdown. Negotiations over a solution to the CAP's problems within the Council and Commission were difficult (Hallstein 1973: 144). The members of the EU finally settled on a compromise that required the other members of the EU to subsidize their agricultural exports to France at the same time as French agricultural exports were subjected to a special export tariff in order to keep the European agricultural market in equilibrium. In effect, these measures implied the (temporary) isolation of the French agricultural market from the rest of Europe (*Frankfurter Rundschau*, 13 August 1969; Tietmeyer 1969). This, of course, contradicted precisely the original intentions behind the formation of the CAP. The result underscored that monetary integration and the CAP were indeed very closely interlinked.

In addition to concerns about the CAP and customs union, incentives to use monetary cooperation as a tool for political integration became increasingly important. With exchange rates repeatedly coming under pressure, a pattern of unilateral decision making developed, without any consultations in EU institutions. This indicated a necessity to strengthen the institutional structure of the EU. Moreover, with the customs union and CAP completed by the late 1960s, the member countries of the EU were looking for further areas of integration. The EMU project appeared as a possible driving force for further political, as well as economic, integration (Kruse 1980: 54–58; Tsoukalis 1977: 82–86). From the perspective of the Commission, a common currency also had the major advantage that it could serve as a symbol of cohesion among the Europeans. And, similar to the British entry negotiations that framed the Action Programme ideas, the likelihood of increasing EU membership facilitated the political dynamics of the Werner Report ideas. With the prospect of Denmark, Great Britain, Ireland, and Norway joining the EU in the early 1970s, the Commission worried that EU expansion would lead to a loss of momentum.[3] It preferred to strengthen the institutional structures before an increase in membership would reduce the efficiency of EU decision making.

The political ramifications of EMU were particularly compelling for Germany. European integration had served as a way to avoid isolation and to integrate Germany into the West (Fratianni and von Hagen 1992: 17; Hrbek and

Wessels 1984). It was the preferred method for Germany to achieve both security and wealth. The particular circumstances of the late 1960s and early 1970s offered multiple possibilities for linking these broader political considerations with monetary cooperation. As Loukas Tsoukalis (1977: 85) observed:

> EMU was for Herr Brandt's government a preponderant political choice. The factors behind this choice were manifold and ranged from the need for a Westpolitik as a counterbalance to the government's Ostpolitik, increasing fears about the reliability of U.S. support in the future in both the political and defence fields, concerns about the state of European integration and a desire to give proofs of its "Europeanism."

External economic developments were also significant in instigating the new monetary initiative. The late 1960s saw the development of a serious—and for the Bretton Woods regime ultimately fatal—breach between the United States and Germany. Especially after the creation of the two-tier gold system in March 1968, German officials lost confidence that the United States would be able to get its balance-of-payments difficulties under control. Moreover, the spillover effects of U.S. domestic policies (Great Society Program) and the Vietnam War further eroded the legitimacy of U.S. leadership in the international monetary system. Germany was unwilling to adjust its domestic economy to these external pressures, that is, to import inflation, and thus became the primary target of speculative dollar flows. In this way, American monetary problems aggravated already existing difficulties for intra-European exchange rates and increased the European sense of vulnerability. Advocates of monetary union "stressed that whereas the member states had become *commercially* integrated with one another, *monetarily* they still communicated with and through the dollar" (Peeters 1982: 4). Under these conditions, the European countries had a general incentive to counterbalance American monetary power through joint action (Kruse 1980 42–44).

After the Werner Report was issued, the French government voiced concerns over the supranational elements in it (*Frankfurter Allgemeine Zeitung*, 16 December 1970; *Neue Zürcher Zeitung*, 20 December 1970). As a consequence, the Commission and the Council weakened the already limited institutional recommendations of the Werner Report. Nevertheless, the Council of Ministers endorsed the basic goals of the Werner Report on 22 March 1971. It also adopted a resolution calling for the realization in stages of a complete EMU by 1980. As a consequence of this decision, EMU became an official goal of the European Community. With these steps, the EU went significantly beyond the achievements of the Action Programme. One contemporary observer—the former president of the Commission, Walter Hallstein—even called the Werner Report "the most important document of European integration since the Treaties of Rome" (Hallstein 1973: 148).

To implement the Council resolution in the field of exchange rate concertation, the governors of the EU central banks decided in April 1971 to narrow the fluctuation margins for intra-EC parities to 1.2 percent. This step was scheduled for June of that year. The breakdown of the Bretton Woods system, however, prevented the start of exchange rate concertation. In May 1971, the German and Dutch governments decided to float their currencies against the dollar, after Germany had become subject to massive capital inflows.[4] While Germany proposed a joint European float of all EU currencies, France and Italy rejected such a step and maintained their peg to the dollar under Bretton Woods rules. The governments of these two countries feared that the German proposal would lead to an appreciation of the franc and lira vis-à-vis the dollar (Tsoukalis 1977: 112–19).

With these decisions, the EU member states abandoned the idea of greater exchange rate stability within Europe for a while. Only the conclusion of the Smithsonian Agreement in December 1971 made it possible for the Europeans to relaunch the ideas of the EMU project. The Smithsonian Agreement increased the margins of fluctuations vis-à-vis the dollar from 1 percent to 2.25 percent and thus the width of the band to 4.5 percent. Consequently, the width of intra-European parity bands increased to 9 percent. The Council of Ministers decided to cut this band in half—an agreement that took effect on 24 April 1972.

This step created the so-called "Snake in the tunnel." The dollar exchange rates of the European currencies would provide the ceiling and the floor (the "tunnel") in between which intra-EU exchange rates would move collectively up and down (describing the curve of a snake). One of the birth defects of the Snake was, however, that the continuing weakness of the dollar did not allow it to perform in a snakelike fashion. Instead of moving up and down around the central parity of the dollar, the Snake was consistently pushed to the ceiling of the Smithsonian tunnel (Hellmann 1979: 25–26). This situation in turn created adjustment pressures on the weaker currencies in the Snake. Within the one year of its existence, Great Britain, Ireland and Italy left the Snake in the tunnel, while Denmark left and rejoined after a few months.

After the breakdown of the Smithsonian Agreement in March 1973, the Snake lost its tunnel. At the Council meeting of 11 March, the remaining members of the Snake decided to preserve the Snake and to float jointly against the dollar. While the breakdown of the Smithsonian Agreement for the first time opened up the chance for a unique Community identity in monetary affairs, these hopes did not materialize. On the one hand, the EU member states that had left the Snake during the preceding year—Great Britain, Ireland, and Italy—did not rejoin the system. On the other hand, two nonmembers of the EU—Norway and Sweden—joined the Snake in order to find a credible peg for their currencies after the breakdown of globally fixed exchange rates. The character of the Snake as a distinct EU institution further eroded as the result of the "revolving door" policy of France. France left the Snake in January 1974, rejoined in July 1975, only to withdraw again nine months later. Without France, the Snake became essentially a "deutsche mark zone" for Germany and its smaller neighbors—sometimes also referred to as the "mini-Snake." Its identity had hardly anything to do with the Community, and decision making within the Snake moved away from EU institutions to separate fora of the Snake members. Snake members abandoned the practice of meeting in EU locations, and the EU Commission discontinued its participation in Snake meetings.

The mini-Snake survived until the remaining EU member countries joined the EMS in 1979.[5] Thus, the evaluation of the Snake's success is mixed. For the remaining members, the Snake provided a framework for a moderate degree of exchange rate concertation—although realignments within the Snake were quite frequent and fraught with controversies and disruptions. However, given its initial objectives, the Snake did not come close to fulfilling the expectations that were associated with the adoption of the Werner Plan in the early 1970s. From the perspective of the Community as a whole, the Snake was a failure. It did not bring the EU closer to the goal of monetary cooperation and integration.

The Politics of European Monetary Cooperation during the 1970s

Domestic Adjustment

The exchange rate crisis of 1968/69 was the strongest indicator of a severe divergence in the balance-of-payments positions of EU member states. Inflation rates varied dramatically between the EU member states, and weak currency countries started to develop significant current account problems. Thus, any attempt at monetary cooperation under these conditions posed a significant distributional problem: Who would bear how much of the necessary adjustment costs to establish macroeconomic consistency? Which standard could possibly serve as the appropriate reference point for macroeconomic coordination among the Europeans?

Table 5.1
A Chronology of the Werner Report and Snake

18 November 1967	Devaluation of British pound by 14.3 percent.
November 1968	Emergency meeting of Group of Ten in Bonn.
12 February 1969	Barre Report.
8 August 1969	Devaluation of French franc by 11.1 percent.
24 October 1969	Revaluation of German deutsche mark by 9.3 percent.
1–2 December 1969	The Hague Summit: decision to launch EMU.
8 October 1970	Werner Report issued.
22 March 1971	Council decision to attain EMU.
9 May 1971	Floating of deutsche mark and guilder.
15 August 1971	Suspension of dollar convertibility.
17/18 December 1971	Smithsonian Agreement.
24 April 1972	Launching of the "Snake in the tunnel"; members: Belgium, France, Germany, Italy, Luxembourg, the Netherlands.
2 May 1972	Denmark, Great Britain, and Ireland join the Snake.
23 May 1972	Norway joins Snake as associated member.
23 June 1972	Great Britain and Ireland withdraw.
27 June 1972	Denmark withdraws.
10 October 1972	Denmark rejoins Snake.
13 February 1973	Italy withdraws.
19 March 1973	Breakdown of the Smithsonian Agreement: the Snake loses the "tunnel": decision to float jointly against the dollar. Sweden joins as an associated member. Deutsche mark is revalued by 3 percent against other Snake currencies.
29 June 1973	Deutsche mark is revalued by 5.5 percent.
17 September 1973	Guilder is revalued by 5 percent.
10 October1973	Norwegian crown is revalued by 5 percent.
19 January 1974	France withdraws.
10 July1975	France rejoins.
15 March 1976	France withdraws.
18 October 1976	Deutsche mark is revalued by 2 percent against Dutch guilder and Belgian franc, by 3 percent against Swedish and Norwegian crowns, and by 6 percent against Danish crown.
1 April 1977	Danish and Norwegian crowns are devalued by 3 percent; Swedish crown is devalued by 6 percent.
28 August 1977	Sweden withdraws from Snake. Danish and Norwegian crown are devalued by 5 percent.
13 February1978	Norwegian crown is devalued by 8 percent.
17 October 1978	Deutsche Mark is revalued by 4 percent; Dutch guilder and Belgian franc are revalued by 2 percent.
12 December 1978	Norwegian decision to withdraw from Snake.
13 March 1979	End of the Snake; remaining members join the European Monetary System.

Sources: Deutsche Bundesbank, *BAP*; Gros and Thygesen 1992; Hellmann 1979; Kruse 1980; van Ypersele and Koeune 1984.

The discussion over these issues took the familiar form of the "monetarist" versus "economist" dispute (Kruse 1980: 62–70; Tsoukalis 1977: 90–98). Again these differences were rooted not so much in different philosophical assumptions or tactical considerations but rather in significantly divergent material interests and circumstances. Facing balance-of-payments difficulties, France emphasized the establishment of financing mechanisms, the pooling of currency reserves and drawing rights, and a fast reduction of fluctuation bands as the first steps toward monetary union. Indeed, France's partners in the EU viewed the proposals for monetary support mechanisms as the true core of the Barre initiative. From their perspective, the other proposals for closer coordination of economic policies were simply designed to make the financing mechanisms more acceptable to them (Tsoukalis 1977: 73).

At the same time, however, French officials rejected giving European institutions decision-making power over a common monetary policy (Vereinigte Wirtschaftsdienste 1970). Their proposals for an EU monetary institution "more closely resembled the IMF than a European central bank" (Dillingham 1991: 48). These conditions would have given France the chance to force Germany into accepting a higher inflationary standard. In addition to the question of adjustment costs, the "monetarist" position also had a significant symbolic advantage from the French perspective: it highlighted the "correct" source of monetary instability. While the German-backed "economist" position in its essence emphasized intra-European differences and the need for convergence between them, the "monetarist" strategy would allow the EU member states to by-pass these issues and turn immediately to external concerns, increase European leverage in international monetary negotiations, and to put pressure on the United States, the "true" source of all European monetary problems.

The Germans argued for convergence first, exactly because they wanted to force the others to adjust to their standard. The "economist" stand reflected Germany's position as a strong currency country. Had the "monetarist"

Table 5.2

Inflation Rates of EU Member States, 1969–1979 (Percentage Increase of Consumer Price Index)

	1969	1970	1971	1972	1973	1974	1975	1976	1977	1978	1979
Belgium	3.7	3.9	4.3	5.5	7.0	12.7	12.8	9.2	7.1	4.5	4.5
Denmark	3.6	6.5	5.8	6.6	9.4	15.2	9.6	9.0	11.1	10.1	9.6
France	6.1	5.9	5.5	6.2	7.3	13.7	11.8	9.6	9.4	9.1	10.8
Germany	1.9	3.4	5.2	5.5	7.0	7.0	5.9	4.3	3.7	2.7	4.1
Ireland	7.4	8.2	9.0	8.6	11.4	17.0	20.9	18.0	13.6	7.6	13.2
Italy	2.6	5.0	4.9	5.7	10.8	19.1	17.1	16.7	18.5	12.0	14.8
Luxembourg	2.3	4.6	4.7	5.2	6.1	9.4	10.8	9.8	6.7	3.1	4.5
Netherlands	7.3	3.8	7.4	7.9	8.0	9.6	10.5	8.8	6.4	4.1	4.2
United Kingdom	5.5	6.4	9.5	7.1	9.2	15.9	24.3	16.6	15.8	8.3	13.4

Source: International Monetary Fund, *International Financial Statistics*, Washington, D.C.: various years: world tables.

Table 5.3
Current Account Balances of EU Member Countries, 1969–1979 (in millions of U.S. Dollars)

	1969	1970	1971	1972	1973	1974	1975	1976	1977	1978
Belgium	242	717	647	1,308	1,395	831	181	435	-554	-823
Denmark	-410	-544	-424	-63	-468	-981	-490	-1,914	-1,722	-1,502
France	-1,660	-204	165	-99	1,437	-3,857	2,743	-3,373	-408	7,064
Germany	1,890	840	1,020	1,230	5,120	10,610	4,430	3,700	4,050	9,160
Italy	2,402	798	1,603	2,053	-2,466	-8,007	-523	-2,839	2,484	6,252
Ireland	-204	-198	-200	-150	-254	-688	-124	-428	-522	-849
Netherlands	73	-489	-96	1,370	2,449	3,037	2,390	3,464	1,196	-1,218
United Kingdom	1,157	1,970	2,717	533	-2,412	-7,448	-3,465	-1,380	145	2,163

Source: International Monetary Fund, *International Financial Statistics Yearbook*, 1993.

position prevailed, Germany would have had to finance the balance-of-payments difficulties of the deficit countries and accept a higher inflation rate. Thus, the German proposal for the realization of a monetary union started out from the necessity to harmonize economic policies and goals and mentioned fixed exchange rates only as a by-product of successful convergence (Bundesregierung 1970). In addition, the Germans, in contrast to the French, wanted a common monetary institution to be strong in order to be able to enforce the rules of the game and preserve a low inflationary standard.

At first sight, the Italian position in the early phase of the Werner Report negotiations seems to deviate from the typical split between strong and weak currency countries. Italy sided with the "economists,"although its version was weaker than that of the Germans and Dutch (Tsoukalis 1977: 91–111). As a much weaker currency country than France, a forced convergence through a monetary union would have been very costly for Italy.[6] Instead it preferred a gradual convergence, if possible softened by financial assistance from the wealthier EU members. In addition, it shared Germany's pro-Atlanticism and preferred to go slow because it did not want to achieve separate European monetary cooperation at the expense of U.S.-European ties (Tsoukalis 1977: 81). However, Italy moved to the monetarist side once its balance-of-payments problems intensified in the early 1970s. Under these conditions, it favored Community responsibility for interventions in foreign exchange markets and a progressive pooling of reserves (Tsoukalis 1977: 144).

Overall, the absence of any specific rules in the Werner Report reflected these unresolved disagreements between strong and weak currency countries. The Werner Report was essentially the "lowest common denominator" between the two groups of countries (Tsoukalis 1977: 110). While the chances for any consensus were low to begin with, the oil crisis of 1973/74 ultimately destroyed any prospect for a successful solution to the consistency problem. Germany introduced restrictive policies to deal with the shock, whereas other Snake members allowed their inflation rates to jump upwards in 1974. Thus, by the mid-1970s inflation differentials had widened further. For all practical purposes, the oil crisis finally sealed the fate of the Werner Report.

External Adjustment, Financing and Side Payments

Bargaining over the rules of the Action Programme did not feature issues of external adjustment and financing. Since the only idea there was to establish a monetary union, financing would have been automatic, and external adjustment would not have been possible anymore. The Werner Report process, however, represents not merely an attempt at constructing a monetary union but also at creating a pegged exchange rate regime as a first step toward that goal. Thus, the member states of the EU needed to negotiate rules for external adjustment and for the financing of balance-of-payments difficulties. These issues remained quite contentious throughout the 1970s.

The main items for bargaining in this area were the rules governing the access to financing assistance and the procedures for setting central rates and fluctuation margins. With respect to the financing mechanisms, strong currency countries in general favored rules that implied minimal obligations on their part and provided them with a significant degree of control over loan terms. Weak currency countries, of course, preferred generous schemes with few restrictions. During the 1970s, the EU member states institutionalized three different types of financing mechanisms: the very-short-term financial support facility, the short-term financial support facility, and the medium-term financial support facility (Scharrer 1973: 117–29; Willgerodt et al. 1972: 124–55). The very-short-term and the short-term financial support were agreements between the central banks on monetary support for balance-of-payments difficulties.[7] The very-short-term facility provided unlimited credit lines between the central banks, to be used automatically for mandatory interventions to defend the fluctuation bands of the Snake. These credits had to be repaid at the end of the month following the intervention. An extension of three months was possible. While the very-short-term facility had no quantitative limits for monetary support, the short repayment period was designed to limit the borrowing activities of central banks.

The unlimited character of very-short-term support did not precipitate a domestic debate within Germany during the Snake negotiations. This is remarkable in comparison to the EMS negotiations a decade later, when precisely this issue triggered one of the more tumultuous controversies. Two factors help explain this difference. First, the EMS established longer repayment terms and easier ways to extend credits than the Snake; therefore, the temptation to use these facilities increased. Second, the financing mechanisms of the Snake were established on an explicitly experimental basis (*Süddeutsche Zeitung*, 9 March 1972). At the time of the Snake's inception, interventions were expected to be much smaller than the deutsche mark interventions under the rules of Bretton Woods and the Smithsonian Agreement. The Snake rules seemed the "lesser evil" compared to contemporary international obligations under Bretton Woods to support the dollar (*Süddeutsche Zeitung*, 19 March 1973). In reality, however, the weaker Snake currencies did not rise as strongly as the deutsche mark vis-à-vis the dollar after the breakdown of the Smithsonian Agreement, forcing the Bundesbank to intervene on their behalf often to the same extent as interventions on behalf of the dollar under Bretton Woods. Thus, the Bundesbank soon felt that the experimental Snake rules for the very-short-term facilities were not a success (Scharrer 1973: 120).

Under Snake rules, it was possible to transform the very-short-term credit into a short-term credit, which had a term of three months and was renewable up to six months. Short-term credit, however, was limited. The member states of the EU agreed on specific quotas for each central bank. Medium-term credit was based on the same quotas but had repayment terms of two to five years. These credits were beyond central bank control and required a decision by the Council of Ministers. This situation allowed creditor countries to impose specific policy restrictions on debtor countries, a fact strongly resented by weak currency countries (*Frankfurter Rundschau*, 16 February 1972).

Another controversial feature of these financing mechanisms was their bilateral character. Weak currency countries opposed bilateralism because they became directly dependent on strong currency countries. Moreover, weak currency countries deemed the repayment conditions for the very-short-term facility as too constraining and the supply of short- and medium-term credit as insufficient. Strong currency countries favored the ability to control credit conditions as well as the limitations on borrowing facilities and repayment schedules. German officials, in particular, rejected any attempts to multilateralize financing mechanisms. They were especially concerned about losing control over their money supply and their ability to impose policy restrictions on creditor countries in a multilateral institution (Vereinigte Wirtschaftsdienste 1972a). Despite the intentions of the weak currency countries, the European Monetary Cooperation Fund (EMCF) never developed into an independent institution for the financing of balance-of-payments difficulties (Gros and Thygesen 1992: 21). Ultimately, the German desire to keep as much control as possible over the money supply did succeed over French and Italian pressure to loosen credit conditions in the negotiations over the EMCF (*Frankfurter Allgemeine Zeitung*, 13 September 1972; *Die Zeit*, 15 September 1972).[8]

In addition to the financing facilities, rules for external adjustment also remained controversial. Exchange rate changes during the operation of the Snake were frequent and, more important, remained largely unilateral. Moreover, within the seven years of the Snake's operation, there were eight decisions to withdraw from the system. Most spectacularly, the French even decided to leave the Snake twice. These withdrawals were ultimately nothing but hidden devaluation decisions. Thus, the Snake did not improve multilateral coordination of exchange rate policies over the conditions that existed under Bretton Woods. The degree of consensus among the participants remained fairly low.

An especially contentious issue during the Snake negotiations concerned the fluctuation bands. Italy and France rejected the narrow bands preferred by the Germans to insert greater discipline into the system (Vereinigte Wirtschaftsdienste 1972b: 6–7). The fluctuation bands were set at 2.25 percent around the central rates—a margin that Italy, in particular, viewed as too rigid, which was the most important reason for Italy's exit from the Snake (Hellmann 1979: 39). It is, therefore, not trivial that EU member states could find a more consensual agreement on this issue a decade later in the EMS negotiations.

International developments further aggravated the controversial character of external adjustment issues. The move from the "Snake in the tunnel" to the "Snake without the tunnel" contributed to a shift in adjustment burden among Snake members. As long as the tunnel existed, Germany was obligated to maintain its dollar parity within the bands of the Smithsonian Agreement. However, the breakdown of the Smithsonian Agreement removed this constraint on Germany. While the other Snake members were now effectively obligated to follow the deutsche mark, a corresponding German obligation did not exist anymore. Germany became the nth currency in the Snake, liberating it from any balance-of-payments constraints. The costs of maintaining exchange rates now shifted even more clearly to the other members of the Snake.

Germany's Pivotal Role in the Werner Report and Snake Episodes

The remaining task for this chapter is to analyze the pivotal role Germany played in the Werner Report and Snake negotiations. My account of this role, of course, is informed by historical knowledge about the role Germany assumed a decade later in the EMS process. While conditions in the early 1970s were quite different from those in the late 1970s, the variance in Germany's bargaining behavior emphasized here is intriguing and represents an important piece in the puzzling patterns of European exchange rate cooperation.

Standard Setting

In the negotiations over the Werner Report, the EU member states were clearly unable to find a consensual solution to the problem of establishing domestic macroeconomic consistency. Most important, Germany was not willing to compromise its own domestic macroeconomic standard to facilitate closer monetary cooperation. Instead, German policymakers made clear that Germany's own priorities would have to set the standard for the other members in the system. In the view of German policymakers, the main cause of the monetary problems in Europe during the late 1960s and early 1970s was indeed the differences in inflation.[9] Under the conditions of divergent inflationary standards, German monetary officials insisted that monetary union required a unified economic policy and a convergence in other areas of economic and social activity (Gleske 1968). As Hans Tietmeyer (1969: 12), then a leading official in the ministry of economics and the German member of the Werner group, argued: "A monetary union and more importantly a common EC currency can exist without frictions only if the different economic and social structures of the EC member countries have assimilated to each other and if a largely common economic and monetary policy is secured. . . . A European currency has to remain a Fata Morgana . . . as long as we have not realized the coordination of economic policies." Coordination, of course, did not imply a compromise of German macroeconomic objectives, but rather the setting of the German standard as the target for the coordination process. As Tietmeyer (1969: 13) continued:

> Even if we can achieve a real coordination of the basic parameters and goals of credit policies, fiscal policies and wage policies, there remains an important

question: *coordination on what level?* . . . If German
policy would pursue economic and monetary union
without any qualifications, one cannot overlook the possible dangers of such policy, in particular for price stability. The economic policy that would result from
majority decisions among the six EC members would
certainly not satisfy our current measures of price stability (my emphasis).[10]

The German minister for economics, Karl Schiller,
pointed in the same direction: "The European Community
is so far neither a political community, nor is it a stable
community in economic terms. Some member states accept
inflation rates of 6, 7 or 8% and do not even view these price
increases as a violation of the Treaty of Rome. . . . We have
observed that other EC member states are very quick in
forcing inflation onto us" (quoted in *Handelsblatt,* 28/29
November 1969). Similarly, Chancellor Brandt, upon his
return from The Hague summit, noted that real convergence among the EU member states was weak and that
Germany was not willing to accept a higher inflation rate
to create EMU (Bundesregierung 1969).

Consequently, in the negotiations to reach the Council
decision on the Werner Report in March 1971, Germany did
not offer any substantive sacrifices to reach a compromise
(Schiller 1971). The Werner Report itself reflects this
German insistence on standard setting, but it does so only
in vague and unspecified terms. The report acknowledged
the general "economist" principle of moving toward EMU *in
stages* but did not describe specific rules for moving from
one stage to the next. It accepted the need to coordinate
domestic policies prior to monetary unification, but it did
not set specific targets for the coordination process. It
embraced the principle of convergence without setting
explicit goals for convergence. And the report reflected
Germany's insistence on a strong institutional structure,
but without describing it in any specific fashion. Thus,
while Germany did not sign on to principles to which it was
vehemently opposed, it was unable to shape them strongly
enough to produce clear rules. Similarly, the 1973 negotia-

tions over the establishment of a European central bank system faltered because Germany's partners were unwilling to agree on procedures for establishing economic policy convergence and because of Germany's corresponding fear that a system without convergence requirements would only increase the German money supply (*Neue Zürcher Zeitung*, 30 June 1973). In other words, Germany did not serve as a "constitutional architect" for EMU, as it would two decades later in the Maastricht process.

In contrast to the EMU aspect, the Snake component of the Werner Report indeed saw the expected solution to the standard-setting problem. Given the fact that negotiators were unable to agree on any officially binding domestic policy obligations or specifically chosen reference point, the strongest currency country was in position to serve as the nth country in the system. Facing no reserve constraint, German macroeconomic policies effectively set the standard for the other Snake members. Among the bigger Snake members, this position rested simply on the strength of the deutsche mark. During the operation of the mini-Snake, however, Germany's nth country function also reflected the natural differences in size. Clearly, the other large EU member states had difficulties accepting Germany's nth country status as the solution to the standard-setting problem. At the time, floating seemed to many of them a viable alternative. Thus, the fact that floating exchange rates proved to be very costly in terms of economic adjustment during the 1970s emerges in retrospect as an important factor for the French and Italian decisions to accept Germany's nth country position a decade later in the EMS.

Overall, German policymakers had problems gaining legitimacy for Germany's nth country status among Snake members. The economic costs of following the German standard were very high during this period—higher in fact than during the early phase of the EMS. Despite the fact that the German inflation rate was lower than those of its neighboring countries, it was high measured by its own standards. As a consequence, German monetary authorities pursued rigid monetary policies that put pressure on its European neighbors.[11] Great Britain, Italy, and France were not willing to adjust to high German interest rates and the stringent stabilization policies of the government. One after another, they left the Snake because their exchange rates had fallen to the floor of the band, and they were unable and unwilling to support them (Kruse 1980: 146–47, 165–68).

By comparison, the EMS had much more favorable starting conditions. During the early 1980s, the peg of the European currencies to the deutsche mark provided a partial shield for the EMS member states against the high interest rate policy of the United States. Thus, the costs of following the deutsche mark were much lower after 1979 than they were during the operation of the Snake. Moreover, all countries started to attach greater importance to the goal of containing inflation, resulting in less accommodating policies to the second oil shock in 1979. Later, of course, the reversal in French policies and the attempt by weak currency countries to "tie their own hands" further improved the legitimacy of Germany's nth currency status during the mid-1980s.

Concessions and Side Payments

Despite the fact that the German bargaining position appeared rigid and inflexible for the most part, the Snake episode also featured a number of German concessions and side payments to its partners. While Germany would make more notable concessions later during the EMS negotiations, the few conciliatory gestures of the Snake period fit the pattern of Germany's bargaining position, namely, an inflexible stance on domestic adjustment combined with greater flexibility on external adjustment, financing, and side payments. In this context, accepting the principle of separate European financing mechanisms appears as the most meaningful German concession. Until The Hague summit, Germany had resisted this idea. Conceding to French pressure on this issue, which had been growing since the franc crisis of 1968/69, German policymakers agreed to the creation of financing facilities during the summit.

Italian negotiators also elicited a few German concessions. To protect their own gold reserves, the Italians were able to negotiate the use of dollars as a means of settlement for intervention debt (Hellmann 1979: 34–35; Kruse 1980: 115; Vereinigte Wirtschaftsdienste 1972c). Giving in to pressure by other Snake members for reciprocity on this point, the Germans later also agreed to extend the Italian repayment conditions to the other members (Vereinigte Wirtschaftsdienste 1973). Similarly, Italy was able to link its participation in the Snake to the introduction of particular regional policy programs within the EU (Tsoukalis 1977: 120–22; *Neue Zürcher Zeitung*, 9 March 1972; *Süddeutsche Zeitung*, 9 March 1972).

The setting of parities also became an item of explicit bargaining among the member states of the Snake. The crucial compromise that made it possible for the Snake to continue as a joint float after the breakdown of the Smithsonian tunnel was the revaluation of the deutsche mark within the Snake on 19 March 1973 (Kruse 1980: 130–31). For France, this was the only way to defuse the costs of the upward trend of the deutsche mark vis-à-vis the dollar and the condition for its continued participation in the Snake, although this compromise saved French membership for less than a year.

Overall, however, Germany showed very little inclination to make significant side payments or concessions. The mechanisms for external balance-of-payments adjustments and financing remained controversial throughout this period, and the weak currency countries viewed them as insufficient and too strict. In particular, the British remained dissatisfied with the prevailing financing arrangements of the Snake (Kruse 1980: 130–31). German policymakers rejected both the extension of repayment schedules and the expansion of facilities (Tsoukalis 1977: 142–46). Similarly, the German government insisted on keeping narrow fluctuation margins notwithstanding Italian demands to widen them.

Table 5.4
Bargaining Issues in Werner Report
and Snake Negotiations

INTERNAL ADJUSTMENT ISSUES

Weak Currency Country Demands	Strong Currency Country Demands	Solutions	German Concession?
1) General: monetarist Strategy early monetary union	General: economist Strategy: monetary union after convergence	None	No
2) No convergence criteria	Introduction of convergence criteria	None	No
3) Weak institutional structure of common monetary institutions	Strong institutional structure of common monetary institutions	None	No

EXTERNAL ADJUSTMENT AND FINANCING IN THE SNAKE

1) Extended borrowing periods for financing facilities	Short borrowing periods to maintain discipline	Very short term support: 30 days	No
2) Expansion of monetary facilities	No change after initial agreement	No change after initial agreement	Yes in accepting the initial agreement; No for later attempts to extend
3) Use of dollars for repayment of financing aid	At first resistance	Allow use of dollars	Yes
4) Widen fluctuation margins	No widening of bands to maintain discipline	No widening of bands	No

Conclusion

Despite numerous changes in the international environment and in the incentives for monetary cooperation, the bargaining interaction between EU member states on the Werner Report and Snake clearly resembles that of the Action Programme. As summarized in table 5.4 strong and weak currency countries disagreed over how to establish macroeconomic consistency among them. Germany insisted on its own macroeconomic standard as the focal point for cooperation, while the other large EU member states were for the most part not willing to follow. The EMU aspect of the Werner Report dissolved under these controversies, while the Snake saw the development of a German nth country (albeit fragile) solution to the problem. In addition, the Snake exhibited a few examples of Germany's willingness to treat certain questions of external adjustment and financing as negotiable. These concessions, however, remained much more limited than they would be later during the EMS negotiations.

6

Asymmetry and Bargaining Exchanges in the European Monetary System

In marked contrast to earlier attempts at monetary cooperation, the European Monetary System, established in 1979, represents an example of quite successful exchange rate cooperation in the EU. While parities within the EMS had to be realigned several times until 1987, the system functioned by and large smoothly. Overall, exchange rate crises remained on a small scale between 1979 and 1992. And the EMS significantly reduced exchange rate fluctuations between realignments. In addition to its fairly stable operation, the EMS showed other signs of success. Membership in the system became attractive to outsiders and increased until the early 1990s. All member states exhibited some degree of convergence toward lower levels of inflation, although there is little evidence that this was directly due to the EMS. The narrowing of the gap in monetary policies between the EU countries—most important between France and Germany—during the late 1980s served as a major driving force behind attempts at a transformation of the EMS into a monetary union. Thus, notwithstanding their early skepticism, most observers soon viewed the EMS as a successful regime for exchange rate cooperation.

However, the relative stability deteriorated rapidly in 1992. After large speculative attacks in currency markets, Italy and Great Britain left the Exchange Rate Mechanism (ERM) of the EMS in September 1992. The following year witnessed numerous exchange rate crises and realignments. In August 1993, the remaining ERM members agreed to widen fluctuation margins from +/–2.25 percent to +/–15 percent after a speculative attack against the French franc and other EMS currencies. In the wake of these decisions, the level of uncertainty over the future of monetary cooperation in Europe remained fairly high. The EMS never returned to narrow fluctuation bands. However, despite these problems the EMS survived as an institution, a fact that ultimately served as a necessary precondition for the move toward EMU.

Despite the obvious differences between the EMS and earlier attempts at monetary cooperation, this chapter contends that bargaining over the rules of the EMS was structurally very similar to these earlier attempts. Again, the bargaining setting was shaped by the contrast between strong and weak currency countries. Strong currency countries once more resisted efforts to compromise their domestic macroeconomic standard and were willing to make concessions only on questions of external adjustment, financing, and side payments. Concessions on some of these issues went further than during the Snake. While this fact is certainly not the only reason for EMS stability and longevity, it nevertheless helps to explain why weak currency countries were more satisfied with the distributional aspects of the EMS than the Snake.

Overall, this chapter challenges the prevailing view in the literature that the EMS was *intended* as a symmetric system and that only later developments turned the EMS into an asymmetrical institution. Even if the EMS agreement itself did not specify Germany as the center country of the system or adopted the deutsche mark as numeraire, I argue that asymmetry is structurally implied by the way EMS rules were adopted. The analysis reveals that all attempts to agree on binding rules for a symmetric solution to the redundancy problem in the EMS failed. In the absence of explicit policy rules, however, the system would have to feel the impact of the differential balance-of-payments position in its operation. With domestic adjustment left unregulated, the principal strong currency country in Europe necessarily acquired the central position within the EMS.

Emphasis on countries' relative balance-of-payments positions also helps to understand the bargaining tradeoffs made in designing the EMS rules. While asymmetry in the EMS was inevitable, successful completion of the EMS negotiations was in part made possible by the ability of the participating countries to shift bargaining from the intractable issue of internal adjustment to questions of external adjustment and financing. The narrowing of countries' balance-of-payments positions starting in the second half of the 1980s also helps to illuminate why monetary union became a feasible and attractive alternative to replace an apparently quite successful regime.

Historical Overview

The first ideas for a renewed attempt at monetary cooperation in the EU emerged in 1977 with an initiative by Roy Jenkins, then president of the EU Commission. In a speech at the European University Institute in Florence on 27 October 1977, he proposed to restart the EMU process (Jenkins 1991: 456–73; Jenkins 1989: 175–203).[1] The Jenkins proposal, however, received no support among member states, and the idea of a renewed attempt at exchange rate cooperation in the EU became viable only after French President Valery Giscard d'Estaing and German Chancellor Helmut Schmidt seized the initiative in the spring of 1978. Giscard and Schmidt presented their early thoughts to the European Council on 7 April 1978. Instead of reforming the Snake, they planned to set up a completely new system. Two major new features of the regime were to be (1) a strengthened system of financing assistance for its members, including the founding of a European Monetary Fund, and (2) the creation of a European unit of account (later to be called "ECU") for intra-EC bookkeeping purposes, the settlement of intervention debt, and as a reserve asset of EMS central banks. At first, negotiations proceeded under a veil of secrecy among central economic advisors to Schmidt, Giscard, and the British prime minister, James Callaghan—although the British very quickly dropped out of serious participation in the negotiations. Except for EU Commission President Roy Jenkins himself, both the EU Commission and the Bundesbank Council were left in the dark during the first few months of the negotiations.[2]

Several broader considerations triggered this renewed monetary initiative. Schmidt and Giscard both felt that the currency instability that followed the breakdown of Bretton Woods was a main factor in the lack of growth in the industrialized world. Their hope was that exchange rate cooperation would impove Europe's economic performance (*Financial Times*, 11 July 1978; Loriaux 1991: 253). In their view, the dismal economic performance of the EU member states during the 1970s had discredited flexible exchange rates, and it seemed time to launch a renewed attempt at European exchange rate cooperation. Moreover, exchange rate instability and balance-of-payments problems posed a more direct threat to the functioning of free trade within the customs union. In the mid-1970s, monetary problems spilled over into the customs union when Denmark, France, and Italy adopted import restrictions on various products in violation of EU rules. Most consequential was Italy's adoption of an import deposit scheme to deal with its balance-of-payments problems. (*Neue Zürcher Zeitung*, 3 May 1974; *Der Spiegel*, 19/1974). The threat these measures posed for free trade contributed greatly in particular to German incentives to use exchange rate cooperation as a tool to safeguard its trading interests (Lahnstein 1978; Schmidt 1978).

In the view of many policymakers, the largely negative experience with flexible exchange rates affected not only trade but also balance-of-payments adjustments (van Ypersele and Koeune 1984: 17–29). From their perspective, the experience of the 1970s indicated that flexible exchange rates did not automatically restore equilibrium to a country's balance-of-payments. Weak currency countries largely saw persistent deficits despite depreciating currencies, and strong currency countries maintained surpluses despite appreciating currencies. Flexible exchange rates added fuel to the vicious circle of inflation, depreciation, and balance-of-payments deficits and to the "virtuous" circle of appreciation, low inflation, and balance-of-payments surpluses. Thus, flexible exchange rates still implied significant external pressures for weak currency countries (Balladur 1988). Moreover, during the late 1970s, even German policymakers became increasingly concerned over the potential downsides of flexible exchange rates, namely, the real effective appreciation of the deutsche mark against the other larger European currencies and the dollar and the competitiveness problems this implied for Germany's economy (Kaufmann 1985; Ludlow 1982). Under these circumstances, a new exchange rate regime promised two benefits for the logic of balance-of-payments adjustments. First, a commitment to keep parities within limited bands could help to slow down vicious or virtuous cycles. Second, regulated access to financing facilities would increase the availability of reserves, improve the position of weak currency countries vis-à-vis financial markets, and provide breathing space to implement domestic policy measures or simply to keep exchange rates stable between realignments.

Another motivation for lauching the EMS had to do with the dynamics of European integration. Retrospectively known as the age of "Eurosclerosis" and "Europessimism," the 1970s saw a significant deterioration in cooperation among the EU member states. Monetary relations were in disarray, economic divergence between countries had increased, costs of the Common Agricultural Policy ballooned, and the member states were unable to agree on any new initiatives (Taylor 1983). In this context, the EMS was seen as a tool to safeguard some of the EU's achievements and to facilitate renewed integration in other areas. This line of thought was politically vindicated during the mid-1980s, although it is difficult to prove the exact *causal* role of the EMS. The main elements of European integration, the customs union and the Common Agricultural Policy, did not unravel. Moreover, the EU engaged in new initiatives. It is unlikely that the EU would have embarked on the pursuit of the Single Market project without the success of the EMS. Roy Jenkins later, for example, would describe the EMS as the "central channel from which most subsequent European advance has flowed" (1991: 490). These internal EU considerations were supplemented by broader geostrategic issues (Schmidt 1990: 247–72). An unraveling of the EU would have considerably weakened the European pillar of Germany's integration into the West. Thus, the creation of the EMS provided an additional way of tying Germany to Western Europe (Dell 1994: 2; Marsh 1992: 233 and passim).

Probably the most important incentive for this renewed initiative came from developments in the international realm (Ludlow 1982: 64–69). This factor is most visible in Helmut Schmidt's changing position between October 1977 and February 1978. Originally, he had reacted coolly to Roy Jenkins' initiative on monetary cooperation in his Florence speech during the fall of 1977. However, at the end of February, Schmidt presented his own ideas for a new monetary initiative to the EU Commission president. While Schmidt's proposal fell short of the full monetary union envisioned by Jenkins, Schmidt's general attitude had radically changed over the preceding four months (Jenkins 1991: 456–78; Jenkins 1989: 198–224). The most important development during this short period was clearly the depreciation of the dollar. The drop in the value of the dollar put competitive pressures on Germany not only in non-EU trade but also vis-à-vis its European neighbors because the dollar dragged other non-Snake currencies (franc, sterling, and lira) down with it (*Stuttgarter Zeitung*, 25 July 1978). Thus, the specific timing of Schmidt's plan for monetary cooperation can be explained as a response to the dollar problem. The idea was that a broader-based exchange rate system would distribute the burden of speculation against the dollar onto more shoulders. And while Schmidt did not anticipate that the

EMS would stabilize European exchange rates completely, it offered a better chance to contain the influence of the dollar as an additional source of intra-European currency instability.

The dollar problem, however, was not the only source of Schmidt's dissatisfaction with U.S. policies in the late 1970s. Rather, in his view, it represented the most visible sign of an increasing loss in American leadership under the Carter administration.[3] The so-called locomotive debate with the American attempt to induce Germany to reflate introduced serious disagreements over the management of the global economy. Furthermore, Schmidt rejected the foreign policy approach of the Carter administration, which he saw as destabilizing East-West relations and as a constant source of uncertainty in international relations. German and American officials in particular clashed over the strategies for arms control negotiations. In addition, the question of introducing the neutron bomb and the conflict over Germany's export of nuclear reactors to Brazil created tensions.

Thus, the environment for a renewed monetary initiative was quite conducive during the late 1970s. However, out of fear that early publicity may easily destroy the initiative, it was only at the European Council in Bremen in July 1978 that the heads of governments went public and officially announced their decision to set up a European monetary system by the end of the year. At that point, however, most of the important issues still needed more precise definition. The major bargaining problems concerned the rules for intervention, the role of the ECU, the design of the proposed EMF, the rules governing exchange rate changes, and the repayment conditions for financing assistance. In addition, Italy and Ireland established a link between the EMS negotiations and the question of structural funds. In retrospect, the Aachen summit on 14 September 1978 between Giscard and Schmidt appears as the main breakthrough in the negotiations, when France, to the dismay of other weak currency countries, accepted Germany's demand for a bilateral grid to determine intervention obligations and relegated the ECU grid to the role of divergence indicator. Other significant steps toward agreement were Schmidt's grudging acceptance of a larger fluctuation band for the Italian lira during the Siena Summit of 1 November and the decision of the Council of Economics and Finance Ministers on 21 November to increase the sizes of the short- and medium-term financing facilities. The European Council in Brussels of 5 December 1978 adopted a resolution containing the rules for the European Monetary System, and the system went into operation on 13 March 1979 after struggles over the CAP had delayed the start of EMS operations for a few weeks.

The EMS began operation with the following key rules. Fluctuation margins around the central bilateral parities were established at +/–2.25 percent (although Italy and later newly participating countries were free to choose +/–6 percent fluctuation margins temporarily). In terms of the official rules, reaching the margins would trigger unlimited, mandatory intervention on the part of both affected countries. As later sections of this chapter will point out, this obligation was limited in practice by several aspects. Most important, the Bundesbank had achieved agreement with the German federal government that it would not be bound by an unlimited intervention obligation if that conflicted with its domestic tasks (the so-called Emminger letter).

In addition, participants agreed on a "divergence" indicator, based on the multilateral ECU grid, which was supposed to function as an early warning system to induce intervention, consultation, or policy coordination before bilateral exchange rates reached their margins. According to official rules, the realignment of parities required the consent of all EMS participants. Short-term and medium-term financing facilities were significantly increased compared to those of the Snake arrangement. Borrowing periods for all forms of financial assistance were also extended (most important, the very-short-term period was extended from thirty to forty-five days). Terms of repayment allowed the partial use of ECUs and dollars. Agreement on the creation of an EMF was initially postponed for two years, although the goal was later more or less quietly dropped from the bargaining agenda. And, unrelated to the official rules but included as part of the package deal, the EU member states granted loans to Italy and Ireland.

The two most important episodes of rule changes were the so-called Basle-Nyborg reforms of 1987 and the changes in response to the ERM crisis of 1992/93.[4] The Basle-Nyborg Accord of 18 September 1987 introduced four innovations (Committee of Central Bank Governors 1987). EMS rules now allowed more explicitly the use of the very-short-term facility for intramarginal interventions. While use of these facilities through the EMCF was possible before Basle-Nyborg, it required concurrence by the respective central banks.[5] From now on, debtor countries could "presume" agreement by the creditor central bank that up to 200 percent of the quota for short-term financing could be used for intramarginal interventions. However, such use was still not considered automatic. Second, the repayment period for the very-short-term facility was extended by an additional month, allowing now a maximum of seventy-five days for the settlement of intervention debt. Third, the terms of repayment after Basle-Nyborg allowed settlement in ECUs up to the full amount of debt, as opposed to only 50 percent prior to the 1987 agreement. In exchange for these German concessions, the Basle-Nyborg Accord urged the defense of exchange rates through the use of interest rate policies and stated explicitly the goal of convergence toward low inflation.

Until 1992 the rules of the system functioned more or less properly. In 1992, however, exchange rates in the ERM—which had not been changed for more than five years—became volatile. Several factors contributed to the instability: The divergences in the macroeconomic needs of the various member states following German reunification,[6] the inflation differentials that had accumulated between strong and weak currency countries over the previous five years, the weakness of the dollar in international financial markets, and uncertainties over the future of the

Maastricht Treaty following its rejection in the Danish referendum of 2 June 1992. The crisis expressed itself in several events and developments. The lira was devalued on 13 September 1992. Three days later, the pound and the lira exited the ERM. Between September 1992 and August 1993, all ERM currencies except for the deutsche mark and the guilder came under speculative pressure at some point in time. There were also five realignments between 1992 and 1995. And finally, in August 1993, severe pressure on the French franc led to the most significant change in explicit EMS rules, a widening of fluctuation bands from 4.5 percent to 30 percent. While exchange rates among the core EMS members returned to their pre-crisis values quickly and showed very limited fluctuations, EMS member states never officially returned to narrow fluctuation bands.

Bargaining Asymmetries and the Politics of Monetary Cooperation in the EMS

Obviously, the EMS was for the most part more successful than its predecessor regime. Despite this difference, however, the underlying bargaining dynamics did not vary significantly. Again, differences in balance-of-payments positions shaped the logic of designing EMS rules. Distributional concerns over the costs of macroeconomic adjustment informed the bargaining positions of weak and strong currency countries both during the initial negotiations to set up the EMS and during subsequent bargaining over EMS reforms. Consequently, the positions of strong currency countries succeeded on all aspects of domestic adjustment and bargaining compromises were feasible only on issues of external adjustment, financing, and side payments.

Domestic Adjustment

The issue of domestic adjustment remained as contentious a bargaining item in the EMS as it was during the

Snake period. There existed no consensus among the EU member states in the late 1970s on an appropriate macroeconomic standard for the new exchange rate system. Moreover, strong currency countries did not leave any room for possible bargaining compromises on this issue. The rules of the EMS had to come on their terms, or they would not come at all. This claim appears at least in part controversial from the perspective of two competing interpretations of the EMS experience. One line of argument follows logically from the contention that the EMS was supposed to function as a symmetrical regime and that only later developments transformed the EMS into an asymmetrical system (Gros and Thygesen 1992; van Ypersele and Koeune 1984). From this viewpoint, asymmetry in the EMS would appear unintentional. The second competing claim is based on the view that the EMS was designed as a deliberate tool for policy convergence. This perspective essentially perceives domestic adjustment issues as nonconflictual, in the sense that weak currency countries willingly accepted the asymmetry of the EMS as a device for convergence to the standard of the strong currency countries in the system (e.g., McNamara 1998). I will address the analytical problems of these claims later in this subsection after reviewing both the macroeconomic policies and bargaining behavior of EMS member states relevant for this issue.

The most visible sign that controversies over domestic adjustment issues continued to exist during the late 1970s and early 1980s was the fact that inflation rates continued to diverge significantly between strong and weak currency countries (table 6.1). While the French government under Giscard's prime minister, Raymond Barre, embarked on more restrictive macroeconomic policies in 1976/77, it did not achieve much convergence with Germany (Artus and Nasse 1985; Cameron 1995a; Sachs and Wyplosz 1986). The commitment to continued restrictive policy remained vague, and further disinflationary efforts by the Giscard presidency even during the first few years of EMS operations between 1979 and 1981 were not forthcoming. German-French inflation differentials actually increased during the first two years of EMS operations. Contemporary observers concluded early that economic convergence did not progress during the first four years of the EMS' existence (Matthes 1983). In retrospect, the true reversal in French macroeconomic policy priorities and clear commitment to German-style restrictive policies did not come before the Mitterrand turnabout of 1982/83. As Russo and Tullio (1988: 63) observe, until 1982/83 there existed "no agreement (not even implicit) on inflation. . . . After 1983 an implicit agreement on inflation emerged—namely, to converge toward the German inflation rate and to let the Federal Republic of Germany determine the anchor inflation rate of the system."

Thus, there existed no common understanding about the macroeconomic goals of the system during the negotiations to set up the EMS. The gap over coordination goals between Germany, on the one hand, and Italy and Great Britain, on the other, remained even larger than the French-German difference. During the EMS negotiations, the British chancellor of the exchequer, Denis Healey, explicitly demanded a monetary system that would have no deflationary tendencies and rejected an arrangement that would force weaker countries into excessive deflation (*Die Zeit,* 27 October 1978; Andersen 1979: 10; *Neue Zürcher Zeitung,* 13 July 1978; *Financial Times,* 27 October 1978; Healey 1989: 438–40; Dell 1994). In other words, strong and weak currency countries continued to view domestic adjustment issues as fraught with severe distributional concerns.

Not only did strong and weak currency countries pursue different macroeonomic policies, but their bargaining objectives in the EMS negotiations diverged significantly. All of the weak currency countries negotiated for some concessions from Germany on standard-setting issues. During the early phase of the negotiations, Giscard clearly envisioned an explicit exchange between disinflationary policies in the weak currency countries and reflationary policies in the strong currency countries as the foundation for the new system (*Frankfurter Allgemeine*

Table 6.1
Inflation Rates in EU Member Countries (CPI)

	1979	1980	1981	1982	1983	1984	1985	1986	1987	1988	1989	1990	1991	1992	1993
Belgium	4.5	6.7	7.6	8.7	7.7	6.3	4.9	1.3	1.6	1.2	3.1	3.5	3.2	2.4	2.8
Denmark	9.6	12.3	11.7	10.1	6.9	6.3	4.7	3.7	4.0	4.6	4.8	2.6	2.4	2.1	1.3
France	10.8	13.3	13.4	11.8	9.6	7.4	5.8	2.5	3.3	2.7	3.5	3.4	3.2	2.4	2.3
Germany	4.1	5.4	6.3	5.3	3.3	2.4	2.2	-0.1	0.2	1.3	2.8	2.7	3.5	4.0	4.1
Greece	19.0	24.9	24.5	20.9	20.2	18.4	19.3	23.0	16.4	13.5	13.7	20.4	19.5	15.9	14.4
Ireland	13.2	18.2	20.4	17.1	10.5	8.6	5.4	3.8	3.1	2.2	4.1	3.3	3.2	3.1	1.4
Italy	14.8	21.2	19.5	16.5	14.7	10.8	9.2	5.8	4.7	5.1	6.3	6.4	6.3	5.2	4.5
Luxembrg	4.5	6.3	8.1	9.4	8.7	5.6	4.1	0.3	-0.1	1.5	3.4	3.7	3.1	3.2	3.6
Netherlds	4.2	6.5	6.7	5.9	2.8	3.3	2.2	0.1	-0.7	0.7	1.1	2.5	3.9	3.7	2.1
Portugal	23.6	16.6	20.0	22.7	25.1	29.3	19.3	11.7	9.4	9.6	12.6	13.4	11.4	8.9	6.5
Spain	15.7	15.6	14.6	14.4	12.2	11.3	8.8	8.8	5.2	4.8	6.8	6.7	5.9	5.9	4.6
United Kingdom	13.5	18.0	11.9	8.6	4.6	5.0	6.1	3.4	4.1	4.9	7.8	9.5	5.9	3.7	1.6

Source: International Monetary Fund, *International Financial Statistics Yearbook*, 1994.

Zeitung, 3 July 1978). Most visibly, weak currency countries emphasized the need for greater "symmetry" in European exchange rate politics. No other phrase distinguishes the launching of the EMS so distinctly from the Snake experience than that of symmetry.[7] All of the weak currency countries participated in the EMS negotiations because they believed that it would result in a significantly different system than the Snake. As officials of weak currency countries stated explicitly, their countries could have rejoined the Snake at any time if they had believed this to be in their interest (Dell 1994: 27). Their clear impression at the time was that they were negotiating a system that would distribute adjustment costs more evenly. Their goal was to meet the strong currency countries somewhere "in the middle."

The centerpiece of the early French strategy was to implement intervention rules based on the ECU basket instead of a bilateral parity grid (Dell 1994: 24–31; Ludlow 1982: 159–66). The approach was explicitly intended as a way of putting pressure on the strong currency countries to adjust. The basket solution was designed to make the average performance the reference point for intervention obligations. Unlike the bilateral grid, which always identifies two outliers (namely, one on the upper end of the fluctuation margin, and one on the lower end), the basket system could have allowed for the identification of just one currency as an outlier. This possibility existed because the margins of exchange rates would have been identified, country by country, in reference to its ECU central rate. The hope of weak currency countries was obviously that the ECU indicator would more often identify a strong currency—in particular the deutsche mark—as the outlier than a weak currency. According to a French official, "in the Snake . . . three times out of four, problems had arisen because the strongest currency, in almost every case the DM, had reached its upper limits" (quoted in Dell 1994: 27). Thus, the target of the ECU grid was explicitly the deutsche mark, even if the basket also allowed for the possibility that weak currencies could be identified as the outliers.[8]

The identification of an outlier in the ECU grid was supposed to trigger mandatory interventions by the respective country and possibly other adjustment measures, such as domestic policy changes or an exchange rate change. If the ECU indicator indeed identified the deutsche mark as an outlier, Germany would have to take adjustment measures without any corresponding obligation on the part of a weak currency country. In this sense, weak currency countries hoped that the ECU indicator would relieve pressures on them and establish a more symmetrical system.

The bilateral grid, by contrast, identifies pairs of countries simultaneously. Under a bilateral grid, intervention occurs when *two* currencies reach the margins of their fluctuation bands—one of them its upper limit, the other one, its lower end. Despite the mutual obligation for intervention, however, the economic adjustment logic of the bilateral grid is asymmetrical. The weak currency country can run out of currency reserves, whereas the strong currency country can potentially finance its interventions indefinitely. Thus, limited currency reserves, the obligation to repay financing debt, and the better ability of strong currency countries to sterilize their interventions restrict the policy options of weak currency countries. In other words, symmetrical *intervention* obligations (i.e., compulsory interventions when bilateral exchange rates reach their margins) do not necessarily entail symmetrical *adjustment* obligations. Thus, weak currency countries face much stronger constraints than strong currency countries. The fact that the Bundesbank had served notice in the form of the so-called Emminger letter that it did not feel obligated to intervene perpetually on behalf of weak currencies if that conflicted with its domestic obligations—an issue I will address shortly—only aggravated this asymmetry. From the perspective of the weak currency countries, these constraints would always come into play under the bilateral grid, while there was a chance that the ECU grid would occasionally allow them a reprieve.

Germany rejected the ECU grid and advocated the bilateral grid precisely because it feared that a basket system would force it to compromise its domestic economic priorities. President Giscard acquiesced to the German position at the Aachen summit on 14 and 15 September 1978. He agreed that intervention rules would be based on bilateral parities. Most participants and observers recognized at the time that this concession contradicted the original goal of symmetry. German commentators and policymakers noted after the Aachen summit that the new system would be based essentially on the same rules as the Snake (*Frankfurter Allgemeine Zeitung*, 19 September 1978; *Süddeutsche Zeitung*, 19 September 1978). Italian and British officials severely criticized the French government for its concession, arguing like the Germans that the new system would simply be a copy of the Snake (*Financial Times*, 19 September 1978; *The Times*, 19 September 1978; Jenkins, 1991: 481–82; Spaventa 1980: 77–80). Officials from both countries labeled the French retreat from the ECU basket as a "sellout" and "capitulation" to the Germans and continued to push for the ECU grid into the later stages of the negotiations (*Börsen-Zeitung*, 1 November 1978; Ludlow 1982: 164). Even the governor of the Banque de France and chief French negotiator Bernard Clappier continued to pursue the basket solution long after Giscard's concession, which stemmed from his personal conviction that it represented the core idea of a more symmetrical system and that a new regime without the ECU grid would merely repeat the asymmetry of the Snake (Dell 1994: 29).

To uphold at least the appearance that the EMS would be a distinctly different system, Schmidt and Giscard agreed that the ECU basket would become the "divergence indicator"—a solution that is often referred to as the "Belgian compromise."[9] The divergence indicator was supposed to function as an early warning signal and trigger consultation or possible adjustment measures. However, it was not designed to initiate automatic interventions or to require other adjustment measures by the country that reached the margins of the ECU basket. The importance of the divergence indicator was largely psychological. It allowed all participants to claim that the EMS was differ-

ent from the Snake. This rationale was particularly significant for the terms of the French and Italian domestic
debates over the EMS (Hellmann 1979: 57–58). The adoption of the divergence indicator permitted countries to
cooperate without losing face. In substantive terms,
however, the divergence indicator was hardly significant.
As German government officials explicitly predicted at the
time, the divergence indicator would be irrelevant to the
functioning of the EMS.[10]

Judging from the initial goals of the French bargaining
strategy, the Aachen compromise is puzzling. Clearly,
Giscard was aware that his concession meant an end to any
attempt at creating a more symmetric system. However, a
focus on bargaining leverage of weak and strong currency
countries allows for a quite straightforward explanation:
the decision to accept the parity grid was owed to the
absence of any meaningful bargaining alternatives. The
uncompromising German position left France with no
leverage on this issue (*Frankfurter Rundschau*, 15 September 1978). The choice Giscard faced at Aachen was essentially that between the parity grid and no EMS at all (Dell
1994: 29–30). German policymakers exercised leverage
because there was no chance of credibly excluding them
from the eventual exchange rate regime and because the
costs of possible bargaining failure did not match the costs
of losing policy autonomy. Thus, the French reversal on the
basket- or parity-grid question had little to do with a
sudden reversal in French priorities but rather reflected
bargaining realities at the time.

In addition to the basket question, weak currency
countries pursued a number of other goals to achieve
German compromises on the consistency issue. The British
favored an external orientation on the dollar—for example,
by assigning a specific weight to the dollar in the ECU
basket. Not only were British oil-exporting interests behind
this proposal, but, judging from the experience of the
1970s, the dollar promised to provide a less rigid focal point
for the rest of Europe than the deutsche mark. This coin-
cided neither with German interests in a rigorous system

nor with the long-running objective of Britain's weak currency ally, France, to liberate European monetary politics from U.S. dominance. The historical outcome of this issue also puts an ironic twist on this aspect of the British bargaining position. The deutsche mark weakened in the early 1980s and at least in part actually protected the weaker currencies from the high interest rate policy of the United States during the early 1980s. In other words, deutsche mark orientation achieved quite the opposite of the initial expectations and in that respect de facto helped to alleviate some potential tensions.

A special issue that would normally belong under the heading of financing rules nevertheless deserves attention in this context, namely, the provision of unlimited automatic very-short-term financing assistance. Bundesbank officials clearly saw this issue as potentially the most important threat of externally induced inflation in Germany. However, as Bundesbank and other German officials were well aware, three aspects of the financing mechanisms severely limited their threat to domestic macroeconomic conditions in Germany. First, financial assistance needed to be repaid. While that obligation in itself provided constraints on the amounts weak currency countries could prudently borrow, the fact that short- and medium-term financing assistance had explicit upper limits prevented them from infinitely converting very-short-term obligations into these types of debt. Second, the EMS rules did not explicitly prevent sterilization. Without a rule against sterilization, the Bundesbank could continue to intervene in financial markets and safeguard its domestic objectives. Hans Tietmeyer (1994: 34) describes this logic in the following fashion: "From a German monetary policy point of view such intervention was more or less 'neutral', i.e. its effects on bank liquidity and the money supply in Germany were practically non-existent. The success of such interventions rested essentially on the respective partner's own monetary policy action, i.e. interest rate adjustment." Only when the amount of intervention would start to strain its capacity to sterilize did the Bundesbank have to resort to the third possibility of limiting interventions, namely, its threat to stop interventions. During the EMS negotiations, the Bundesbank obtained the government's explicit permission to stop interventions if that conflicted with its domestic goals, the so-called Emminger letter (Emminger 1986: 356–71; Kaufmann 1985: 68). As Economics Minister Otto Graf Lambsdorff (1978) declared publicly at the time in the German parliament, the Bundesbank had the "option of not carrying out interventions, if the Bundesbank believed it could not do so because of concern over its money supply policy or other considerations." Similarly, Finance Minister Hans Matthöfer publicly agreed that the Bundesbank was free to stop intervention and that the German government would attempt to negotiate a realignment in the EMS if intervention obligations threatened domestic goals in Germany (Emminger 1986: 361–62; Kaufmann 1985: 68).[11]

The importance of the Emminger letter, however, should not be overstated. First of all, the other two limitations on financing—the limits of prudent borrowing and the possibility of sterilization—in themselves represented significant constraints until the 1992 crisis. Indeed, the 1992 crisis was the first occasion when the content of the Emminger letter became relevant for the operation of the EMS. In September 1992, the Bundesbank's intervention obligations fundamentally collided with its domestic objectives. Tables 6.2 and 6.3 illustrate the volume of interventions during the September 1992 and July/August 1993 crises. Table 6.2 provides figures for the overall amount of interventions in deutsche mark by the EMS central banks. It shows a significant increase in compulsory interventions during 1992 and 1993 compared to previous years, as well as in intramarginal interventions. Table 6.3 lists outstanding Bundesbank claims against the EMCF at the end of the respective period. These claims represent a measure of the debt other central banks incurred through the very-short-term and short-term facilities of the ERM. The table indicates a rise in the use of these facilities in September 1992 and again in August 1993 to unprecedented levels. For the

Table 6.2
Deutsche Mark Interventions by All Participating Central Banks in the EMS (in DM billion)

		Compulsory	Intramarginal	Total		Compulsory	Intramarginal	Total
Purchases	1979	-	2.7	2.7	1987	-	47.8	47.8
Sales		3.6	8.1	11.7		15.0	61.7	76.8
Balance		-3.6	-5.4	-9.0		-15.0	-13.9	-28.9
Purchases	1980	5.9	.9	11.8	1988	-	26.8	26.8
Sales		-	1.0	1.0		-	16.3	16.3
Balance		+5.9	+4.9	10.8		-	+10.5	+10.5
Purchases	1981	2.3	8.1	10.4	1989	-	20.4	20.4
Sales		17.3	12.8	30.1		5.0	8.6	13.6
Balance		-15.0	-4.7	-19.7		5.0	+11.8	+6.8
Purchases	1982	-	9.4	9.4	1990	1.5	32.5	34.1
Sales		3.0	12.8	15.8		-	12.3	12.3
Balance		-3.0	-3.4	-6.4		+1.5	+20.2	21.8
Purchases	1983	16.7	19.1	35.8	1991	-	6.4	6.4
Sales		8.3	12.9	21.2		-	21.9	21.9
Balance		+8.4	+6.2	+14.5		-	-15.5	+15.5
Purchases	1984	-	28.9	28.9	1992	-	75.1	75.1
Sales		4.7	7.6	12.3		63.7	199.7	263.4
Balance		-4.7	+21.4	+16.6		-63.7	-124.6	-188.3
Purchases	1985	-	29.1	29.1	1993	-	92.0	92.0
Sales		0.4	30.8	31.1		25.1	168.8	193.9
Balance		-0.4	-1.6	-2.0		-25.1	-76.8	-101.9
Purchases	1996	19.0	33.6	52.6				
Sales		4.1	74.0	78.1				
Balance		14.8	-40.4	-25.5				

Source: Deutsche Bundesbank, *Annual Report*, various years.

Table 6.3
Bundesbank Claims against the EMCF and (beginning in 1994) the EMI (very-short-term and short-term facilities in the EMS; in DM million)

	Jan.	Feb.	Mar.	April	May	June	July	Aug.	Sept.	Oct.	Nov.	Dec.
1980	–	–	–	–	–	–	–	–	–	1022	4292	4228
1981	4077	5520	3301	–	–	–	–	–	–	–	–	–
1982	–	–	–	–	–	–	–	–	–	–	–	–
1983	–	–	–	–	–	–	–	–	–	–	–	–
1984	–	2397	3958	3032	779	601	129	–	–	–	–	–
1985	–	–	–	–	766	–	–	–	–	–	–	–
1986	–	–	–	758	–	–	–	–	–	–	–	–
1987	–	–	–	–	–	–	–	–	–	–	–	–
1988	–	–	–	–	–	–	–	–	–	–	–	–
1989	–	–	–	–	–	–	–	–	–	3006	–	–
1990	–	–	–	–	–	–	–	–	–	–	–	–
1991	–	–	–	–	–	–	–	–	–	–	–	–
1992	–	–	–	–	–	–	–	–	46674	36499	34924	6834
1993	18	398	382	142	–	–	–	20545	20545	20545	4415	4300
1994	–	–	–	–	–	–	–	–	–	–	–	–

Source: Deutsche Bundesbank, *Zahlungsbilanzstatistik*, Statistisches Beiheft zum Monatsbericht 3, various years.

first time, it seemed conceivable that sterilization would not be sufficient to prevent unwanted growth in Germany's domestic money supply. As the then Bundesbank President Helmut Schlesinger admits, "The amount was extraordinarily high, higher than ever before in a speculation crisis. We were in a situation in which we, with the strongest EMS currency and thus having to absorb all the funds, were really no longer in a position to continue our monetary policy" (quoted in *Financial Times*, 15 September 1992). As a result, the Bundesbank requested the federal government to negotiate a realignment in the EMS.[12] Nevertheless, it took thirteen years of operations before events tested the content of the Emminger letter.

Another reason not to overstate the importance of the Emminger letter is the fact that EMS rules did not establish multilateral procedures for its financing facilities. In order not to lose control over the German money supply, the Bundesbank consistently refused to pool reserves among the EU member states prior to entry into EMU. In particular, the proposal for the creation of a European Monetary Fund (EMF) envisioned in the EMS agreement was never implemented. In the negotiations over the EMF, the German government insisted on strict rules for the creation of reserves and the access rights of member states to the financing facilities (Kloten 1981 and Schlüter 1982). In addition, German officials demanded greater macroeconomic convergence as a necessary prerequisite for the establishment of the EMF (*Börsen-Zeitung*, 18 December 1979 and 22 November 1980). In essence, an early creation of an EMF would have violated Germany's preference for the "economist" path to monetary integration. As a result, negotiations over the EMF never succeeded.

Summarizing these issues, during the late 1970s no agreement existed among the EU member states on the question of macroeconomic consistency. While most of the weak currency countries had in one way or another embarked on a course of disinflationary policies, all of them aimed at softening the German macroeconomic standard during the EMS negotiations. Germany actively sought to protect its own domestic policies against infringements by the EMS. It was clearly unwilling to compromise its domestic standard for the sake of successful exchange rate cooperation. Ultimately, the German stance on these issues was successful. As one of the British participants observed: "German interests were well protected in the EMS. Indeed Germany gave away nothing about which the Bundesbank needed to be seriously worried" (Dell 1994: 30). However, this unwillingness to compromise was due not only to Bundesbank pressure, but was clearly shared by most decision makers in Germany's political system. In particular, officials from the economic and finance ministries drafted early positions in the negotiations that allowed for no compromise on these issues.[13]

The idea of convergence only became relevant in the mid-1980s. In this context, the EMS was seen as an instrument possibly to "borrow" credibility (Giavazzi and Pagano 1988; Svensson 1994; Woolley 1991). By maintaining a target exchange rate against the deutsche mark, governments of the weak currency countries could signal disinflationary resolve to their domestic constituencies. In addition, reference to the "imposed" constraint of a fixed exchange rate could help governments to dispel partially the domestic costs of restrictive policies. Ultimately, however, the idea of borrowing credibility could only facilitate, but not replace, basic domestic policy decisions in these countries. Despite increasing convergence after the mid-1980s, the EMS did not truly function as a tool for joint policy *coordination*. The degree of convergence in the EMS was the result of individual policy decisions by member states (most important, France, and less explicitly Italy) to follow the German standard. It was not the outcome of joint decision making in macroeconomic policies.

The convergence during the 1980s, of course, reduced some of the tensions that surrounded the domestic adjustment issue. Nevertheless, the German position remained uncompromising. The Basle-Nyborg reforms offer a paradigmatic example of this logic. The French government sought greater symmetry in the EMS through a joint European exchange rate policy toward the dollar and yen and the coordination of money supply targets (*Financial Times*, 9 September 1987). Following previous patterns, Germany rejected these demands and exchanged concessions only on questions of intervention and financing rules (Pöhl 1987; *Die Welt*, 16 September 1987; *Frankfurter Allgemeine Zeitung*, 16 September 1987). Indeed—and this tends to get overlooked in conventional descriptions of the agreement—the Basle-Nyborg Accord gave even greater recognition to asymmetry in the EMS because the explicit emphasis to use interest rate policy implied that responsibility for defending a weak currency resided chiefly with the weak currency country. In this sense, the bargaining logic of European monetary negotiations had not changed.

The bargaining interaction during the EMS negotiations contradicts the assertion that EMS asymmetry was unintentional and that the EMS was meant to function as a symmetric regime. If EU member states had really been committed to the construction of a symmetric regime, this would have entailed some form of a compromise between weak and strong currency countries on the standard-setting problem. The evidence presented here suggests that weak currency countries were unable to solicit any meaningful concessions on these issues from their strong currency country partners. Most important, their attempt to install the ECU grid as the trigger mechanism for mandatory interventions failed. Also, they did not achieve a multilateralization of financing facilities. Moreover, strong currency countries retained their ability to sterilize their interventions and therefore their ability to counteract the effects of interventions on their domestic economy.

German policymakers knew at the time that the EMS would not force Germany to compromise its domestic macroeconomic objectives. EMS rules as agreed upon in the 1978 negotiations left strong currency countries free to set the macroeconomic standard for the new system. The reactions of weak currency countries to the Aachen summit and "Belgian compromise" leaves no doubt that policymakers of weak currency countries were aware of the structural asymmetry these decisions would introduce into the EMS. If EMS rules gave the appearance of greater symmetry at the time, it resulted from the fact that strong currency countries were more willing to accommodate the concerns of weak currency countries on issues of external adjustment, financing, side payments, and symbolic issues.

The politics of bargaining over EMS rules also contradicts the analytical claim made in the literature on policy ideas (McNamara 1998) that weak currency countries were willing to accept EMS asymmetry because they were committed to a policy of disinflation and macroeconomic convergence by the late 1970s. The compelling aspect of the convergence argument is indeed that it seems to offer an explanation for EMS asymmetry. *Convergence*, in the sense of the high inflation countries moving closer to the priorities of strong currency countries, is distinct from *coordination* through a process of bargaining. Convergence as opposed to coordination is a one-sided policy commitment of the weak currency countries. It does not impose a corresponding obligation on the strong partner in this relationship. Viewed from the convergence argument then, asymmetry appears almost as intentional.

However, there are at least five analytical problems associated with the convergence argument. First of all, it is doubtful if convergence became a really important goal before 1982 or 1983. As argued above, evidence of a firm commitment to policy convergence before the Mitterrand turnabout is scarce. Thus, while the commitment to policy convergence can help us to understand the success of the EMS in the second half of the 1980s, it provides little insight into the bargaining process over the rules.

Second, even if one acknowledges that the weak currency countries were seriously committed to a policy of disinflation in 1978, this is not to say that the *German* macroeconomic standard necessarily served as the focal point of convergence. Rather, it seems more plausible to assume that most of the weak currency countries sought to establish some form of compromise somewhere between theirs and Germany's preferences. The debate over the

ECU indicator underscores this intention on the part of the high-inflation countries.

This means, third, that the convergence argument cannot account for the occurrence of distributive bargaining on the part of the EU member states. If convergence was the reason for cooperation, all member states should have readily endorsed the standard set by the deutsche mark. This, however, was hardly the case. The EMS negotiations featured significant distributional negotiations among the member states.

Fourth, if convergence toward the German standard had really been central, there was hardly any need to negotiate a new regime for monetary cooperation in Europe in the late 1970s. The Snake would have been quite sufficient to serve the purpose of convergence (Dell 1994). This suggests that bargaining for a new regime was driven by concerns over the distribution of adjustment burden in the Snake. While weak currency countries ultimately did not achieve their goals of changing the logic of standard setting, the EMS provided more favorable rules on financing, external adjustments, and side payments.

Finally, the convergence argument cannot explain the reemergence of the EMU project in the late 1980s. If convergence is the goal, EMU seems hardly necessary. Rather it is more persuasive to interpret the goal of EMU as a reflection of distributional concerns over the asymmetrical adjustment burden imposed by the EMS.

External Adjustments, Financing, and Side Payments

In this subsection I will only address some general features of external adjustment and financing in the EMS. A specific analysis of the bargaining exchanges over the EMS rules on these issues will be saved for the next section since the German role of brokering agreement in this area became particularly important for the success of the EMS negotiations. As mentioned above, the regular EMS fluctuation margins were set at +/–2.25 percent, with a special

+/–6 percent fluctuation band for Italy (which was later also applied to new entrants into the EMS). One important aspect of the actual EMS operations was that members usually did not use the whole range of fluctuation margins. Rather, there was a pervasive tendency to employ intra-marginal interventions in order to keep exchange rates comfortably within their bands and to forestall speculative attacks in case of temporary weakness. Since intramar-ginal interventions were carried out in dollars, the danger of an increase in the German money supply remained small. In addition, realignments usually took place well before currency values reached their margins (Gros and Thygesen 1992: 72–85; Ungerer et al. 1990). Since this practice kept mandatory interventions at a fairly low level, weak currency countries avoided extensive confrontations with the Bundesbank.

Realignments within the EMS followed a clearly dis-tinguishable pattern (Gros and Thygesen 1992: 67–97; Ungerer et al. 1990). During the first four years of opera-tion, convergence between the EMS members remained minimal. Despite a period of relative DM weakness, seven realignments were necessary until March 1983. Increasing convergence, in particular the turnabout in French macro-economic policies, and the strength of the dollar were largely responsible for a decline in the number of realign-ments (four) between 1983 and 1987. And from 1987 to 1992, the EMS saw no major realignment, except for a largely technical change in the lira's central rate in the context of its move to narrower fluctuation bands. All realignments were carried out with comparatively limited disruptions and turbulences in financial markets.

The development of operational procedures for realign-ments is also unique. Until 1981, member states arranged realignments largely on an informal and ad hoc basis. This changed with the realignment of 5 October 1981. While the core of this realignment was a change in the deutsche mark–French franc parity, the French sought to arrange a "face-saving" deal for domestic political purposes. The result was a simultaneous devaluation of some of the other EMS currencies, despite the fact that none of these countries had initially asked for a devaluation. The second face-saving element of this particular realignment was the German agreement to accept a larger *re*valuation of the deutsche mark (+5.5 percent) than a *de*valuation of the franc (−3.0 percent). Thus, it was not the previously agreed norm of multilateral negotiations, but rather the need for the French government to preserve its prestige that facilitated the implementation of explicit bargaining over realignments. From that time until 1987, most realignments followed this pattern of a negotiated package deal. The result of this explicit bargaining was that the actual devaluations turned out to be smaller than requested by the respective member state and that devaluing countries explicitly agreed to certain domestic policy changes (Ungerer et al. 1990). Most prominent were the French decisions to cut government spending in exchange for realignments from 1981 to 1983 (Hall 1986; Loriaux 1991: 261).

Thus, EMS operations with regard to external adjustment and financing turned out to be much smoother for many years than they were during the Snake period. While subsequent convergence is certainly part of this story, it cannot be ignored that bargaining over the rules on external adjustment and financing produced more consensual solutions than a decade earlier. These were in part due to a greater German willingness to broker agreement among EMS members and to address at least some of their distributional concerns.

Germany's Role in EMS Bargaining

Standard Setting

As explained previously, member states did not adopt any specific *rules* to regulate domestic adjustment. Germany successfully protected its priorities for domestic adjustment against the demands of weak currency countries and favored noncooperation on this issue over any eventual constraints on the pursuit of its macroeconomic policies. With no rules in place, however, the absence of a reserve constraint necessarily meant that the standard of the strong currency country would become the effective answer to the consistency problem. As during the operation of the Snake, Germany became the nth country in the EMS by controlling the one free monetary policy instrument in the EMS. As explained earlier, Germany did not face a reserve constraint and was therefore in position to choose much more freely its adjustment options than weak currency countries. This forced other EMS members to maintain equilibrium in their balance-of-payments, while Germany was relieved of an external constraint and free to choose its macroeconomic policies in line with domestic objectives.

While this indicates at first sight an imposed solution to the consistency problem, the provision of a stable focal point nevertheless eased the bargaining problems that would arise in the absence of such a solution. In that sense, the egoistic behavior of Germany in protecting its domestic priorities was ironically also a contribution to cooperation. This logic became even more pronounced during the 1980s when the other EMS members started to use the German standard as a reference point for their own disinflationary efforts.

One important expression of Germany's standard-setting position is its ability to set the interest rate floor within the EMS. As table 6.4 demonstrates, the Benelux countries almost completely succeeded in converging to German interest rate levels. France tested its autonomy in 1991 and 1992 and was able briefly to hold short-term rates below German levels. However, the French central bank had to intervene with more than Ffr 50 billion in support of the franc between October 1991 and January 1992 (Thygesen 1993: 456). In other words, the French attempt lacked credibility in capital markets, a situation that repeated

itself in a more pronounced fashion during the spring of
1993. As the deutsche mark briefly depreciated, the French
authorities again lowered interest rates below German
levels. In addition, French politicians openly claimed that
the French franc could replace the deutsche mark as the
anchor currency (*Financial Times*, 23 June 1993, 26/27
June 1993; *Der Spiegel*, 14 June 1993, pp. 98–104). French
tactics became so irritating for German authorities that
German Minister of Finance Theo Waigel canceled a scheduled meeting with his French counterpart, Edmond
Alphandéry, in June 1993 (*Frankfurter Allgemeine Zeitung*,
25 June 1993). However, this strategy ultimately backfired
when the French franc came under severe pressure, and
EMS rules had to be changed in August 1993.

The patterns of intervention policy in financial
markets underscore the logic of Germany's nth country
status. In their analysis of EMS-related interventions,
Francesco Giavazzi and Alberto Giovannini (1989:67) con-
clude that "[m]ost of the intramarginal intervention was
carried out by countries other than Germany, while Germany intervened only when bilateral fluctuation margins
were reached." This behavior supports the contention that
Germany did not concern itself with the relative position of
exchange rates within the band (Mastropasqua, Micossi,
and Rinaldi 1988). It intervened only when EMS rules
required such intervention. This relatively passive attitude
vis-à-vis the exchange rate meant that Germany maintained a large degree of control over its domestic policy
objectives.

The 1992/93 crisis in the EMS, however, underscores
the faultlines of this standard-setting solution in exchange
rate cooperation. Germany's position as the standard setter
lost legitimacy because other EMS members became
unwilling or unable to adjust to Germany's standard
through the traditional means of domestic or external
adjustment. Germany's high interest rate policy produced
externalities unacceptable for its partners. Its freedom
from balance-of-payments constraints started to destabilize
the system.

Table 6.4
Short-term Interest Rates, 1979–1992

	1979	1980	1981	1982	1983	1984	1985	1986	1987	1988	1989	1990	1991	1992
Belgium	10.9	14.2	15.6	14.1	10.5	11.5	9.6	8.1	7.1	6.7	8.7	9.8	9.4	9.4
Denmark	12.5	16.9	14.9	16.4	12.0	11.5	10.0	9.1	9.9	8.3	9.4	10.8	9.5	11.5
France	9.7	12.0	15.3	14.6	12.5	11.7	10.0	7.7	8.3	7.9	9.4	10.3	9.6	10.4
Germany	6.9	9.5	12.4	8.8	5.8	6.0	5.4	4.6	4.0	4.3	7.1	8.4	9.2	9.5
Greece	-	-	16.8	18.9	16.6	15.7	17.0	19.8	14.9	15.9	18.7	19.9	22.7	24.5
Ireland	16.0	16.2	16.7	17.5	14.0	13.2	12.0	12.4	11.1	8.1	9.8	11.4	10.4	12.4
Italy	12.0	16.9	19.3	19.9	18.3	17.3	15.0	12.8	11.4	11.3	12.7	12.3	12.2	14.0
Netherlands	9.6	10.6	11.8	8.2	5.7	6.1	6.3	5.7	5.4	4.8	7.4	8.7	9.3	9.4
Portugal	16.1	16.3	16.0	16.8	20.9	22.5	21.0	15.6	13.9	13.0	14.9	16.9	17.7	16.2
Spain	15.5	16.5	16.2	16.3	20.1	14.9	12.2	11.7	15.8	11.6	15.0	15.2	13.2	13.3
United Kingdom	13.9	16.8	14.1	12.2	10.1	10.0	12.2	10.9	9.7	10.3	13.9	14.8	11.5	9.6

Source: Commission of the European Communities, 1993.

Concession Making and Side Payments

While Germany maintained an uncompromising position on domestic adjustment issues, its bargaining strategy on rules for external adjustment and financing, as well as on side payments, showed much greater flexibility. The most important items on the bargaining agenda here were the procedures for setting central rates in the ERM, the width of fluctuation margins, and the conditions for financing assistance. Given the fact that Germany succeeded with all of its demands on internal adjustment, German concessions on some of these issues were essential to avoid bargaining deadlock and to alleviate at least some of the distributional concerns of weak currency countries. Thus, while overall German bargaining behavior on EMS rules was clearly self-interested and rigid, on these issues Germany performed a function similar to that of a broker in establishing a zone of agreement among participants.

The rules governing the setting of central rates were crucial for the successful implementation and development of the EMS. With the German refusal to accept any obligation to reflate its economy, it was inevitable in 1978/79 that realignments had to become a tool of adjustment for the foreseeable future. The idea of exchange rate stability in Europe was viable at the time only for more or less extensive periods between discreet realignments. In particular, German policymakers never conceived of the EMS as a rigid fixed exchange rate regime (Schmidt 1990: 259–60). During the initial negotiations, the German government reached an understanding with its partners that realignments would be carried out in a swift, timely, and discreet fashion (Hellmann 1979: 79–80; *Süddeutsche Zeitung*, 14 July 1978; *Die Zeit*, 28 July 1978; Dell 1994: 57). In essence, this meant that covergence was not one of the core concepts of the early EMS operations. Rather, there existed a consensus that realignments were a legitimate tool for adjustment among a group of countries that was still characterized by significant divergence. While still controversial, realignments and devaluations had clearly lost some of their political stigma. The experience of floating during the 1970s had shifted the costs and benefits of exchange rate decisions: in the eyes of many policymakers, orderly realignments were now superior to currency chaos.

The fact that realignment decisions after 1981 became the subject of multilateral negotiations further strengthened their largely consensual character. While technical requirements for the functioning of the ECU played a role, the original decision to establish multilateral procedures also reflected political considerations (Hellmann 1979: 76–80). Since a deutsche mark revaluation had historically been the only form of real adjustment Germany would accept for itself, it was mandatory that German policymakers kept this option open. Despite fears voiced within the Christian-Democratic opposition that the provision for multilateral procedures might prevent realignments, German policymakers in general viewed this stipulation as a tool to gain influence over the policies of their partner countries and to aid in the process of convergence.[14] Even Bundesbank officials were not worried that the rule of multilateral bargaining over realignments would constrain the pursuit of Germany's domestic priorities. The ability to stop interventions effectively amounted to a unilateral device for coercing other EMS participants into a realignment (Emminger 1979). Indeed, the 1992 crisis underscores this rationale.

A factor that helped to establish realignments as consensual means of adjustments was the frequent willingness of Germany to "concede" revaluations of the deutsche mark rather than to force complete devaluations upon the weak currencies, ultimately a largely psychological measure with little economic impact. The two primary bargaining objectives for Germany in realignment negotiations were to get other strong currency countries also to revalue their currencies and to limit the actual range of parity changes. These objectives reflected two simultaneous policy goals. Germany could maintain its competitiveness as much as possible, by limiting the range of the exchange rate changes and by keeping other strong currencies tied to the deutsche mark. Second, Germany could exert pressure for domestic adjustment in the weak currency countries, by preventing them from putting the whole weight of adjustment on external measures. Under these conditions, a deutsche mark revaluation had the intended economic consequences and allowed Germany to pursue its domestic objectives. Politically, it helped governments of the weak currency countries to "save face" with their domestic constituencies.[15] In particular, deutsche mark revaluations allowed them to "blame" Germany as the main source of divergence.[16] The habit of deutsche mark revaluations was thus a "concession" to keep France in the EMS and to keep EU markets open (*Stuttgarter Zeitung*, 6 October 1981; *Die Welt*, 14 June 1982; *Frankfurter Allgemeine Zeitung*, 22 March 1983; *Handelsblatt*, 22 March 1983).

The commitment to consensual realignments weakened during the late 1980s. Increasing convergence and the absence of major global monetary crises after 1987 seemed to make realignments unnecessary. In addition, the early prospects and later the concrete negotiations on moving toward EMU promoted a reluctance among EMS members to change exchange rates because that could be seen as a sign that countries were not ready to join the monetary union. Between 1987 and 1992, the EMS became increasingly viewed as a quasi-monetary union. This view, however, not only reflected an inherent strength of the EMS. It also constituted the core of problems that ultimately led to its breakdown. The unwillingness to consider any realignment prior to September 1992 clearly contributed to the turmoil that followed. One of the basic prerequisites for the smooth operation of the EMS, namely, consensual realignments, disappeared during these years.

This environment induced the EMS participants to reject early German requests for a revaluation of the deutsche mark after reunification. Similarly, both Great Britain and France resisted devaluations of their currencies during periods of severe turmoil in financial markets after the summer of 1992—ultimately triggering the British ERM withdrawal and the widening of fluctuation bands in the ERM. These developments indicated that the assumptions behind the absence of realignments between 1987 and 1992 were in reality quite problematic. First, while the weak currency countries had undoubtedly progressed in their convergence efforts, inflation levels still diverged among the EMS members. Italy, in particular, accumulated a significant inflation differential in these years, and Great Britain entered the ERM during a period of high domestic inflation and at an exchange rate that was generally perceived as overvalued.[17] Second, dollar stability remained only a temporary phenomenon. During the summer of 1992, the dollar hit record lows against the deutsche mark, aggravating and fueling the tensions that culminated in the September crisis. And third, the crisis of 1992/93 unmasked the "quasi-monetary union" of 1987 through 1991 as a myth. As long as exchange rates are not permanently and reliably fixed in a full monetary union, financial markets can test the stability of parities. In this sense, the 1992/93 crisis in part expressed the failure of the EMS members to determine adequately the divergence that German reunification would introduce among them and the appropriate adjustment measure for the EMS, namely, an early revaluation of the deutsche mark.[18]

It is therefore not surprising that the operating procedures for exchange rate adjustments changed again with the 1992 crisis. Realignments essentially reverted from multilateral negotiations back to more ad hoc arrangements. Over the weekend of 11 through 13 September, German and Italian authorities negotiated the devaluation of the lira largely bilaterally. The Monetary Committee was bypassed, and the Council of Finance Ministers essentially lost control of the issue and simply rubberstamped the German-Italian deal (*Financial Times*, 12–13 December 1993). The failure of the EMS members to negotiate a comprehensive realignment is in part responsible for fueling further turbulences in financial markets. Only three days later, on 16 and 17 September 1993, Great Britain and Italy respectively withdrew from the Exchange Rate Mechanism after sustained interventions and interest rate increases could not lift their currencies from the ERM floor. In addition, the Spanish peseta was devalued on 17 September. Subsequent devaluations of the Spanish, Portuguese, and Irish currencies followed the pattern established by the 1992 lira devaluation. They were ad hoc arrangements, and they were no longer accompanied by specific domestic policy measures in the devaluing countries (Thygesen 1993: 456). Overall, the deterioration in the legitimacy of the realignment tool contributed to the crisis and near-demise of the EMS. The crisis, thus, demonstrates the importance of the earlier consensus on realignments for the stability of the EMS in its initial years.

Another bargaining item during the initial negotiations concerned the size of fluctuation bands in the EMS. Italy negotiated successfully for larger bands of 6 percent on each side of the central parity. After the Aachen Summit removed the ECU grid from the bargaining table, the question of fluctuation bands indeed became the highest priority on the Italian agenda. According to most observers, it is unlikely that Italy would have participated in the EMS without a compromise on this question (*Neue Zürcher Zeitung*, 10 September 1978; Spaventa 1980; Ludlow 1982). Helmut Schmidt himself was very hesitant to make this concession because of the lack of discipline that this would entail for the new monetary system. He feared that the wider margins would loosen external constraints on weak currency countries (Schmidt 1990: 364). In the immediate aftermath of the Brussels summit, he described the acceptance of the larger fluctuation bands as the most significant German concession during the EMS negotiations but as a compromise that needed to be made in order for the system to come into existence (Schmidt 1978). The concession of larger fluctuation bands not only enabled Italy to join the EMS but was also a prerequisite for French participation. During the negotiations, the French government was anxious to avoid being the weakest country in the new system (*Neue Zürcher Zeitung*, 10 September 1978; Dell 1994: 31). While France acted as a leading force in the EMS negotiations, its ultimate decision to join came only after Italy and Ireland had accepted the terms of the EMS agreement.

As it turned out, the decision to allow Italy to use larger fluctuation bands is a very significant factor in explaining the survival of the EMS during its early years. The large bands allowed Italy to keep the lira within specified parameters for longer periods of time and to use devaluations only about once a year on average during the first eight years of the EMS. At the same time, the larger fluctuation bands discouraged currency speculation because in the case of a realignment they allowed EMS members to fix new central rates within the margins set by the old fluctuation bands. Thus, the market rate of the lira would not suddenly jump to a new level as a result of a devaluation and therefore prevent currency speculators from cashing in on "one-way-bets" (de Grauwe 1994).

A comparable bargaining setting occurred during the ERM crisis of July/August 1993. Among the various alternatives discussed for solving this crisis, the widening of fluctuation margins provided the lowest common denominator for all parties involved. The political logic of European monetary politics simply foreclosed other options. For example, the preferred French option would have been a rapid reduction in German interest rates. Following the typical pattern, however, Germany was unwilling to adjust through a change in domestic policy. Similarly, during late July 1993, it became increasingly unlikely that the Bundesbank would indefinitely continue to intervene on behalf of the French franc, despite the much greater verbal support that Bundesbank officials gave to the franc than to the lira and pound a year earlier. Thus, a choice of prolonged interventions in financial markets did not exist.

Another option discussed during the July 1993 crisis was a temporary exit of the deutsche mark from the ERM. Since Germany was the main source of divergence in the EMS from the French perspective, a temporary float of the deutsche mark would have presumably eliminated the major cause of monetary instability at the time. But the Netherlands, Denmark, and Belgium rejected the proposal to suspend German ERM membership temporarily (*Süddeutsche Zeitung*, 3 August 1993; *Financial Times*, 3 August 1993). Since the other strong currency countries threatened a joint float with the deutsche mark, the EMS would have consisted of the French franc and the remaining weak currencies. This scenario was politically infeasible, in particular in competition with a joint float of the EU's strong currencies.

French opposition thwarted another potential solution to the July 1993 crisis, namely, a devaluation of the French franc and other weak currencies. Reflecting their typical preference for adjustment, German policymakers had since 1990 promoted a realignment to absorb the shock of German monetary unification. The French government, however, did not want to endanger the credibility it had accumulated for its *franc fort* policy over the past few years. A realignment would have unfairly stigmatized the weak currency countries. Given the fact that a change in German domestic policy, financing, a German withdrawal, or a realignment could not serve as consensual adjustment options, the widening of fluctuation margins became the policy of choice in August 1993. While the +/–15 percent margins agreed upon during the crisis involved a significant change in the essence of EMS rules, the decision formally preserved the EMS as an institution. It made it possible to maintain central rates, and financing facilities continued to exist. Thus, given the options available in July/August 1993, the decision to widen fluctuation margins preserved some of the presumed benefits of exchange rate cooperation. In particular, it prevented even greater damage to European integration. And given the fact that exchange rates among the EMS core members returned quickly to the precrisis range, the decision also allowed governments to underscore their political commitment to the EMU project by maintaining exchange rate stability despite large fluctuation bands.

In addition to questions of external adjustments, the other major bargaining objects in the history of the EMS have always been the rules governing the system's financing facilities. During the initial EMS negotiations, the main French goal, after Giscard dropped the demand for the ECU-based intervention system, was to achieve more favorable rules on the EMS financing mechanisms. Simultaneously, it became a prominent item on the Italian bargaining agenda. Both governments pursued two goals in particular: first, to enlarge the financial assistance available under the prevailing Snake rules, and, second, to establish favorable repayment conditions.

These goals were not trivial. At the time of negotiations in the late 1970s, the weak currency countries believed that more favorable financing rules than the Snake's were necessary to alleviate some of their distributional concerns. Throughout the post–World War II period, British, French, and Italian governments had relied heavily on the financing of balance-of-payments difficulties. They were convinced that financing was an important element of easing the adjustment process (Walsh 1994). This belief motivated demands for a significant increase in the quotas for short- and medium-term financing compared to the Snake quotas. The French government pursued a combined goal for both facilities of 25 billion ECU (about $34 billion at the time) and preferred a higher allotment of the total to the short-term as opposed to the medium-term facility. Given the fact that the then-highest central bank credit ever granted was the $5 billion IMF loan to Great Britain in 1976, the French demand was quite substantial (*Die Zeit*, 27 October 1978). Germany originally rejected both the expansion of these quotas and a larger amount for the short- over the medium-term support mechanism because they could potentially reduce discipline in the system. In the end, however, the German government agreed to the French demands. Short-term monetary support was set at 14 billion ECU, medium-term financing at 11 billion ECU. According to many observers, this concession was crucial to make the membership of France and Italy possible (Hellmann 1979: 51; Ludlow

1982: 239–43). On the other hand, it was not a very costly
compromise from the German perspective because the
enlargement of these credit facilities would have little
impact on Germany's domestic economic priorities.

Even after these initial compromises the question of
financing facilities remained consistently on the bargaining
table, although in a different form than originally anticipated. Weak currency countries ultimately underutilized
the short- and medium-term facilities during the actual
operation of the EMS. This fact, however, does not demonstrate the irrelevance of financing in the EMS. Rather, it is
the pattern of intervention that changed significantly
during the operation of the EMS. Instead of marginal intervention, which allowed the use of the EMS financing facilities, intramarginal interventions became the dominant
mode of exchange rate management. By 18 September 1992,
intramarginal interventions in the EMS since its creation
had reached a total of 770 billion DM (Nölling 1993: 57). The
original EMS, however, did not allow for an automatic use
of financing facilities for intramarginal interventions. Thus,
if countries wished to intervene intramarginally, they either
had to bargain explicitly with other EMS governments or
central banks, or they had to use their own dollar reserves.
The first alternative was burdensome and constraining and
was not in accordance with the incentive of the weak currency countries to multilateralize financing rules. The
second one contradicted the incentive of liberating European monetary relations from American dominance. The
EMS member states addressed these developments and
considerations in the Basle-Nyborg reforms of 1987 by
allowing the use of the very short-term facilities for intramarginal interventions. The quid pro quo in the extended
use of the financing facilities was the greater reliance on
interest rate changes for exchange rate stabilization. In
essence, the result of the Basle-Nyborg arrangement was
thus quite ironic: the weak currency countries were supposed to rely less on intramarginal intervention in order to
obtain more liberal access to it.

A similarly important bargaining issue for the weak currency countries was the question of extended borrowing periods. Great Britain and Italy both felt that the repayment periods of the Snake were insufficient to allow them to replenish their reserves after a balance-of-payments crisis. Some observers noted that the British exit from the Snake in 1972 was in part triggered by its looming inability to meet repayment obligations. Ultimately, the weak currency countries succeeded in the initial EMS negotiations in extending the borrowing period for very-short-term assistance from thirty to forty-five days. The Basle-Nyborg agreement again extended repayment periods to seventy-five days. Both outcomes came against earlier German resistance. They were possible because these concessions were not costly for German domestic economic priorities.

A peculiar instance of German concessions concerns the more or less symbolic issue of the name for the common unit of account within the EMS (Hellmann 1979: 44–45). The name *ecu* was psychologically important to the French since a currency with that name was used in thirteenth-century France. Because the German translation of the Council resolution of 5 December 1978 still used the German abbreviation EWE for the common unit of account, and the English and Italian versions spoke of ECU in capital letters, the French attached notes to all versions of the EMS agreement that they called it "Ecu" in the singular and "Ecus" in the plural. That was supposed to indicate that Ecu meant more to the French than the simple abbreviation of the term *European Currency Unit* (spelled ECU in capital letters). Following this episode, Schmidt conceded the introduction of the term *ECU* (i.e., as the English abbreviation in capital letters) into the German language, but as a special concession to France, he promised the use of the French pronunciation for the term (Schmidt 1979).[19]

The construction of side payments to weaker countries also aquired some significance in the EMS bargaining process. While structural aid is not an inherent aspect of exchange rate cooperation, the weaker countries feared that disinflationary policies could increase some of their problems. Italy and Ireland, therefore, demanded an increase in regional funds. It is noteworthy that on this issue the alliance of weak currency countries fell apart. France rejected an increase in the Regional Development Fund (Statler 1979: 222–23). Germany, on the other hand, became the principal spokesperson for Italian and Irish interests and was willing to accept much larger obligations than those that were ultimately implemented (Schmidt 1979; Jenkins 1989). Because of French resistance, Italy and Ireland had to accept loan and interest rate arrangements with the EMS and the European Investment Bank. Direct capital transfers—their original goal—remained disappointing.

In summary, Germany played a leadership role during the EMS negotiations in two ways. Uncompromising insistence determined the specific standard-setting solution found for domestic adjustment issues. On the other hand, Germany showed greater flexibility on questions of external adjustment, financing, structural aid and symbolic issues. This allowed for the emergence of a "zone of agreement" among the EU member states (see table 6.5).

Conclusion

Despite visible differences in success and policy outcomes, the rules of the EMS reflect a consistent pattern of bargaining among EU member states. As in earlier attempts at monetary cooperation, strong currency countries rejected any form of compromise on issues of domestic adjustment. However, they demonstrated greater willingness to alleviate weak currency countries' concerns over adjustment costs on issues of external adjustment, financing, and side payments. Table 6.5 summarizes this bargaining exchange. The upper part of the table indicates the absence of German concessions on all major negotiating items dealing with internal adjustment. In contrast, the lower part of table 6.5 depicts significantly greater German

Table 6.5
EMS Bargaining Issues

INTERNAL ADJUSTMENT ISSUES

Weak Currency Country Demands	Strong Currency Country Demands	Solutions	German Concession?
1) General goal: compromise on macroeconomic standard	General goal: No constraints on the pursuit of domestic policies	Standard setting according to nth currency solution	No
2) ECU grid (France, Italy, Great Britain)	Parity grid	Parity grid triggers interventions; ECU grid becomes "divergence indicator"	No; officials viewed divergence indicator as irrelevant
3) Dollar orientation (Great Britain, Italy)	Dollar independence (support by France)	Dollar independence	No
4) Multilateralization of credit in EMF	Binding rules for EMF; possibility to stop interventions; no rules against sterilization	no agreement on EMF; countries are free to cease interventions and to sterilize	No

EXTERNAL ADJUSTMENT, FINANCING, AND SIDE PAYMENTS

1) Larger fluctuation bands (Italy)	Small fluctuation bands maintain discipline	6% fluctuation bands	Yes
2) Revaluation of strong currencies	Consensual realignments if exchange rates are unsustainable	Variable forms of realignments	Yes, if necessary for domestic political reasons in devaluing country
3) Extension of financing facilities	Takeover of Snake facilities	Extension of financing facilities	Yes
4) Use of very-short-term facilities for intra-marginal interventions (Basle-Nyborg)	No change	Use of very-short-term facilities for intramarginal interventions	Yes
5) Extended borrowing periods: a) 60 days (EMS agreement) b) 75 days (Basle-Nyborg)	No change (keep previous periods) a) 30 days b) 45 days	a) 45 days b) 75 days	Yes
6) Side payments: extension in structural funds (Italy, Ireland)	Germany more willing to make concessions than France	Loans (but no direct capital transfers)	Yes (and willing to go further)

flexibility on issues of external adjustment, financing, and side payments. While macroeconomic convergence later became the most important stabilizer for the EMS, the bargaining exchanges EU member states engaged in help to explain the survival of the EMS during its early years.

7

The Politics of European Monetary Union: Bargaining over the Maastricht Rules

Two statements by a French and a German official, respectively, strikingly illustrate the range of bargaining problems involved in the Maastricht process toward monetary union (EMU).[1] In 1988 French Finance Minister Edouard Balladur stated that the EMS should be reformed "to prevent one country from determining the objectives of economic and monetary policy for the group as a whole" (quoted in McCarthy 1993: 58). Reimut Jochimsen, president of the Landeszentralbank of Northrhine-Westphalia and member of the Bundesbank Council, said of the German position on EMU: "a stable currency takes precedence over a common one (though the objective naturally remains to achieve both simultaneously)" (Jochimsen 1993: 198). While the French hoped to prevent Germany from dominating the other EU member states, German policymakers—while in principle supportive of the idea of monetary union—sought to avoid any form of cooperation that would compromise their own domestic economic priorities.

This chapter depicts the process toward the Maastricht Treaty as a struggle to find common ground for cooperation under these circumstances. Both Balladur and Jochimsen describe the primary distributional concerns that each of these two leading countries brought to the EMU bargaining table. The primary French incentive for EMU was dissatisfaction over the asymmetrical functioning of the EMS. Successful French convergence toward German macroeconomic goals had eroded the legitimacy of any asymmetry in the EMS. Germany, however, was from the outset of the EMU process clearly unwilling to accept a common currency that would be less stable than its own. While French convergence created the basis for Germany to take seriously the demand for monetary union, the Maastricht process toward EMU still featured distributional conflicts similar to those that arose in earlier attempts at monetary cooperation, and bargaining followed familiar patterns. Bargaining leverage increasingly separated from real macroeconomic divergence, and the advantage of strong currency countries rested now primarily on their longer track record and greater credibility in financial markets. Nevertheless, their remaining bargaining leverage was still sufficient to install their preferred monetary constitution in Europe.

This argument already hints at the main irony of the Maastricht process. Despite the initial French incentive to challenge the asymmetry of European monetary relations, the solution of the Maastricht Treaty in many aspects was not equitable. Germany pushed through its own vision on all important domestic macroeconomic issues, from the convergence criteria to the constitution of the European Central Bank. Ultimately, there was only one way to bridge the rift between Balladur's and Jochimsen's statements quoted at the beginning of this chapter. If Germany's ability to pursue unilateral decisionmaking was the core objection of the others, the only chance to multilateralize monetary policymaking was to do it on German terms. Following the patterns exhibited in earlier examples of European monetary cooperation, Germany was willing to make concessions only on issues that did not infringe on its domestic macroeconomic priorities. Even on those other issues, however, the German room for compromise was limited. German negotiators achieved successful bargaining outcomes even on a number of symbolic questions, such as the seat of the European Central Bank in Frankfurt and the name of the eventual European currency, *Euro* (instead of the French-backed *ecu*). Thus, while the French achieved their goal of a treaty commitment to monetary union, the concrete rules for monetary union are distinctly German.

Historical Overview

During the first half of the 1980s, a renewed attempt at forming a monetary union along the lines of the Action Programme and Werner Report initiatives was essentially a nonissue. The EMU topic, however, reappeared in the second half of the 1980s.[2] Numerous factors created a favorable environment for the reemergence of the topic. Among the more conventional incentives were the anticipated trade and investment effects of monetary union. A common currency would completely eliminate exchange risks. If firms are risk averse, this would stimulate the growth of trade and investment. The available evidence indicates that the business community supports the goal of monetary union, even if it is difficult to determine the influence of other potential concerns on this preference, for example, stable prices or competitiveness. Even for Germany, surveys and anecdotal evidence show significant support among business leaders for monetary union.[3] In addition to exchange risk, a common currency would eliminate all transaction costs and the costs associated with currency hedging. Despite these considerations, however, trade and investment gains from monetary unification remain relatively small. The EU Commission calculated overall economic gains of 0.25 to 0.5 percent of GNP. While such increases are not insignificant, their small order suggests that they are not the decisive incentive for the Europeans to pursue EMU.

In addition, however, EMU could help to safeguard the trade and investment effects of previous projects in European integration. During the 1980s the EU embarked on a major new initiative of market integration, the Single European Act (SEA).[4] The SEA program seeks to abolish all internal frontiers among EU member states and to allow for the free movement of goods, services, people, and capital across national borders. While the increase in transactions as a result of the customs union and single market projects had been substantial, policymakers and observers voiced the fear that spillover from monetary crises could cause governments to reintroduce protectionist measures (Eichengreen 1993). According to Wolfgang Schäuble, then chairman of the CDU/CSU faction in the German Bundestag, monetary turbulence could create situations in which "the single market is not irreversible" (*Der Spiegel* 7, 12 February 1996). Similarly, representatives of German business continuously warned against spillover of monetary problems into the single market and used this argument in favor of EMU (*Financial Times*, 27 April 1995). From this perspective EMU could serve as a tool to maintain and facilitate the trade and investment effects of the Single European Act program.

Another fortunate circumstance was the appointment of Jacques Delors to the presidency of the EU Commission in 1985 (Ross 1995). This decision put a politician in charge of the central EU bureaucracy who was strongly attached to the idea of greater monetary cooperation in Europe and whose policies as French finance minister during the early 1980s had built the foundation for greater French-German macroeconomic convergence. In his inauguration speech as president of the Commission, Delors advocated a single European currency (*Wall Street Journal*, 15 January 1985), a goal he pursued with great persistence in the following years.

More important, however, the early part of the EMU debate was mostly driven by the incentive to stabilize and safeguard the achievements of the EMS. Despite the relative success of the EMS, the second half of the 1980s witnessed two potentially destabilizing tendencies. The first was the liberalization of capital movements in the context of the SEA. Put in terms of Robert Mundell's (1968) renowned theorem, governments now faced the problem that they could no longer pursue simultaneously the three objectives of exchange rate stability, capital mobility, and independent macroeconomic policy. Earlier chapters have already raised questions about the causal significance of capital mobility in this theory. I suggested there that the crucial and more basic incompatibility obtains between the objectives of exchange rate stability and macroeconomic policy independence. Capital mobility is merely a framing condition. A higher degree of capital mobility simply speeds up the process of adjustment. It denies governments time to adjust, whereas a lower degree of capital mobility allows states to postpone adjustment for periods of time. In this sense, it is necessary to guard against attributing too much causal signifcance to the liberalization of capital flows for the emergence of EMU.

Nevertheless, economists in general viewed the possibility for governments to impose capital controls prior to the introduction of the SEA as an important stabilizing element for exchange rates in the EMS. Clearly, liberalization of capital flows would strain the capacity of the EMS to stabilize exchange rates (Eichengreen 1994). Moreover, without capital controls, it would no longer be possible to separate onshore and offshore financial markets and to allow the French and Italian central banks to force up Eurocurrency interest rates without experiencing a corresponding increase in their domestic interest rates. Thus, the economic costs of defending their currencies would increase after the dismantling of capital flows. In this sense, the SEA provided an incentive to devise strategies that would stabilize the achievements of the EMS. The so-called Padoa-Schioppa Report provided the intellectual rationale for moving from the pegged exchange rate system of the EMS to a full monetary union (Padoa-Schioppa 1988). And while a single currency is not necessarily a technical concomitant for the functioning of the single market, the common currency would further integrate and symbolize the single market in Europe.

The second, and ultimately most important concern over the future stability of the EMS resulted ironically from the system's very success. Increasing convergence eroded the legitimacy of Germany's central position. Since Germany's nth country status in the EMS was policy-based rather than resource-based, its continued role as the standard setter now rested merely on its longer historical record of low inflation, not on its policy edge. Under these circumstances, asymmetry in the EMS had to become controversial and potentially threatening to the stability of the EMS. Thus, French concerns over the asymmetric distribution of obligations in the EMS corresponded with Germany's realization that an asymmetric EMS was politically untenable in the long run. Consequently, the German debate increasingly focused on the question of how to maintain the benefits of monetary cooperation under potentially increasing EMS instability. In this context, EMU appeared as an escape route from long-term EMS instability.

The question of policy domain is related to this issue.[5] While the Bundesbank pursued price stability for Germany, the asymmetric logic of the EMS forced the other members to adjust to the Bundesbank's policy. This logic was compelling as long as the other EMS members tried to gain credibility for their disinflationary policies. After successful convergence, however, the rationale for following Bundesbank preferences became questionable. German economic conditions and needs do not always and necessarily fully overlap with European conditions and needs as a whole (Matthes 1988). The Bundesbank could not possibly function as a European central bank. Thus, political tensions were bound to increase if the Bundesbank took only German domestic conditions into account for its monetary policy decisions—most visibly expressed, of course, in the economic divergence following German reunification. Only a common central European monetary institution would pursue a monetary policy geared toward the EU as a whole.

French Finance Minister Edouard Balladur's memorandum on reform of the EMS in early 1988 represents the crucial initiative of transforming the question of domain into an explicit political issue. Deploring the asymmetric functioning of the EMS, Balladur's statement clearly criticized Germany's standard-setting role in the EMS. Germany's ability to determine the macroeconomic standard for the system as a whole had become unacceptable. Instead,

Balladur demanded that EU member states develop procedures to establish economic priorities collectively.

Despite this critical intention, the Balladur initiative did not receive a completely hostile reception in Germany. While Chancellor Helmut Kohl and Finance Minister Gerhard Stoltenberg worded their responses cautiously, Foreign Minister Hans-Dietrich Genscher emerged as the primary advocate of monetary integration in Germany. He reacted to Balladur's initiative with a memorandum of his own, proposing the creation of a common European monetary area and European central bank (Genscher 1988; *Frankfurter Allgemeine Zeitung*, 27 January 1988; *Wirtschaftswoche*, 29 January 1988).

Genscher's positive reaction, however, was not as surprising as some observers suggest (e.g., Gros and Thygesen 1992: 311–17). First, Genscher's memorandum contained the well-known German demands for macroeconomic convergence before moving toward monetary integration and for the independence of a European central bank according to the Bundesbank model. Thus, while the relatively friendly tone of Genscher's response contrasts with the anti-German sentiment of Balladur's initiative, its substance did not deviate from the well-established "economist" strategy of Germany. Second, a debate over further monetary integration had already been well under way in Germany at the time Balladur and Genscher issued their respective memoranda (Schönfelder and Thiel 1994: 22–28).

One source of this brewing domestic debate in Germany over monetary union derived from the abovementioned concerns over the long-term stability of the EMS. Even in the eyes of German policymakers, increasing convergence by other EMS members had eroded the legitimacy of asymmetry in the EMS. These thoughts were supplemented by broad foreign policy considerations. Using the positive impact of the SEA negotiations, German policymakers sought to push for new initiatives in European integration during the second half of the 1980s. Genscher, as one of the main creators of the SEA, feared that future difficulties would erode the single market if monetary cooperation could not keep up with the speed of integration under the SEA (Genscher 1995: 387–99). Most important, Genscher used the idea of monetary unification as a theme for Germany's agenda during its term in the EU presidency. The most crucial step during Germany's EU presidency was the decision at the Hannover Summit of June 1988 to appoint a commission under the chairmanship of Jaques Delors to study the issue of monetary union. Eighteen months later, the fall of the Berlin Wall and pending reunification provided additional political stimulus for the EMU debate. To reassure its European neighbors and avoid isolation, the German government became even more openly committed to the goal of monetary unification.

The Delors Commission issued its report in April 1989 (Committee for the Study of Economic and Monetary Union 1989). The report designed a process toward monetary union in three stages. The first stage was to consist of closer macroeconomic coordination between the EU member states and the complete liberalization of capital flows in the EU. For the second stage, the report envisaged a tightening of fluctuation margins, the creation of a European system of central banks, and the gradual transfer of monetary policymaking responsibility to the Community level. The third stage would consist of setting up a European central bank, the irrevocable fixing of exchange rates, and ultimately the introduction of a single European currency. At the Madrid Summit in June 1989, the governments of the EU member states endorsed the Delors Report, chose July 1990 as the starting date for stage one, and decided to convene an intergovernmental conference (IGC) to discuss specific rules for monetary union. The notable exceptions to this general approval were the reservations expressed by the British government.

The crucial event that intervened between the Madrid Summit and the start of the IGC was the fall of the Berlin Wall in November 1989. The prevailing literature often treats the prospect of German reunification as the main causal factor for the Maastricht Treaty (Baun 1995–96;

Baun 1996; Garrett 1993; Martin 1993; and Sandholtz 1993a). That, however, overstates the impact of these pending geopolitical changes in central Europe. While reunification may have been an important push for successfully completing the negotiations, it was not the cause of the EMU process (see also Moravcsik 1998). Rather, it is more appropriate to see German reunification as accelerating and intensifying the Maastricht process. While the German government was committed to the goal of EMU in general terms—at the latest since Genscher's response to the Balladur memorandum—the specifics of any eventual process toward monetary union were subject to an intense domestic debate in Germany.[6] This domestic debate, however, led to the impression that Germany was dragging its feet on the specific timetable for EMU negotiations (*Süddeutsche Zeitung*, 28 June 1989, 10 September 1990; *Frankfurter Rundschau*, 28 June 1989; *Frankfurter Allgemeine Zeitung*, 8 September 1989; *Financial Times*, 21 September 1990).

Thus, while the prospect of German reunification was not responsible for the emergence of the EMU issue, it was crucial for ending this period of German indecision. During the winter of 1989/90, serious divisions occurred between France and Germany over the question of German reunification. The French government became reluctant to endorse it. In particular, President Francois Mitterrand's visits to Kiev and East Germany represented deliberate attempts to slow down the rapid speed of the unification process (Baun 1996: 41–44; Teltschik 1991). Chancellor Helmut Kohl perceived the French strategy as a potential threat to isolate Germany. This prospect was crucial in pushing Kohl to agree on a firm timetable for the IGC negotiations on EMU (Schmidt 1990: 262). Initially settled at a French-German Summit on April 19, the European Council adopted the timetable at its summit in Dublin on 28 April 1990. With this step, Germany was seriously committed to concrete negotiations over EMU. In exchange, Mitterrand dropped his resistance to German reunification (Methfessel 1996: 35). A side aspect of this bargain was the agreement simultaneously to convene an intergovernmental conference on *political* union (EPU) in order to prepare the EU for the impending changes after the end of the cold war.

Post-1990 interpretations, however, exaggerate the causal significance of the Kohl-Mitterrand deal. Neither the argument that reunification would have been impossible without Germany's commitment to Maastricht nor the assertion that Germany's "sacrifice of the deutsche mark" was only the result of French pressure on the reunification question is correct. Both processes already had their own dynamics by the spring of 1990; their interaction simply accelerated each other. Given the internal political processes in East and West Germany, the open support of the Bush administration and Gorbachev's waning resistance to it, reunification became inevitable at least in the medium term, no matter how long France attempted to resist. Furthermore, Germany had accepted the principle of EMU before reunification became an issue at all. The events during the spring of 1990 simply provided greater urgency for Germany to accept a definitive timetable for negotiations and then later during the Maastricht Summit itself to accept the so-called automaticity clause.

The Rome Summit of December 1990 formally launched the intergovernmental conferences on political and economic union. IGC negotiations on EMU had to decide a number of significant issues: the scope of and the precise rules for stage two of monetary union, the rules governing common monetary institutions and monetary relations in stages two and three, and the conditions for a transition from stage two to a full monetary union.[7] While bargaining ultimately found a successful outcome in the Maastricht Treaty, a definitive agreement was not reached until the heads of governments finalized some important deals at the Maastricht Summit of December 1991.

While I will review various aspects of the bargaining process and its results later in this chapter, the substantive provisions of the Maastricht Treaty (Council and Commission of the European Communities 1992) can be summarized as follows:

1. The treaty scheduled stage two of the EMU process
   to begin in January 1994. During this phase, monetary coordination was supposed to increase among
   the European countries in order to prepare for the
   transfer of monetary decision-making power to the
   European Central Bank (ECB) and the fixing of
   exchange rates in stage three.

2. The primary institutional element of stage two was
   the establishment of a European Monetary Institute
   (EMI) (Art. 109f and "Protocol on the Statute of the
   European Monetary Institute"). It took over the
   functions of the EMCF and of the Committee of
   Central Bank Governors. Its major task was the
   technical preparation of the unification of currencies
   in stage three. While it served as the predecessor of
   the new European Central Bank (ECB), its authority was limited. Monetary policymaking responsibilities remained with national central banks during
   stage two.

3. The treaty and its Protocols established the following convergence criteria for participation in stage
   three of EMU:[8] Governments needed to achieve a
   sustainable financial position, which the "Protocol
   on Excessive Debt Procedure" defined as a budget
   deficit below 3 percent of GDP and an overall debt
   below 60 percent of GDP. Member states needed to
   achieve a high degree of price stability, which the
   "Protocol on the Convergence Criteria" defined as an
   "average rate of inflation . . . that does not exceed by
   more than 1 1/2 percentage points that of, at most,
   the three best performing Member States in terms of
   price stability." Countries' long-term interest rates
   were supposed to indicate the durability of convergence, which the "Protocol on the Convergence Criteria" defined as an "average nominal long-term
   interest rate that does not exceed by more than two
   percentage points that of, at most, the three best
   performing Member States in terms of price stability." Moreover, member countries' exchange rates
   were compelled to respect the normal fluctuation
   margins of the ERM "without severe tensions" in the

two years prior to the examination of eligibility for stage three of EMU.

4. The treaty explicitly set deadlines for a decision to move to stage three. The first deadline mentioned in the treaty was the year 1997. EMU would enter stage three if the "Council, meeting in the composition of the Heads of State or Government" decided that "a majority of the Member States fulfill the necessary conditions for the adoption of a single currency" and that "it is appropriate for the Community to enter the third stage" (Art. 109j(3)). The EU officially abandoned this deadline after the 1992/93 turmoil in the EMS. The second target date was 1999, when all those countries fulfilling the convergence criteria were supposed to move to stage three. This provision has often been referred to as the "automaticity clause," since it required monetary unification regardless of whether the group of eligible countries constituted a majority of EU member states (as required by the 1997 deadline) or merely a small group.

5. Great Britain and Denmark received "opt-out clauses" from monetary union. They notified the European Commission about their intentions not to join EMU, despite the fact that they fulfilled most of the convergence criteria in the spring of 1998.

6. The rules governing the ECB itself were largely structured according to the model of the Bundesbank (Art. 104–109c and "Protocol on the Statute of the European System of Central Banks and the European Central Bank"). Most important is its political independence and the explicit policy goal of low inflation.

Ratification of the Maastricht Treaty was much more difficult than expected. The Danish electorate rejected the treaty in a referendum in June 1992. Only after the Danish government received a number of special supplements at the Edinburgh Summit did the treaty survive a second referendum in May 1993. The French referendum of September 1992 resulted in an extremely close victory for the treaty, and many observers merely attribute this result to the sympathy effect for President Mitterrand, who had revealed in the days leading up to the referendum that he was suffering from cancer. In Germany, the goal of monetary union was very controversial, although the treaty survived constitutional challenges and faced little opposition in parliamentary votes. The vote of the British Parliament in favor of ratification, however, was extremely slim, and any future British participation in EMU is still uncertain. Overall, the Maastricht Treaty survived its ratification process only very narrowly.

The currency crisis of 1992/93 also raised doubts over an eventual move toward a common currency. Financial markets remained jittery for a long time, and many observers feared renewed turmoil in the run-up to the eventual final fixing of parities in EMU. In addition, EU member states were experiencing severe problems meeting the official convergence criteria of the Maastricht Treaty. Most important, due to the continentwide recession, the chances for most EU member states to fulfill in particular the fiscal requirements were seen as very low during the mid-1990s. For several years, Luxembourg was the only EU member to comply with all criteria. Even Germany exceeded the deficit ceiling in 1995 and 1996. Nevertheless, the economic upswing, various austerity and one-time fiscal measures allowed all EU members—except Greece—to push their 1997 budget deficit below the 3 percent GNP margin of the Maastricht Treaty. Similarly, inflation rates stayed low, and calm financial markets allowed interest rates to converge close to the reference value. Under these conditions, the Heads of Governments decided that eleven EU member states would join in the third stage of EMU starting on 1 January 1999, despite the fact that many of them had overall debt levels of above 60 percent GNP (see table 7.1). While Great Britain, Denmark, and Sweden decided on their own not to seek admission to the common currency, Greece was the only EU member state judged not to be in compliance with the Maastricht convergence criteria.

Bargaining Asymmetries and the Politics
of the Maastricht Negotiations

As in the case of previous attempts at monetary cooperation, the problem of reaching agreement over domestic macroeconomic adjustment formed a significant part of the EMU negotiations. Theoretically speaking, a monetary union could offer a distinct advantage over a pegged exchange rate system in terms of reduced bargaining complexity: it creates consistency automatically. As discussed in earlier chapters, history knows examples of currency unification between quite unequal partners. However, the automatic adjustment process within a currency union can impose substantial costs for its participants. Monetary union between East and West Germany was possible in 1990 because political imperatives clearly outweighed distributional considerations. Within the Maastricht negotiations, this condition did not exist to such an extent. Distributional concerns clearly shaped EMU bargaining. The Maastricht Treaty negotiations featured essentially two main areas in which distributional concerns were at stake: the rules governing the *common monetary institutions* and the rules governing *entry into the monetary union.*

The rules governing the common institutions had three major bargaining items: the political independence of the ECB itself, the independent status of the respective national central banks that comprise the ESCB, and the functions of a common monetary institution during stage two. The strong currency country position was central to the bargaining logic on all three items. First of all, they demanded the political independence of any eventual central bank, following the model of the German Bundesbank, and a constitutionally guaranteed commitment of the ECB to the goal of low inflation. Central bank independence was seen as a central condition and cause for Germany's low inflation record (Goodman 1992). Thus, for the policymakers of the strong currency countries, the status of the European central bank was primarily a stan-

Table 7.1
Maastricht Convergence Criteria for EU Countries in 1997

	Deficit	Debt	Inflation	Interest rates
reference value	-3.00	-60.0	2.7	7.8
Austria	-2.5	-66.1	1.1	5.6
Belgium	-2.1	-122.2	1.4	5.7
Denmark	+0.7	-65.1	1.9	6.2
Finland	-0.9	-55.8	1.3	5.9
France	-3.0	-58.0	1.2	5.5
Germany	-2.7	-61.3	1.4	5.6
Greece	-4.0	-108.7	5.2	9.8
Ireland	+0.9	-66.3	1.2	6.2
Italy	-2.7	-121.6	1.8	6.7
Luxembourg	+1.7	-6.7	1.4	5.6
Netherlands	-1.4	-72.1	1.8	5.5
Portugal	-2.5	-62.0	1.8	6.2
Spain	-2.6	-68.8	1.8	6.3
Sweden	-0.8	-76.6	1.9	6.5
United Kingdom	-1.9	-53.4	1.8	7.0

Source: European Monetary Institute, 1998.

dard-setting issue. They saw any model other than an independent ECB along the lines of the Bundesbank as potentially threatening to their macroeconomic standard.[9]

Other countries were less convinced of the need for central bank independence. Their domestic traditions had differed. France had even achieved disinflation with a government-controlled central bank. Given these circumstances, strong currency country policymakers did not expect the other countries to accept the principle of central bank independence easily. In his comments on EMU prior to the IGC negotiations, French Finance Minister Pierre Bérégovoy rejected the goal of central bank independence for the ECB despite the basic agreement reached in the Delors Report (*Handelsblatt*, 15 November 1990; *Frankfurter Allgemeine Zeitung*, 30 January 1991). The French draft treaty proposed a stronger role for the Council in monetary matters than the German proposals (Italianer 1993: 69–70). Even after Maastricht, President Mitterrand commented during the referendum campaign that the "function of the [ECB] is to implement the resolutions passed by the twelve heads of state and government in its conduct of monetary policy" (Mitterrand 1992). While not backed by the wording of the treaty, the comment still raised concerns among German observers about a reliable French commitment to the goal of central bank independence (*Frankfurter Rundschau*, 5 September 1992; *Süddeutsche Zeitung*, 9 September 1992; Nölling 1993: 194). The Germans saw a stronger role for the European Council as potentially compromising the ECB's independence.

In spite of French reservations, however, acceptance of the principle of central bank independence during the IGC negotiations was unexpectedly easy. Ultimately, a credible exit threat enhanced Germany's bargaining position on this point. The other countries knew well that Germany would not participate without the principle of central bank independence. At the same time, however, participation of the principal strong currency country was essential to the EMU project. Thus, weak currency countries were not in position to reject German demands on this issue. Moreover, strong currency countries had an important tactical advantage. The Committee of Central Bank Governors was in charge of drafting the ECB Statute (Cameron 1995b). Among the governors, of course, the goal of central bank independence was not controversial and represented part of their common institutional interest—independent of the national affiliation of the various central bank governors and the legal status of their own home institution. In the end, the central bank governors' draft was adopted at Maastricht with very few changes.

Following a similar logic, strong currency countries also demanded that all national central banks receive independent political status before they became full constituent members of the ESCB in stage two. Surprisingly, that issue turned out to be more controversial than the question of political independence for the ECB itself. France and Great Britain both rejected a demand that they viewed as an intervention into the domestic politics of EU member states (*Börsen-Zeitung*, 11 September 1990; Baun 1996: 61–62; Bini-Smaghi, Padoa-Schioppa, and Papadia

1994: 10–11). While the compromise reached during the IGC negotiations was to require the independence of national central banks only for stage three but not for stage two, it came at the expense of stronger German opposition to any transfer of meaningful tasks to the European Monetary Institute during the second stage. The irony of this solution was underscored by the fact that the French government decided on its own to make its central bank independent shortly after the Maastricht Summit.

As indicated, the question of national central bank independence had implications for the design of a common monetary institution during stage two (Bini-Smaghi, Padoa-Schioppa, and Papadia 1994: 10–11). Originally, France and Italy demanded a gradual transfer of monetary policymaking power to a common central bank during the second stage of the EMU process, as recommended by the Delors Report (Wilking 1992: 148). The German authorities, however, were worried about a clear delegation of monetary responsibilities during stage two. They feared that the French-Italian proposal would confuse responsibilities between the common monetary institution and national central banks. In their view, a clear sense of monetary accountability was necessary during the transitional phase. There also existed the danger that a strong common monetary institution during stage two would create an open-ended half-way house that would neither require the full commitment of each participant nor be capable to implement rigorous monetary policies. Such an ambiguous separation of responsibilities also could have left the common monetary institution in stage two open to political pressures (Anderson and Goodman 1993: 52–53).

The fact that its partners were unwilling to grant independence to their national central bank as an entry requirement for stage two contributed only to greater German insistence on this point. Ultimately, the German position by and large succeeded in the negotiations, with the one symbolic concession of allowing the provision to choose an outside EMI president (rather than to appoint one of the national central bank governors). The treaty established a weak European Monetary Institute (EMI) for stage two. The EMI took over the tasks of the EMCF and the Committee of Central Bank Governors, but it was devoid of any operational functions, and its primary task was the technical preparation for the third stage (*Handelsblatt*, 30 December 1993; *Financial Times*, 29 December 1993). Monetary decision making remained the domain of the national central banks during stage two.

The choice between a common and a single currency was an interesting subplot to this institutional debate. The British government introduced various proposals for a parallel or hard ECU, which was to compete with national currencies. The idea was that markets would ultimately select the best currency in the process. Politically, however, the hard ECU proposals were merely diversionary tactics. The British hoped these proposals would appeal to the Bundesbank and would reinforce skepticism about the EMU process in Germany (Thatcher 1993: 762). Competition in which the best currency would prevail should have been intriguing to German policymakers, given the strength of the deutsche mark. It came, therefore, as a surprise to the British when the Bundesbank rejected the hard ECU proposal on the grounds that increased currency substitution would undermine the effectiveness of national monetary policies and create accountability problems (*Financial Times*, 11 September 1990, 10/11 November 1990; *The Independent*, 12 November 1990). Overall, the clear diversionary intent of this prolonged debate damaged even further the bargaining strength of the British government in the IGC.

The second substantial set of bargaining items during the IGC negotiations concerned the conditions for entry into EMU. Here, bargaining revived the traditional "economist-monetarist debate." Germany and its strong currency allies insisted that participants of EMU had to meet tough criteria in order to join the monetary union. According to their concerns, a monetary union without tough convergence criteria would impose costs on the strong currency countries in terms of higher inflation. Again, Germany and its strong currency allies were unwilling to compromise their domestic priorities for the sake of a common currency.

In traditional "monetarist" fashion, weak currency countries at first rejected the introduction of convergence criteria into the Maastricht Treaty. They felt that these criteria would simply serve as a tool to exclude them from participation in EMU. The first French proposal for the treaty in fact did not include convergence criteria. And Italian government officials, as well as officials from other weak currency countries, were outraged when the Dutch draft for the treaty, which served as the main framework of negotiations in the later phases of bargaining, contained convergence criteria for entry into stage three with the explicit intention to exclude those countries that did not fulfill the criteria (*The Times*, 10 September 1991; *Süddeutsche Zeitung*, 11 September 1991; *The Economist*, 14 September 1991).

The particular convergence criteria themselves and the reference values chosen for them did not so much reflect clear-cut economic calculations but rather political considerations.[10] First of all, it is unclear what type of criteria would be appropriate. There were discussions during the IGC negotiations and later on to include indicators of real convergence, such as unemployment, GNP per capita, and the flexibility of labor markets. These were dismissed for various reasons, be it practicality of measurement or the intense pressure of Germany to include inflation-related indicators (Bini-Smaghi, Padoa-Schioppa, and Papadia 1994: 20–31; Nölling 1993: 154–61). Similarly, the particular reference values chosen also reflected bargaining rather than pure economic logic. According to Kenneth Dyson (1994: 156), the convergence criteria "were set at their particular levels for two reasons: because the figures were close to the average performance of the best-performing EU countries in 1990, and because the Bundesbank was keen to agree figures that would constitute a prospectively too high hurdle for the EU states collectively to jump." Even if a larger number of countries ultimately qualified for EMU than expected, the inclusion of convergence criteria into the

Maastricht Treaty reflected the "economist" preference for monetary union *after* convergence.

Thus, as in the case of earlier attempts at monetary cooperation, strong currency countries were unwilling to make concessions on issues of domestic adjustment. They made sure that agreement on the rules for the common institutional structure and membership criteria would come on their terms. In contrast to the EMS negotiations, however, participants of the Maastricht negotiations were unable to shift bargaining to questions of external adjustment and financing issues to address some of the distributional concerns resulting from the pervasive influence of strong currency countries on domestic adjustment issues. Within a monetary union, external adjustment through exchange rate changes is impossible, and traditional forms of financing balance-of-payments difficulties are unnecessary. Nevertheless, a number of EMU-related issues more conducive to symmetrical bargaining also required solutions. In particular, this involved the timing of the various stages, the cohesion funds, and various more or less symbolic issues. The next section will address these issues by analyzing Germany's role in using concessions on some of these issues as a vehicle to avoid bargaining deadlock and to alleviate at least some of the concerns that resulted from the decidedly "German" character of the institutional and membership rules for EMU.

Germany's Role in the Maastricht Process

The conventional assumption is that France has driven the process toward EMU. Balladur's initiative had finally put the topic of monetary unification back on the EU's agenda, and EMU was paramount to the French interest in undermining German monetary power. Clearly, France served as the primary agenda setter in bringing the EMU topic to the negotiating table. Nevertheless, Germany ultimately became the linchpin in the EMU bargaining framework and was pivotal in shaping the Maastricht rules.

Following the familiar pattern, Germany served as the standard setter for EMU by taking the role of a "constitutional architect." Similarly, German policymakers performed a "broker"-like function, making a number of side payments and symbolic concessions to prevent deadlock and allowing for the successful conclusion of the Maastricht Treaty negotiations.

Identifying this role also resolves a startling contrast in the current literature on EMU. Some observers point to the overwhelming influence of Germany on the rules governing EMU in the Maastricht Treaty (Marsh 1992). Other analysts have noted a surprising tendency of the German government to make concessions during the EMU negotiations (Sandholtz 1993b; Bini-Smaghi, Padoa-Schioppa, and Papadia 1994; Italianer 1993). The distinction this section draws between German standard setting and German concessions on side payments demonstrates that this contrast is not necessarily puzzling. German officials have consistently insisted on Germany's role as the standard setter of EMU but have been willing to make side payments and to compromise on other EMU-related issues. Separating these issues in that manner makes it possible to gain a more comprehensive understanding of the bargaining interaction in the EMU process.

Standard Setting

As previously argued, standard setting has been the typical solution to the problems associated with domestic adjustment issues in European monetary cooperation. Within the EMS Germany provided the function of standard setting by solving the redundancy problem in nth country fashion. In a monetary union, however, a formal redundancy problem does not exist. A monetary union establishes consistency simply by enlarging the domain of monetary policy. Thus, the EMS solution of keeping rules on internal adjustment open to let Germany establish the macroeconomic focal point in nth country fashion was not conceivable for the members of EMU. Neither could

Germany simply allow just any rules of monetary unification if it was concerned about the distributional implications of a common currency. Under these circumstances,
Germany became the constitutional architect of EMU. The
strong German position resulted from two simultaneous
conditions. Germany had a credible exit threat from EMU
negotiations. At the same time, German participation was
imperative for any functioning monetary union because the
project would otherwise have no credibility. As the *Financial Times* (28 February 1991) noted already during the
early stages of the IGC negotiations: "In the end, EMU will
come on something close to German terms, or not at all. It
is up to Germany's partners to decide whether they want to
pay the price." Thus, the need to secure German participation in EMU at virtually any cost created an asymmetrical
bargaining interaction. In the end, the Maastricht Treaty
met most long-standing German conditions for monetary
union.

Germany's standard-setting role is probably most
visible in the case of the architectural design for the European Central Bank. The ECB Statute imitates in many
respects the laws governing the Bundesbank. In particular,
its independence from national governments and other EU
institutions reflects German demands for a credible safeguard of price stability. In some respects, the ECB rules are
even tougher than those of the Bundesbank. The main aim
is to maintain price stability, whereas the Bundesbank Law
speaks less clearly of "safeguarding the currency." And,
unlike the Bundesbank, the ECB cannot provide credit to
governments (Marsh 1992). Moreover, the German parliament can change the Bundesbank Law, whereas a change
in the ECB Statute would require the renegotiation and
ratification of a treaty among the EU member states. Thus,
its status is more secure than that of the Bundesbank
(Kenen 1995: 39–43; Dyson 1994: 150–51; Teivainen
1997).[11]

The other significant element of standard setting is, of
course, the existence of convergence criteria for monetary
union. As elaborated in the previous section, these conver-

gence criteria were logical components of the "economist" position advocated by the strong currency countries. Convergence criteria ensured that the obligation of adjustment would rest with weak currency countries (otherwise EMU entry would simply be denied) and that the reference point for convergence would be close to the standard set by the strong currency countries.

In addition to the Maastricht agreement itself, the German standard-setting role has also been visible in various post-Maastricht bargaining settings. Most important, perceiving an imbalance between the rules for monetary policies—centralized around the ECB—and the rules for fiscal policies—still decentralized and subject to individual national policy—German policymakers insisted on the adoption of a "stability pact" that would include binding sanctions for governments whose deficit spending went above agreed limits *after* entry into EMU. Again, France initially resisted the idea of a stability pact. When this position became untenable the newly elected Socialist government demanded the inclusion of active employment policies into the eventual stability pact. The ultimate decision amounted to nothing more than a "fig leaf" (*Financial Times*, 17 June 1997) for the French government by adding a largely empty employment chapter into a document that followed more or less German preferences for strict fiscal rules (*Handelsblatt*, 30 December 1997).

A similar post-Maastricht pattern of German standard setting has also characterized the determination of the specific policy tools of the ECB. Following the conclusion of the Maastricht negotiations, the Bundesbank chose the question of monetary targeting for a highly visible discussion (Deutsche Bundesbank, *Annual Report 1992*: 87). Bundesbank officials maintained that money supply targets should be made part of any ECB monetary policy, although Bundesbank officials later softened their position to a more pragmatic mix of both monetary and inflation targeting (*Financial Times*, 23 December 1997). In addition, Bundesbank officials insisted strongly on maintaining a minimum reserve policy along the lines of Bundesbank policies (*Süd-

deutsche Zeitung, 28 December 1995). Well aware of the need to transfer credibility from the Bundesbank immediately to the new ECB, German preferences again benefitted from an asymmetrical bargaining interaction. Ultimately, the ECB could not afford to start operations with a disgruntled Bundesbank as one of its constituent national central banks. Thus, the ECB announced that monetary targeting would be a component of its monetary policy, and it adopted a minimum reserve policy.

Another contentious issue on which the German position prevailed even after the conclusion of the IGC talks was the relationship between the so-called "ins" and "outs" of EMU—an arrangement sometimes also referred to as EMS II (*Süddeutsche Zeitung*, 15 April 1996). France initially sought to establish a relatively rigid pegged exchange rate regime between the "ins" and "outs," including automatic financing assistance through the ECB and strict limitations on devaluations of weak currencies. Following their well-established convictions, German officials rejected the French proposals. Any eventual financing obligations by the ECB vis-à-vis the "outs" was supposed to be limited along lines that reflected the Emminger letter procedure of the Bundesbank for the EMS. As in the original EMS, obligations for adjustment must rest with the weak currency countries, and devaluations must remain an available adjustment instrument for the "outs". The agreement reached at the informal meeting of EU finance ministers and central bank governors in September 1996 in Dublin follows German preferences in this respect (*Die Welt*, 23 September 1996; *Süddeutsche Zeitung*, 23 September 1996; *Financial Times*, 23 September 1996).

The above analysis describes Germany's standard-setting role as very inflexible and uncompromising. There is no doubt that several other EU members resent this situation and view the German position as arrogant and uncooperative. However, German obstinacy in some sense also facilitated agreement at Maastricht. Germany's role as constitutional architect avoided policy conflict among the EU members, since it precluded bargaining over standard-setting issues. The independent status of the ECB and the introduction of convergence criteria were settled quasi-automatically, due to the need of securing German participation. Rather than struggling with Germany over these issues, the energy of the non-German countries was diverted to areas in which Germany was much more willing to make concessions.

Concessions and Side Payments

The situation on standard-setting issues contrasts significantly with bargaining over other issues in the EMU negotiations. During the IGC negotiations, as well as in later bargaining settings, Germany accepted a number of "deals" and made concessions if they were necessary to come to an agreement. According to many observers, the most important concession that allowed EMU to move forward occurred at Maastricht itself, namely, Germany's acceptance of a definitive timetable for moving to stage three in the EMU process. Germany's attempt to avoid distinct deadlines in the EMU process had raised French and Italian uncertainties over Germany's real interests. While the weak currency countries had agreed during the pre-summit negotiations to all German demands for strict convergence criteria and the independence of the ECB, they had not received a corresponding German commitment to move ahead with monetary union at a definitive date. The most familiar story line has it that France's President Mitterrand and Italy's Prime Minister Giulio Andreotti hatched out a last minute deal in the night before the summit to lock in Germany (Marsh 1992: 237–47). Given the asymmetry in the bargaining outcome so far (namely, their acceptance of convergence criteria and central bank independence but the absence of a definite German commitment), they had to make certain that their efforts at convergence would be rewarded eventually. Thus, they proposed to make EMU obligatory in 1999 for all countries that fulfilled the convergence criteria. By accepting Germany's stringent conditions for convergence and central bank independence, "the Maastricht players laid back down on the table trump cards taken from Germany's own hand"(Marsh, 1992: 247). In other words, Germany's leverage on the timetable question was weak. Most important, Germany's "economist" position did not logically preclude a binding timetable.

Ultimately, agreeing on the automaticity of EMU was the necessary bridge between the contrasting "economist" and "monetarist" positions on monetary unification. On the one hand, the deal among Germany, France, and Italy followed the "economist" path of forging convergence between the participants prior to monetary unification. On the other hand, it circumvented the inherent problem of the "economist" approach that convergence requirements could delay monetary union indefinitely by setting a discrete date for the transfer of monetary decisionmaking to a joint institution. The automaticity concession was necessary to underscore Germany's commitment to EMU and to give credibility to the project. It also provided the signal to interested states that costly adjustment policies to meet the convergence criteria would in the end be rewarded through EMU membership.

While the automaticity issue may be the most significant concession, Germany agreed to a number of other compromises on related bargaining items.[12] For example, following French demands, it accepted an outside president for the EMI, rather than insisting on its preferred option to let the EMI function simply as a renamed Committee of Central Bank Governors (*Handelsblatt*, 4 November 1991). Another compromise concerns the rules for the external exchange rate relations of EMU (Kenen 1995: 118–23; for the negotiations, see also Baun 1996: 63). Germany preferred rules that would not force the ECB to intervene in financial markets in a manner inconsistent with the goal of domestic price stability. Bundesbank officials would have liked to see "*sole* responsibility of the ESCB for currency market interventions" (Nölling 1993: 166). Other governments sought to maintain governmental control over external exchange rate policy. Ultimately, the German government conceded to give the Council of Ministers influence on external exchange rate policies. Overall, however, Bundesbank officials are not overly concerned about the implications of these regulations. If the ECB can establish credibility similar to that of the Bundesbank, it expects the actual practice of external exchange rate policies to develop along similar lines as the previous distribution of responsibilities within Germany.

Following the pattern familiar from the EMS negotiations, Germany also accepted the creation of the so-called cohesion fund as a further concession during the Maastricht Summit (Baun 1996: 72–73). The purpose of this fund was to promote and support structural changes within the poorer EU countries. Thus, it was to alleviate the cost concerns of weak currency countries about introducing adjustment policies in order to participate in the common currency. Germany, having to cope with its own reunification costs, rejected the creation of new funds until the Maastricht Summit itself (*Die Welt*, 13 November 1991). Instead, weak currency countries were supposed to achieve convergence through their own means and existing funds in the EU (Bundesministerium für Finanzen 1991; *Börsen-Zeitung*, 27 February 1991). Nevertheless, veto threats by the Mediterranean countries forced Germany to concede this point.[13] Compared to the EMS negotiations in 1978, however, it is noteworthy that German officials were much more reluctant this time around to make this side payment.

A related German concession concerns the relationship between political union and EMU. Germany served as the primary advocate of further political integration in the EU. German policymakers also insisted initially that progress on political union and on monetary union were contingent on each other (*Handelsblatt*, 3 December 1991; *Die Welt*, 5 December 1991). Thus, without progress on political union, Germany seemed unlikely to commit itself to greater monetary integration. During the IGC negotiations, Germany ultimately abandoned this condition. German policymakers, in particular Chancellor Kohl, accepted the necessity of not delaying agreement on monetary union any further just to extract concessions on political union. In effect, Germany acceded to its role as the major "loser" on the political union negotiations (Baun 1996: 97).

All of these concessions were possible because ultimately none of them impeded Germany's ability to protect its own domestic priorities. Interestingly, however, German policymakers have prevailed on more EMU-related items than my argument can explain. Germany's success in making Frankfurt the seat for the EMI (and eventually the ECB) and in pushing through the name *Euro* instead of *ECU* for the common currency speak directly to this point. Both decisions are ultimately of symbolic nature.[14] Given the typical patterns of German bargaining they should have been areas in which Germany was inclined to compromise. However, the paramount importance other countries attached to a credible and satisfied German membership in EMU presented Germany with greater leverage than before. The location and name questions were, even in their symbolism, important issues for Germany to reassure the German public (Sperling 1994). Moreover, the difficult domestic political situation in Germany essentially allowed the government to transform these issues into quasi-standard setting issues. A seat in Frankfurt would provide for the easiest transfer of credibility from the Bundesbank to the ECB (and as a side effect could possibly increase Frankfurt's role as a financial center). And only a new name would avoid the association of the new common currency with the ECU's long-run tendency to depreciate against the strong currencies in Europe.

Germany's ability to succeed not only on the substantive provisions of EMU but also on some of the symbolic issues heightened the French feeling that EMU was coming on purely German terms. This feeling is believed to be behind President Jacques Chirac's determination to extract one more symbolic—but highly visible—concession from Germany, namely, the appointment of the first president of the European Central Bank. Opposed to the Dutch central banker Wim Duisenberg—who was strongly backed by

Germany and the other thirteen EU member states—
Chirac nominated Jean-Claude Trichet, the governor of the
Banque de France, to serve as ECB president. While
Duisenberg ultimately prevailed in the diplomatic struggle,
Chirac obtained Duisenberg's commitment that he would
not serve out the full eight years of his term but would
retire early (presumably after about four years) to make
room for Trichet (or possibly another French candidate) as
ECB president. Observers generally viewed this solution as
a French victory in the bargaining process. Chancellor Kohl
justified the concession based on the fact that France had
been forced to make many more compromises than
Germany throughout the process of EMU bargaining (*Süddeutsche Zeitung*, 7 May 1998). However, despite the high
visibility of this decision, it was again a purely symbolic
concession. As even the most hard-line German policymakers had maintained during the ECB presidency debate, in
real substantive terms there was no difference between
Duisenberg and Trichet (*Financial Times*, 5 January 1998;
Die Tageszeitung, 8 May 1998). Indeed, Chirac's very choice
of Trichet had been influenced by the realization that a candidate with a "softer" reputation would have had no chance
for German approval. In that sense, the prevailing logic of
bargaining in European monetary cooperation had not
changed.

Conclusion

Bargaining over the Maastricht rules for EMU followed a similar pattern as previous attempts at monetary
cooperation. As the upper part of table 7.2 summarizes,
strong currency countries insisted on adopting rules that
reflected their preferences for domestic adjustment. Since
strong currency countries had a credible exit threat and
there was no conceivable alternative to constructing EMU
without their participation, the agreed rules reflect the bargaining asymmetry between weak and strong currency
countries. Issues of domestic adjustment were thus settled

through German standard setting. German concessions on issues that did not affect domestic adjustment issues alleviated some of the concerns of Germany's partners in the EU over the decidedly German character of EMU rules, most notably the automaticity clause and the ECB presidency. However, as shown in the lower half of table 7.2, German leverage over the EMU rules was so strong that even the solution to two purely symbolic issues, namely, the ECB seat and the name of the common currency, fully accommodated German demands.

What do these insights tell us about the future of EMU? The argument developed in this book showed that the Maastricht rules for EMU follow the logic of bargaining leverage based on relative balance-of-payments positions. Strong currency countries shaped the institutional framework and membership criteria for EMU. Thus, the architectual design of Maastricht is asymmetric. However, with the implementation of EMU, the argument seems to have run its course. Under EMU the main bargaining asymmetry between weak and strong currency countries disappears: weak currency countries cannot experience a reserve constraint in a monetary union. Financing of regional balance-of-payments problems becomes automatic in a monetary union. In other words, "weak" currency countries cannot run out of reserves, and "strong" currency countries seem to be losing the primary basis of their leverage in monetary bargaining. It is thus necessary to ask whether the absence of a reserve constraint will indeed produce a symmetrical system, or whether certain asymmetries are likely to continue under EMU?

Of course, monetary cooperation in EMU will be more symmetrical as a result of extending the domain of monetary policymaking. The nth country problem disappears in the monetary union. No single member state is in a privileged position to occupy the one free policy instrument and to impose its standard as the reference point for the system. The Bundesbank will no longer determine interest rates for all of Europe. Rather, the ECB will set policy and in so doing will take overall European economic conditions

Table 7.2
EMU Bargaining Issues

INTERNAL ADJUSTMENT ISSUES

Weak Currency Country Demands	Strong Currency Country Demands	Solutions	German Concession?
1) No convergence criteria	Convergence criteria	Convergence criteria	No (except for flexible wording)
2) Strong ECB in second stage	Monetary accountability during stage two	Creation of EMI during stage two	No
3) Resistance against ECB independence	Strong insistence on ECB independence	ECB independence	No
4) Reject independence of constituent central banks during stage two	Independence of constituent central banks is tied to accountability question	Creation of EMI; accountability with national central banks during stage two	No
5) Subplot: Hard ECU as parallel currency	Monetary accountability	No parallel currency	No
6) No stability pact	Stability pact	Stability pact	No

EMU-RELATED ISSUES AND SIDE PAYMENTS

1) Automaticity of stage three	Open-ended convergence	Automaticity	Yes
2) Cohesion funds	No new funds	Cohesion funds	Yes
3) Outside president of EMI	EMI merely as a continuation of Committee of Central Bank Governors	Outside President of EMI	Yes
4) Resistance to more political integration	Insist on greater political union	EPU negotiations "disappointing"	Yes
5) Influence of Council on exchange rate policy	Sole responsibility of the ESCB for exchange rate policy	Influence of Council on exchange rate policy	Yes
6) Alternative seats for EMI and ECB	Frankfurt as seat for EMI and ECB	Frankfurt	No
7) Maintain name ECU	Name Euro for common currency	Euro	No
8) ECB President: Trichet (France)	ECB President: Duisenberg	Early retirement for Duisenberg	Yes

into account as opposed to the Bundesbank, which had to concern itself only with internal German conditions. It will exist merely as one of the regional components of the European System of Central Banks (ESCB). For a while, the Bundesbank will continue to play informally the role of a higher moral authority within the ESCB, given the ECB's necessity to transfer Bundesbank credibility to itself. However, once the ECB has established its own track record, even this informal asymmetry will most likely disappear. The German government will, of course, remain an important political player among EMU members and will be in a position strongly to influence EU decision making on fiscal policies and other aspects of macroeconomic policymaking. However, its role will reflect more likely its economic and political size, rather than that of the strong currency country not subject to a reserve constraint.

The expected greater symmetry under EMU, however, does not contradict this book's main argument. Developments in the monetary structure of balance-of-payments positions were ultimately the primary condition for EMU to begin with. The fact that differences in relative balance-of-payments positions were narrowing during the late 1980s made EMU a possible choice for EU members to avoid increasing political instability of the EMS. Germany would not have taken demands for EMU seriously without this development. Ironically, the very success of the EMS also meant its own death sentence. Political dissatisfaction with lingering asymmetries in the EMS that were now solely based on the longer German track record were eroding the legitimacy of the whole arrangement. Thus, EMU offered the distinct opportunity for strong currency countries to enshrine their preferred monetary rules more reliably in the European monetary order.

8

Conclusion

Asymmetries in the distribution of power shape the patterns of monetary cooperation. Domestic politics and interests alone are insufficient to account for the enduring features of cooperation in this area. Merely aggregating the preferences of various players will not tell us which outcomes are likely to emerge. Instead we need to understand the bargaining power available to states in monetary relations. Actors pursue interests and make decisions within a broader structural environment, in which power is distributed unevenly and in which the ability of participants to achieve their goals varies. In other words, there exist external forces that are beyond the short-term control of many actors.

A state's relative balance-of-payments position forms the basis for its bargaining power in international monetary politics. Obviously, adjustment to balance-of-payments disequilibria can be costly for both strong and weak currency countries. The key advantage for strong currency countries is not necessarily lower adjustment costs. For example, a revaluation certainly distributes adjustment costs between the import and export sectors of the domestic economy. Instead, the main power asset for a strong currency country is the absence of a reserve constraint. As a result, a strong currency country controls a greater range of macroeconomic adjustment options. Its government can choose at its volition to adjust through domestic or external adjustment or to buy time through financing the disequi-

librium (while sterilizing to prevent real economic adjustment). Weak currency countries do not have that luxury.
Their financing option is limited, and they have difficulties
resisting market pressures for austerity policies.

Everything else being equal, this situation has provided strong currency countries with leverage in monetary
negotiations. Due to their greater latitude in choices,
strong currency countries enjoy a more credible exit threat,
while weak currency countries cannot threaten to exclude
their strong currency country counterparts in an eventual
exchange rate regime. This asymmetry within the European Union has led to a pattern of bargaining, in which
strong currency countries have consistently rejected concessions on domestic adjustment issues. As a result, the
effective rules governing the various exchange rate regimes
have entailed asymmetrical adjustment obligations and
have by and large reflected the interests of the strong currency countries. Embedded within this larger framework
has been Germany's leadership role in designing these
rules. As the principal strong currency country in Europe,
Germany most importantly served as the macroeconomic
standard setter. In addition, German policymakers have
occasionally taken on broker-type functions by constructing
agreement through concessions on external adjustment,
financing and side payments. In this conclusion I will
address a few broader analytical implications of these
insights.

This book's emphasis on structural features of bargaining interaction in monetary politics, supplements and
juxtaposes the prevailing domestic politics perspectives.
Since domestic politics is embedded in a larger structural
framework, governments often are not able to choose the
policies and rules they would want, no matter how strong
certain societal interests are, how independent or dependent their central banks are, or what party is in government.
Instead, the distribution of power constrains the choices
available for countries to pursue their adjustment and to
implement their preferred rules. As mentioned at the
outset, it is remarkable how different the same reality

appears, if viewed from alternative perspectives. Most scholars emphasizing domestic factors, for example, are struck by the *changes* in state interests and policies between the time the Snake was negotiated and the EMS was implemented. Viewed from a structural perspective, however, the *consistency* of the bargaining interaction emerges as the most noteworthy feature. If German decision making toward European monetary coooperation appears more fluctuating than French decision making on the domestic level (Kaltenthaler 1998), embedding this puzzle in its structural environment also helps to find an answer for it. German policymakers simply had more options available, whereas French policymaking was more constrained. In this sense, domestic and structural perspectives contribute different analytical elements to our understanding of a complex reality.

The main conceptual contribution of the bargaining power argument developed here is that it provides analytical clarity and allows us to bring order to observations that would otherwise appear quite disparate. European monetary cooperation has been marked by significant regularities, and the logic of monetary bargaining in Europe has been quite consistent over time. Thus, the preceding investigation is a good example for the traditional strength of structural theories, namely, the explanation of continuity. The argument puts in place two guideposts for the analysis of European monetary cooperation: the significance of monetary power defined as relative balance-of-payments positions and the role of leadership in constructing rules for cooperation. These factors help us to organize the complexity of this issue area in a coherent fashion.

In contrast, there is no agreement on the main driving forces in domestic politics among scholars on that level of analysis. As mentioned earlier, central bank independence, sociopolitical institutional structures, policy ideas, partisan orientations, or sectoral interests have all received significant attention. It is noteworthy that the analysis offered here neither directly supports nor explicitly contradicts any of these domestic politics assumptions. Ultimately, the distribution of monetary power is a crucial shaping force for the process of monetary rule-making, no matter which domestic factors drive policies and interests.

However, this book's emphasis on structural factors may also instigate efforts to specify the domestic factors responsible for preference formation. For example, with respect to the influence of ideas we may want to ask whether French and other European monetary policy makers really had any other choice but to converge to German objectives and a more monetarist policy stance. Given the structural environment that weak currency countries faced, how much of the policy shift toward austerity in the 1980s was voluntary and due to the intellectual persuasiveness of economic policy ideas, and how much of it was dictated by the realities of monetary power in Europe? In other words, this raises the familiar question of how independent ideas can be from their broader structural environment in which the power and the ability of players to shape outcomes is distributed asymmetrically?

Consideration of structural forces may also help us to think more creatively about the process of preference formation in Germany. Even a powerful institution such as the Bundesbank owed most of its significance in this policy area to the fact that Germany was the principal strong currency country in European monetary politics. This should allow for a more realistic assessment of the Bundesbank's role in monetary cooperation. There is no doubt that Germany's central bank played an important part in shaping the European monetary process. Nonetheless, exaggerated notions of its role obfuscate rather than clarify the causal links at stake. The Bundesbank's role was in part also a product of the dynamics identified in this book. Moreover, it also deserves consideration that most of the preferences exhibited by German policymakers—regardless of whether they were central bankers or not—have been quite consistent with those that one would expect from representatives of strong currency countries.

One remarkable aspect should not be forgotten in this theoretical discussion. As historical research demonstrates, a deliberate creation of explicitly rule-based regimes is a rare occurrence in international monetary relations (Eichengreen 1996b). It is, therefore, ultimately quite astonishing and striking that EU members have been cooperating on exchange rates by and large successfully now for about twenty years. The very argument used here to explain the formation of the specific rules governing European monetary relations simultaneously helps to underscore why these types of negotiated regimes are so uncommon. The conflict of interest between weak and strong currency countries poses a significant constraint on successful monetary cooperation. Bridging the gap is very difficult for policymakers. However, the analysis in this book shows that under certain conditions governments may be able to overcome these problems. Whether this insight offers any hope to other nations seeking to stabilize exchange rate relations in an increasingly globalizing international monetary system, however, remains an open question.

In terms of the more general theoretical implications of this book, one should bear in mind that structural assumptions have their natural limitations. While the distribution of power is an important variable in shaping and molding outcomes, it does not determine them. Structural theory serves as a guide to create order amid conceptual confusion and provides an interpretive framework. The key problem is that both proponents and opponents of structural theories tend to overinterpret their explanatory scope and validity. The modest contention in this book is that the logic of monetary cooperation structures the interaction among states independent of their individual identities. A reserve constraint and the N-1 logic characterize monetary interaction, no matter which particular actors are involved. Power asymmetries are bound to exist between those nations that face a reserve constraint and those that do not.

The concept of bargaining power reaches beyond the traditional structural realist emphasis on size and physical capabilities. Differential balance-of-payments positions create power imbalances between states. This fact should motivate exploration of other power resources that states are capable of translating into bargaining leverage in various international settings. In particular, this study points out that an exit threat alone may not be sufficient to create leverage. An exit threat merely underscores that an actor prefers the costs of noncooperation to those of cooperation. In order to successfully *shape* the bargaining outcome, this exit threat must be supplemented by a weak threat of exclusion other players hold in this interaction. The British exit threat from monetary cooperation did not improve its bargaining leverage. It merely isolated the British government, since cooperation was conceivable without British participation. By extension, the U.S. bargaining position on some issues in international relations is strong simply because cooperation without it would not be very meaningful. This includes policy areas ranging from IMF financing facilities over attempts to deal with global climate change to the nuclear test ban treaty.

The fact that power based on balance-of-payments positions seems more inconspicuous and obscure than the overt use of traditional military and political power capabilities may also shed some light on Germany's peculiar relationship to the exercise of power. With respect to traditional forms of great power politics, Germany often appears as a "tamed" power (Katzenstein 1997). Germany's foreign policy emphasizes integration and cooperation and seeks to avoid confrontation. It shies away from offering leadership on controversial foreign policy questions and avoids openly coercive means of diplomacy. This contrasts noticably with Germany's more forceful behavior in monetary affairs. Clearly, Germany's twentieth-century history still imposes much greater constraints on its use of traditional military and political power tools than on its monetary and economic power.

The argument presented in this book should also instigate new reflection about the role of leadership in international cooperation. Close examination of the policymaking process reveals that leadership is a necessary element for successful cooperation and that the widespread dismissal of hegemonic stability theory in the international relations literature may be a bit premature. On the other hand, the analysis here suggests that conventional hegemonic stability theory's emphasis on issues of public goods provision may simply be too narrow. Instead, it is important to pay closer attention to the solution of coordination problems through standard setting as well as the logic of constructing a zone of agreement in complex bargaining situations. As globalization is rising, pressures for coordination in many areas, from global antitrust rules over international accounting practices to technical standardization, will continue to increase. With it, the role of exercising leadership through standard setting is bound to intensify as well.

Along the same lines, this book's distinction between policy-based and capability-based leadership could be the foundation for a reexamination of U.S. hegemony and hegemonic decline. One possible alternative to the debate over whether and how much the United States has experienced hegemonic decline could be the answer to the following question: Is it conceivable that the breakdown of the Bretton Woods system in the early 1970s has more to do with U.S. macroeconomic *policies* than with fading tangible resources? In other words, did American leadership under Bretton Woods depend much more strongly on its ability to set a legitimate standard and focal point of the exchange rate system than on its material capabilities? And was it balance-of-payments problems and inflationary policies that ultimately delegitimized and weakened the U.S. role as the linchpin of the Bretton Woods system? This line of interpretation also offers another variation for conceptualizing the relationship between policies and capabilities. Its size and the continued importance of the dollar saved the United States from experiencing the fate of countries such as France or Italy. Since others were still willing to hold dollars, the United States did not really face a reserve constraint.

In addition to this retrospective perspective, this book offers guideposts for the analysis of future monetary cooperation problems. Globalization and increasing capital mobility have not eroded the enduring logic of bargaining in monetary relations. Rather, the growing volume and speed of financial transactions has actually strengthened the significance of balance-of-payments positions as tools of monetary power. Greater capital mobility means that weak currency countries feel the limits of their reserve constraint much more profoundly than they did under conditions of lower capital mobility. Financing a balance-of-payments deficit becomes more difficult, and the pressure on governments of weak currency countries to adopt restrictive policy measures grows dramatically. In this sense, globalization does not weaken the significance of state power but rather sharpens the power asymmetries between strong and weak currency countries. Even if Europe is now experimenting with an innovative solution to this issue, continuing globalization worldwide assures that the distributional conflicts over the rules of macroeconomic adjustment will become even more pertinent in the future.

Notes

Chapter 1

1. Unless otherwise specified, I will use the terms *European Union, Europe,* and *Western Europe* synonymously. Citations from older documents may refer to the previous names of the institution now known as the European Union, namely, *European Community* (EC) and *European Economic Community* (EEC).

2. Oatley (1997) uses a supplementary "domestic" argument to explain the "choice" of the nth country in the EMS negotiations, namely, the independence of the Bundesbank and its ability to commit itself credibly to the goal of low inflation and thereby to constrain the choices of others. This argument is certainly an important component of Germany's ability to serve as the standard setter in European monetary politics. As I will argue in chapter 3, however, the argument of central bank independence alone is not sufficient to explain the specific patterns of European monetary politics. Most important, central bank independence would be an ineffective variable if Germany were a weak currency country. Ultimately, its strong currency status is the basis of German bargaining leverage.

3. While the term *monetary cooperation* can describe broader issues, if not further specified, I use it synonymously with *exchange rate cooperation.*

4. The contrast between the failure of the Snake and success of the EMS is the starting point for the explanation developed in McNamara (1998).

Chapter 2

1. These years were chosen to allow for a starting point after the end of the Bretton Woods system compatible with the Bundesbank data series and to mark the year of the Maastricht Treaty ratification.

2. One interesting side aspect to this general statement has been Belgium's significant debt load, which stood at 122 percent of GDP in 1997—more than twice the reference value allowed by the Maastricht Treaty. German policymakers have been critical of this aspect without resisting Belgian participation in EMU. The example, however, also demonstrates the limits of the debt criterion itself. Despite the long-running and well-known Belgian debt situation, Belgium's *monetary* conditions—with low inflation and reasonable exchange rate stability after 1993—were not at all problematic.

3. On the asymmetries introduced by the the ability of countries to sterilize their interventions during the operation of the Bretton Woods system, see Obstfeld (1993).

4. To reduce the complexity of the issue here, I will not address monetary unions at this point. However, since the initial bargaining position of those interested in negotiating a monetary union would be either within a pegged exchange rate system (e.g., EMS) or a floating regime, the logic of bargaining asymmetry applies to those kinds of negotiations as well.

5. It is not surprising that the so-called conditionality policy of the IMF has developed along similar lines as suggested here, namely in the sense of trading access to financing for domestic economic concessions by the weak currency country.

6. Heisenberg (1999) and Oatley (1997) come closest to this type of interpretation.

7. For a comparative evaluation of the status of the Bundesbank and the European Central Bank see Teivainen (1997).

8. For a broader treatment of German interests in exchange rate cooperation see Kaelberer (1996).

9. To zero in on the essential elements of European monetary bargaining, I will leave out a number of other options here, such

as capital controls or trade policies. Helpful discussions of adjustment issues can be found in Cohen (1983) and Webb (1991, 1995).

10. For the distinction between the "economist" and the "monetarist" approach to monetary integration see Tsoukalis (1977): 91–93; Kruse (1980): 63–70.

11. To recall the sequence, GMU went into effect before the exact timetable for political reunification was known. At the time, it was thought that reunification would come only several years later. Favorable international developments—in particular the Soviet-German agreement of 16 July 1990 over united Germany's NATO membership—allowed German reunification to proceed much faster.

12. For an overview see Ishiyama (1975), Kawai (1992), and Blejer et al. (1997).

13. In this sense, Germany's rejection of compromise is typical for strong currency country behavior. As Eichengreen (1992a) demonstrates, the United States—believed to be the principal strong currency country in the post–World War II period—rejected any meaningful restrictions on the options of surplus countries during the Bretton Woods negotiations.

14. To avoid some of the complexity involved in these issues, I do not address IMF conditionality, which obviously has developed into a mechanism to attach financing assistance to specific domestic policy measures, even without the existence of a pegged exchange rate regime. Neither do I address the pressure international financial globalization imposes on coordinating or harmonizing domestic policies.

Chapter 3

1. For the creation of the label *hegemonic stability theory,* see Keohane (1980) and (1984). For some of the major works that are often rightly or wrongly subsumed under the label *hegemonic stability theory,* see Gilpin (1975), (1981) and (1987), Kindleberger (1973) and Krasner (1976).

2. See also: Kindleberger (1973): 292, and Cohen (1977): 223.

3. Some of the major contributions are Conybeare (1984), Gowa (1989), Keohane (1984), McKeown (1983), and Snidal (1985).

4. See Katzenstein (1997) for a broader treatment of these issues.

5. Again, these issues are matters of degree. Germany has, of course, been the source of financing assistance in times of exchange rate crisis, but only as long as sterilization would protect the German economy from its repercussions. It has also been a capital exporter, and its domestic economy is the largest market in Europe. In addition, Germany (in cooperation with the United Kingdom) has been the principal advocate of maintaining free trade in the EU even during recessions. Nevertheless, Kindleberger's definition seems to require a more pronounced dominance than the position of Germany within Europe. For an alternative application of Kindleberger's criteria for hegemony, see Overturf (1997): 168–70.

6. This distinction does not necessarily preclude the possibility that the U.S. position under Bretton Woods may have been policy based in addition to its resource base; see, for example Keohane (1980).

7. Some of the most important documents of this debate are de Grauwe (1989); Giavazzi and Giovannini (1989); Hafer and Kutan (1994); Smeets (1990); von Hagen and Fratianni (1990); Weber (1990).

8. For a brief summary of studies on interest rate policies, see Gardner and Perraudin (1993). The classic case for the discipline argument is Giavazzi and Pagano (1988); see also Fratianni and von Hagen (1990), and Wyplosz (1989).

9. Wyplosz (1989) distinguishes between intentional and systemic asymmetry. His claim that EMS asymmetry is systemic because strong currency countries have a greater capacity for sterilized interventions than weak currency countries certainly supports the arguments developed in this book.

10. The literature has remained fairly skeptical about the argument of the EMS as a disciplinary device. See Fratianni and von Hagen (1990) and Wyplosz (1989).

11. For the idea of "focal points" as the essential element of hegemonic stability theories see: Eichengreen (1989): 255–98.

12. This result is similar to those in coordination games with distributive consequences. There the most powerful player determines the outcome of the game; see Krasner (1991). Since there are, however, also external adjustment mechanisms and financing available in exchange rate cooperation, an overall cooperative outcome of exchange rate politics is more complex than the one depicted in coordination games with distributive consequences.

13. Many studies emphasize the importance of its social and political environment for the success of the Bundesbank. See Goodman (1992), Katzenstein (1987), and Kennedy (1991).

14. Among the most important examples for emphasizing the role of the Bundesbank are the following: Goodman (1992), Heisenberg (1999), Henning (1994), Kaltenthaler (1998), Kennedy (1991), Loedel (1999), Marsh (1992), and Oatley (1997). The subtitle of David Marsh's book *The Bundesbank: The Bank that Rules Europe* is programmatic in this respect.

15. Even within the literature that attributes a great deal of significance to the Bundesbank, there are occasional warnings against overemphasizing this aspect. Kaltenthaler (1998), for example, stresses the weight of other societal and political players in the decision-making process and the need for the Bundesbank to forge alliances with these actors. For Loedel (1999), the Bundesbank is best described as preeminent but not as predominant. Moreover, there are clearly other factors conducive to Germany's low inflation record, such as a low degree of labor militancy and moderate wage demands, the corporatist legacy of state-society relations, and a historical record of fiscal responsibility on the part of federal, state, and local governments.

16. Henning (1994) provides a sophisticated interpretation of the complex decision making process.

17. One difference is, of course, that government-officials are more susceptible to international issue-linkage than central bankers, whose task is defined exclusively with respect to the domestic economy.

Chapter 4

1. For an account of some of the pre-Action Programme proposals for monetary cooperation, see Tsoukalis (1977): 53–56.

2. Gehrmann and Harmsen (1972) provide a useful source of monetary texts from this period.

3. For general historical background, see: Loth, Wallace, and Wessels (1995).

4. For a somewhat more positive evaluation of monetary cooperation under the provisions of the Treaty of Rome, see de Wilmars (1963). For an evaluation of monetary policy in the period before the Action Programme from the perspective of the commission, see the analysis of Walter Hallstein, the former president of the EC Commission, in Hallstein (1973): 132–58.

5. For the linkage between the Common Agricultural Policy and the problem of monetary cooperation, see McNamara (1993).

6. On the theme of external influences on European monetary cooperation, see Henning (1998).

7. Compare the proposals of the commission (1963) with the text of the various Council decisions of May 1964 in Gehrmann and Harmsen (1972): 50–54.

8. "Council Decision of 8 May 1964 on cooperation between Member States in the field of international monetary relations." (64/301/EEC) Reprinted in European Communities (1979): 12. For similar conclusions on the importance of the Council decisions in this period, see also Kruse (1980): 18–19.

9. For some of the problems facing the Europeans in this respect, see Kolodziej (1974): 176–231.

10. See, for example, this statement of the Monetary Committee in its seventh report: the committee "concluded that progressive integration of a growing number of products to settle at much the same level throughout the Community, will make devaluation or revaluation increasingly difficult and unlikely. The establishment of a single agricultural market will strengthen this trend. . . . De facto monetary integration is indeed constantly progressing, although the process is not always immediately obvious." In European Economic Community (1965).

11. This position of the Bundesbank found support in the government, as well as broad public support in German society; see, for example, the comments of Deutsche Bank President Abs reported in *Vereinigte Witschaftsdienste, Devisen und Finanzen* (1963): 6–7, as well as the comments in *Frankfurter Allgemeine Zeitung* 29 December 1962; *Neue Zürcher Zeitung* 25 January 1963; Vocke (1966).

Chapter 5

1. This section does not attempt to give a comprehensive description of the history of European monetary cooperation in the 1970s. There are a number of studies that provide rich accounts of the monetary events during the 1970s. Most important among them are Hellmann (1979); Kruse (1980); and Tsoukalis (1977). For a detailed description of the very early part of this discussion, see Coffey and Presley (1971).

2. For a comparison, see Kenen (1995): 11–18.

3. While Denmark, Great Britain, and Ireland indeed joined on 1 January 1973, the Norwegian electorate rejected EU membership in a referendum on 25 September 1972.

4. It is interesting to note in this context that American and European evaluations of the breakdown of Bretton Woods deviate significantly. Whereas, from the American perspective the crucial step was the end of dollar convertibility in August 1971, from the European perspective the German decision to float the deutsche mark in May 1971 was much more important—in the sense that it prevented a timely start of Snake operations.

5. The non-EU members of the Snake were not able to join the EMS officially. Nevertheless, some European countries have over various periods attempted to peg their currencies to one of the EMS member currencies or the ECU.

6. In light of this, it may seem puzzling why Italy exhibited more clearly "monetarist" preferences during the Maastricht negotiations twenty years later. While this is not the place to examine Italian preferences in detail, at least four significant aspects of monetary politics had changed. First of all, Italy had

participated successfully in the EMS prior to the Maastricht negotiations and established some degree of exchange rate stability. Second, partly as a result of this success, the EMS had developed severe asymmetries, and Italy shared French preferences for addressing these asymmetries through monetary union. Third, the number of weak currency countries had increased significantly with the various expansions of the EU, implying that adjustment costs could be distributed onto more shoulders. And fourth, for political reasons Italy desperately sought to avoid a two- or multiple-speed monetary union, a possibility that was not even discussed during the Werner Report negotiations. In order not to be left out, Italy needed to deemphasize the eventual significance of the convergence criteria as entry requirements and stress the virtue of the monetary union in forging convergence.

7. The non-EU members of the Snake, however, did not participate on an equal basis in the Snake system. The rules did not grant them the same privileges for the financing mechanisms as the EU members. Thus, with respect to the financing mechanisms, the Snake retained characteristics of its origin within the EU.

8. See also the strongly worded statement by then Finance Minister Helmut Schmidt on the rules for the EMCF, reprinted in Deutsche Bundesbank, *BAP* 67, 20 September 1972: 4–5. Schmidt's statement is noteworthy in comparison to the much more flexible attitude he demonstrated toward financing rules as chancellor six years later during the EMS negotiations.

9. See, for example, the interview of the president of the Bundesbank, Karl Blessing, with German radio after the franc devaluation, reprinted in Deutsche Bundesbank, *BAP* 60, 14 August 1969: 2.

10. It is noteworthy that Tietmeyer made these comments as a government official, and not as the president of the Bundesbank—a position he was appointed to roughly two decades later. As such, however, it illustrates nicely the close harmony of interests between government and central bank officials.

11. The already tremendous pressures in the Snake led France repeatedly to veto Swiss entry into the Snake out of fear that their participation would only increase the weight of the Snake's core; see *Neue Zürcher Zeitung*, 20 November 1975.

Chapter 6

1. The most thorough historical account of the EMS negotiations is Ludlow (1982). For the later institutional development of the EMS see Gros and Thygesen (1992).

2. See Schmidt's own account of these early negotiations in Schmidt (1990): 247–59.

3. Schmidt's own account of his relations to the Carter administration is openly critical; see Schmidt (1987): 222–81. Other observers have noted a deep hostility of Schmidt toward Carter; see Jenkins (1989): 224, 247, and passim.

4. In addition, there were the small steps taken by the Council of Economic and Finance Ministers in May 1985 to increase the use of ECUs; see Gros and Thygesen (1992): 89.

5. Since intramarginal interventions in EMS currencies required the "concurrence" of the issuing central bank(s), dollars remained the main intervention currency for a long time in the EMS. One aspect of encouraging the use of the VSTF for intramarginal interventions was the greater use of EMS currencies.

6. The Bundesbank's fight against the inflationary consequences of German reunification collided with the onset of recession in various EMS member states. Financial markets perceived that the resolve of most non-German members to follow the Bundesbank's interest rate policy lacked credibility.

7. Noticeably, the notion of symmetry retreated somewhat into the background during the second half of the 1980s, when the strategy of "borrowing credibility" (which rested explicitly on asymmetry) became important. Incidentally, the problem of symmetry reemerged prominently toward the end of the 1980s after the more or less successful French convergence to the German macroeconomic standard.

8. One of the technical difficulties of the basket grid was that the weight of currencies in the ECU basket needed to be adjusted periodically. This meant that, over time, the weight of the strong currencies would increase, making it more likely that the ECU grid would actually identify weak currencies as outliers. One of the possible alternatives presented by weak currency countries was to fix the weight of currencies in the ECU permanently; see Ludlow (1982): 162–64.

9. The Belgians had presented the formula of pairing the parity grid with the divergence indicator in the days before the Aachen summit. Thus, the fact that Belgium ultimately became the first country to trigger the divergence indicator represents a curious historical irony (*Frankfurter Allgemeine Zeitung*, 16 June 1979).

10. See Schmidt's own largely dismissive evaluation of the divergence indicator in Schmidt (1978). Matthöfer offers a similar evaluation in his interview with *Wirtschaftswoche*, 8 January 1979. For further comments by German officials asserting the insignificance of the divergence indicator, see *Frankfurter Allgemeine Zeitung*, 19 September 1978; *Süddeutsche Zeitung*, 19 September 1978; Hellmann (1979): 49–58; Andersen (1979): 11. On the divergence indicator, see also van Ypersele and Koeune (1984).

11. Thus, Gros and Thygesen's (1992: 51) assertion that this agreement was referred to in public much later is historically incorrect. The issue was well known at the time and referred to numerous times in public. See also Emminger's own early assessment of the EMS, in which he explicitly points to the Bundesbank-government agreement as one of the critical elements that alleviated Bundesbank concerns over the EMS: Emminger (1979).

12. Observers and officials disagree as to whether the events of September 1992 truly followed the Emminger letter procedure. These disagreements overlook the fact that the Emminger letter distinguishes a two-step procedure for such a crisis (see Emminger's interview with *Die Zeit*, 30 March 1979). Step one consists of approaching the government to ask for a realignment. Terminating interventions is only the policy of "last resort" for the Bundesbank. Clearly, in September 1992, Bundesbank officials only took the first step and did not fully escalate the crisis.

13. See the "position paper" on the EMS drafted in the Economics Ministry: *Vereinigte Wirtschaftsdienste-Finanzen*, 25 August 1978. See also Finance Minister Matthöfer's interview comments: *General-Anzeiger*, 11 August 1978.

14. On the position of the CDU on this point, see Andersen (1979): 11. See also: *Frankfurter Allgemeine Zeitung*, 28 February 1979. Schmidt (1990): 260–66, acknowledges the broader political intention of influencing the decisions of weak currency countries behind the multilateralism rule.

15. That was true in particular for the 1982/83 realignments; see Hall (1986): 201–2. The 12 January 1987 realignment represents an even clearer example in the sense that the French government rejected any responsibility for exchange rate turbulences, which resulted in a (technically) pure 3 percent revaluation of the deutsche mark and other strong currencies; see *Die Welt*, 13 January 1987.

16. During the March 1983 realignment negotiations, the French government used the divergence indicator to underscore Germany's responsibility for the divergence between Germany and France; see Hellmann (1983).

17. Ironically, the EMS turmoil erupted when German inflation rates were high. In a sense, speculators attacked the "wrong" currencies. Nevertheless, the Bundesbank policy of fighting domestic inflation forced Italy and Great Britain to pursue policies that neither one of them was able to maintain credibly.

18. It is, of course, a moot point to speculate as to whether an early deutsche mark revaluation would have really prevented turmoil in the EMS. Other factors besides German reunification intervened. As mentioned, inflation differentials had accumulated over five years. In addition, the European economies went into recession at different times, and the referenda on the Maastricht Treaty in Denmark and France created uncertainty over the future of European monetary cooperation.

19. Interestingly, Germany's position on this kind of symbolic issue was much less compromising during the Maastricht EMU process. The first published version of the Maastricht Treaty text used the term *ECU* for the existing basket and *Ecu* for the new currency. After German objections, an erratum was issued, substituting *ECU* for *Ecu* throughout. At the Madrid summit in 1995, the Germans finally pushed through their proposal for the name *euro*.

Chapter 7

1. Technically, *EMU* refers to Economic and Monetary Union. In this chapter I will use the initials *EMU* often in the conventional meaning of European Monetary Union.

2. The literature on the Maastricht process is quite diverse and detailed. Among the most informative studies on the subject are Baun (1996); Dyson (1994); Heisenberg (1999); McCormick (1996); Moravcsik (1998); Sandholtz (1993a); and Cafruny and Rosenthal (1993). For the most comprehensive discussion of the economic rules for EMU, see Kenen (1995).

3. German business interests are also clearly influenced by concerns over the negative competitive effects of DM appreciation. According to a survey by the Allensbach Institute in January 1996, 77 percent of business leaders favored monetary union; reported in *Die Welt*, 14 February 1996. See also the survey in *Ifo-Schnelldienst* 11/89. For anecdotal evidence, see Fröhlich (1991) and the statements by German industrial leaders in *Der Spiegel* 45, 11 November 1995: 32–33; *Der Tagesspiegel*, 4 July 1996.

4. On the SEA, see Cameron (1992); Moravcsik (1991); Sandholtz and Zysman (1989).

5. On the issue of currency domains, see Cohen (1998) and Kenen (1995): 6–11.

6. It is noteworthy that the German domestic debate was not over the goal of EMU itself but rather concerned the monetary unification process and the specific rules that should govern an eventual monetary union. Even among Bundesbank officials, outright rejection of the principle of monetary union is hard to find. For the German domestic debate, see Schönfelder and Thiel (1994); Nölling (1993).

7. For the various draft proposals and related documents produced during the IGC negotiations, see Corbett (1993).

8. The relevant treaty articles are Council and Commission of the European Communities (1992), Art. 104c and Art. 109j; the two protocols specifying the criteria are the "Protocol on the Excessive Deficit Procedure" and the "Protocol on the Convergence Criteria."

9. One of the interesting side aspects of this point is the narrow interpretation of Germany's low inflation record. While the role (and for that matter legal status) of the Bundesbank is certainly an important explanation of that fact, it ignores other institutional and policy-making aspects that have been conducive

for Germany's low inflation record, such as the corporatist character of German domestic politics with its consensual wage bargaining and fiscal restraint on the part of the government. See Cameron (1984): 143–78; see also Dyson (1994).

10. For an extensive discussion of the Maastricht criteria, see Kenen (1995): 80–107 and 124–134.

11. There are, of course, potential problems associated with this particular constitutional construction of the ECB. The political and societal substructure of EMU is not as clearly developed as the constitutional architecture of EMU itself. This could raise legitimacy and policy-making problems for the ECB in the future. However, I will not further address these issues here, since they have not yet become explicit items for negotiations over the rules of monetary cooperation.

12. For a more explicit treatment of these issues, see Sandholtz (1993b).

13. Technically, the cohesion fund is not a treaty provision but rather part of an understanding reached by the heads of government during the summit. Only the Edinburgh Summit a year later agreed on the exact amount of the fund (15 billion ECU); see Methfessel (1996): 60.

14. For a domestic critique of German insistence on these symbolic issues, see Schmidt (1993): 203–7.

Bibliography

Books and Articles

Andersen, Uwe. 1979. "Das Europäische Währungssystem: Eine Initiative zur europäischen Integration." *Aus Politik und Zeitgeschichte* B16/79: 3–21.

Anderson, Jeffrey J., and John B. Goodman. 1993. "Mars or Minerva? A United Germany in the Post-Cold War Europe." In *After the Cold War: International Institutions and State Strategies in Europe, 1989–1991.* Ed. Robert O. Keohane, Joseph S. Nye, and Stanley Hoffmann. Cambridge: Harvard University Press: 23–62.

Andrews, David M. 1994. "Capital Mobility and State Autonomy: Towards a Structural Theory of International Monetary Relations." *International Studies Quarterly* 38 (2): 193–218.

Artus, Patrick, and Philippe Nasse. 1985. "Exchange Rates, Prices, Wages, and the Current Account in France." In *Stabilization Policy in France and the Federal Republic of Germany.* Amsterdam: North-Holland: 145–80.

Balassa, Bela. 1973. "Monetary Integration in the European Common Market." In *Europe and the Evolution of the International Monetary System.* Ed. Alexander K. Swoboda. Leiden: A.W. Sijhoff: 93–128.

BAP. Various years. Deutsche Bundesbank: *Auszüge aus Presseartikeln.*

Balladur, Edouard. 1988. "Lost Illusions of the Floating Rate System." *The Wall Street Journal*, (European Edition), 20 January.

Baun, Michael J. 1995–96. "The Maastricht Treaty as High Politics: Germany, France, and European Integration." *Political Science Quarterly* 110 (4): 605–24.

————. 1996. *An Imperfect Union: The Maastricht Treaty and the New Politics of European Integration*. Boulder: Westview.

Bergsten, Fred C. 1975. *Toward a New International Economic Order*. Lexington, Mass.: Heath.

Bini-Smaghi, Lorenzo, Tommaso Padoa-Schioppa and Francesco Papadia. 1994. *The Transition to EMU in the Maastricht Treaty*. Essays in International Finance 194, Princeton: International Finance Section, Princeton University, November.

Blejer, Maria I., Jacob A. Frenkel, Leonardo Leiderman, and Assaf Razin. 1997. *Optimum Currency Areas: New Analytical and Policy Developments*. Washington, D.C.: International Monetary Fund.

Blessing, Karl. 1963. "Ausführungen über Währungsfragen im Aktionsprogramm der EWG-Kommission im Norddeutschen Rundfunk." Hamburg, 27.1.1963. In *BAP* 9, 29 January.

————. 1964. "Integration und Währung," Vortrag bei dem Europäischen Treffen für Chemische Technik, Achema, 1964" am 27.Juni 1964 in Frankfurt am Main. In *BAP* 39, 1 July.

————. 1966. *Im Kampf ums gute Geld*. Frankfurt am Main: Fritz Knapp Verlag.

Block, Fred L. 1977. *The Origins of International Economic Disorder: A Study of United States International Monetary Policy from World War II to the Present*. Berkeley: University of California Press.

Bulmer, Simon J. 1993. "Germany and European Integration: Toward Economic and Political Dominance?" In *Germany and the European Community: Beyond Hegemony and*

Containment. Ed. Carl F. Lankowski. New York: St. Martin's Press: 73–99.

Bundesministerium für Finanzen. 1991. "Grundpositionen der Bundesregierung für die Regierungskonferenz zur Wirtschafts- und Währungsunion und Verhandlungsstand." Bonn, 10 September 1991. Reprinted in *BAP* 69, 19 September 1991: 5–7.

Bundesregierung. Bulletin des Presse- und Informationsamtes der Bundesregierung. Various years.

———. 1969. "Erklärung der Bundesregierung zur EWG-Gipfelkonferenz in Den Haag am 1. und 2. Dezember 1969." Bulletin des Presse- und Informationsamtes der Bundesregierung. 4 December.

———. 1970. "Deutscher Stufenplan zur Verwirklichung der Wirtschafts- und Währungsunion im Gemeinsamen Markt." Reprinted in *BAP* 15, 27 February: 12–13.

Burdekin, Richard C. K., Jilleen R. Westbrook, and Thomas D. Willett. 1994. "Exchange Rate Pegging as a Disinflation Strategy: Evidence from the European Monetary System." In *Varieties of Monetary Reforms: Lessons and Experiences on the Road to Monetary Union.* Ed. Pierre L. Siklos. Boston: Kluwer Academic Publishers: 45–72.

Butschkau, Fritz. 1963. "Keine Beschleunigung im Währungs- und Kreditbereich." In Deutsche Bundesbank, *BAP* 5, 16 January 1963: 7–9.

Cafruny, Alan W,. and Glenda G. Rosenthal, eds. 1993. *The State of the European Community, Vol. 2: The Maastricht Debates and Beyond.* Boulder: Lynne Rienner.

Cameron, David R. 1984. "Social Democracy, Corporatism, Labor Quiescence and the Representation of Economic Interest in Advanced Capitalist Society." In *Order and Conflict in Contemporary Capitalism.* Ed. John H. Goldthorpe. Oxford: Clarendon Press: 143–78.

———. 1992. "The 1992 Initiative: Causes and Consequences." In *Europolitics: Institutions and Policymaking in the "New" European Community.* Ed. Alberta M. Sbragia. Washington, D.C.: Brookings Institution: 23–74.

————. 1993. "British Exit, German Voice, French Loyalty: Defection, Domination, and Cooperation in the 1992–93 ERM Crisis." Manuscript, Yale University.

————. 1995a. "From Barre to Balladur: Economic Policy in the Era of the EMS." In *Remaking the Hexagon: The New France in the New Europe*. Ed. Gregory Flynn. Boulder: Westview Press: 117–57.

————. 1995b. "Transnational Relations and the Development of European Economic and Monetary Union." In *Bringing Transnational Relations Back In: Non-State Actors, Domestic Structures and International Institutions*. Ed. Thomas Risse-Kappen. New York: Cambridge University Press: 37–78.

————. 1996. "Exchange Rate Politics in France, 1981–1983: The Regime-Defining Choices of the Mitterrand Presidency." In *The Mitterrand Era: Policy Alternatives and Political Mobilization in France*. Ed. Anthony Daley. New York: New York University Press: 56–82.

Camps, Miriam. 1966. *European Unification in the Sixties: From the Veto to the Crisis*. New York: McGraw-Hill.

Claassen, Emil-Maria. 1989. "IMS, EMS, and the (N-1) Problem." *The Economic and Social Review* 20 (2): 91–96.

Coffey, Peter, and John R. Presley. 1971. *European Monetary Integration*. London: Macmillan.

Cohen, Benjamin J. 1963. "The Euro-Dollar, the Common Market, and Currency Unification." *The Journal of Finance* 18 (4): 605–21.

————. 1977. *Organizing the World's Money: The Political Economy of International Monetary Relations*. New York: Basic Books.

————. 1983. "Balance-of-Payments Financing: Evolution of a Regime." In *International Regimes*. Ed. Stephen D. Krasner. Ithaca: Cornell University Press: 315–36.

————. 1993. "Beyond EMU: The Problem of Sustainability." *Economics and Politics* 5 (2):187–203.

————. 1998. *The Geography of Money*. Ithaca: Cornell University Press.

Commission of the European Communities. 1962. "Action Programme for the Second Stage." In Gehrmann and Harmsen, 1972: 36–39.

―――. 1963. "Mitteilung der Kommission an den Rat über die währungspolitische Zusammenarbeit in der Europäischen Wirtschaftsgemeinschaft (vom 19.Juni 1963)." In Gehrmann and Harmsen, 1972: 39–50.

―――. 1969. "Commission Memorandum to the Council on the Coordination of Economic Policies and Monetary Cooperation within the Community" (Barre Report). In *Bulletin of the European Communities* Supplement 3–1969. Reprinted in Gehrmann and Harmsen, 1972: 59–72. References to this document use the original paragraph numbering system of the commission.

―――. 1990. "One Market, One Money: An Evaluation of the Potential Benefits and Costs of Forming an Economic and Monetary Union." *European Economy* 44 (October).

―――. 1993. "Annual Economic Report for 1993." *European Economy* 54.

Committee for the Study of Economic and Monetary Union. 1989. *Report on Economic and Monetary Union in the European Community*. Luxembourg: Office for Official Publications of the European Communities.

Committee of Central Bank Governors. 1987. "Pressemitteilung des Ausschusses der Präsidenten der Zentralbanken der Mitgliedstaaten der Europäischen Wirtschaftsgemeinschaft—Europäischer Fonds für währungspolitische Zusammenarbeit -, Basel, vom 18. September 1987." Reprinted in Deutsche Bundesbank. *BAP* 68, September 23: 3.

Conybeare, John A. C. 1984. "Public Goods, Prisoners' Dilemmas and the International Political Economy." *International Studies Quarterly* 28 (1): 5–22.

Corbett, Richard. 1993. *The Treaty of Maastricht: From Conception to Ratification: A Comprehensive Reference Guide*. London: Longman.

Council of Economics and Finance Ministers. 1974. "Statement of May 7, 1974." Reprinted in *BAP* 26, May 13.

Council of the European Communities and Commission of the European Communities. 1992. *Treaty on European Union*. Luxembourg: Office for Official Publications of the European Communities.

de Grauwe, Paul. 1989. "Is the European Monetary System a DM-Zone?" *CEPR Discussion Paper* No. 297. London: Centre for Economic Policy Research.

―――. 1994. *The Economics of Monetary Integration*. Oxford: Oxford University Press, 2nd rev. ed.

de Wilmars, Jacques Mertens. 1963. "Währungsperspektiven des Gemeinsamen Marktes." *Weltwirtschaftliches Archiv* 90(2): 350–76.

Dell, Edmund. 1994. "Britain and the Origins of the European Monetary System." *Contemporary European History* 3(1): 1–60.

Deutsche Bundesbank. *Auszüge aus Presseartikeln*. (BAP). Various years.

―――. *Annual Report*. Various years.

―――. *Zahlungsbilanzstatistik*. Various years.

Deutscher Bundestag. *Sitzungsberichte*. Various years.

Dillingham, Alan J. 1991. "Shielding the Franc: French Diplomacy and European Monetary Integration, 1969–1988." Dissertation. Georgetown University.

Dixit, Avinash K., and Barry J. Nalebuff. 1991. *Thinking Strategically: The Competitive Edge in Business, Politics, and Everyday Life*. New York: W.W. Norton.

Dyson, Kenneth. 1994. *Elusive Union: The Process of Economic and Monetary Union in Europe*. London: Longman.

Eichengreen, Barry. 1989. "Hegemonic Stability Theories of the International Monetary System." In *Can Nations Agree? Issues in International Economic Cooperation*. Ed. Richard N. Cooper, et al. Washington: Brookings Institution: 255–98.

―――. 1992a. *Golden Fetters: The Gold Standard and the Great Depression, 1919–1939*. New York: Oxford University Press.

———. 1992b. "Is Europe an Optimum Currency Area?" In *The European Community after 1992: Perspectives from the Outside*. Ed. Silvio Borner and Herbert Grubel. London: Macmillan: 138–61.

———. 1993. "European Monetary Unification." *Journal of Economic Literature* 31 (September): 1321–57.

———. 1994. *International Monetary Arrangements for the 21st Century*. Washington: The Brookings Institution.

———. 1996. *Globalizing Capital: A History of the International Monetary System*. Princeton: Princeton University Press.

Emminger, Otmar. 1979. "Das Europäische Währungssystem und die deutsche Geldpolitik." In *BAP* 20, 23 March:1–4. (Original Essay for *Handelsblatt*)

———. 1986. *D-Mark, Dollar, Währungskrisen: Erinnerungen eines ehemaligen Bundesbankpräsidenten*. Stuttgart: Deutsche Verlags-Anstalt.

European Communities. 1970a. "Report to the Council and the Commission on the Realisation by Stages of Economic and Monetary Union in the Community: 'Werner Report' (definitive text)." *Bulletin of the European Communities*. Supplement 11–1970: 1–29.

———. 1970b. "Integral Text of the Final Communiqué of the Conference of the Heads of State or Government on 1 and 2 December 1969 at The Hague." *Bulletin of the European Communities*. Supplement 11–1970: 31–34 (#8).

———. 1970c. "Decision of the Council of 6 March 1970 Regarding the Procedure in the Matter of Economic and Monetary Cooperation." *Bulletin of the European Communities*. Supplement 11–1970: 35.

———. 1978. *Treaties Establishing the European Communities*. Luxembourg: Office for Official Publications of the European Communities.

———. 1979. *Compendium of Community Monetary Texts*. Luxembourg: Office for Official Publications of the European Communities.

European Economic Community. 1962. *Fourth Report on the Activities of the Monetary Committee.* Brussels, 23 March (1010/5/V/1962/5).

———. 1963. *Fifth Report on the Activities of the Monetary Committee.* Brussels, 5 April (8085/5/IV/1963/5).

———. 1964. *Sixth Report on the Activities of the Monetary Committee.* Brussels, 15 April (1018/5/IV/1964/5).

———. 1965. *Seventh Report on the Activities of the Monetary Committee.* Brussels, 12 February (1021/5/II/1965/5).

European Monetary Institute. 1998. *Convergence Report: Report Required by Article 109j of the Treaty Establishing the European Community.* Frankfurt.

Fratianni, Michele, and Jürgen von Hagen. 1990. "Asymmetries and Realignments in the EMS." In *The European Monetary System in the 1990s.* Ed. Paul de Grauwe and Lucas Papademos. London: Longman: 86–116.

———. 1992. *The European Monetary System and European Monetary Union.* Boulder: Westview.

Frieden, Jeffry A. 1991. "Invested Interests: The Politics of National Economic Policies in a World of Global Finance." *International Organization* 45 (4): 425–51.

Fröhlich, Hans-Peter. 1991. "Die Europäische Währungsunion aus der Sicht der Unternehmen." In *Europa auf dem Weg zur Währungsunion.* Ed. Manfred Weber. Darmstadt: Wissenschaftliche Buchgesellschaft: 276–95.

Gardner, Edward H., and William R. M. Perraudin. 1993. "Asymmetry in the ERM: A Case Study of French and German Interest Rates Before and After German Unification." *IMF Staff Papers* 40 (2): 427–50.

Gardner, Richard N. 1956. *Sterling-Dollar Diplomacy.* Oxford: Clarendon Press.

Garrett, Geoffrey. 1993. "The Politics of Maastricht." *Economics and Politics* 5 (2): 105–23.

Gehrmann, Dieter, and Sabine Harmsen, eds. 1972. *Monetäre Integration in der EWG: Dokumente und Bibliographie.* Hamburg: Verlag Weltarchiv.

Genscher, Hans-Dietrich. 1988. "Memorandum für die Schaffung eines europäischen Währungsraumes und einer Europäischen Zentralbank." Reprinted in *BAP* 15, March 1: 6–7.

———. 1995. *Erinnerungen*. Berlin: Siedler.

Giavazzi Francesco, and Alberto Giovannini. 1986. "The EMS and the Dollar." *Economic Policy* 2 (April): 456–85.

———. 1989. *Limiting Exchange Rate Flexibility: The European Monetary System*. Cambridge: MIT Press.

Giavazzi, Francesco, and Marco Pagano. 1988. "The Advantage of Tying One's Hands: EMS Discipline and Central Bank Credibility." *European Economic Review* 32: 1055–82.

Gilpin, Robert. 1975. *U.S. Power and the Multinational Corporation: The Political Economy of Foreign Direct Investment*. New York: Basic Books.

———. 1981. *War and Change in World Politics*. New York: Cambridge University Press.

———. 1987. *The Political Economy of International Relations*. Princeton: Princeton University Press.

Giscard d'Estaing, Valery. 1962. "Die Währungspolitik der EWG—Erst koordinieren, dann unifizieren." *Europa* (July). Reprinted in Deutsche Bundesbank, *BAP* 52, 27 July: 2–4.

Glees, Anthony. 1994. "The Diplomacy of Anglo-German Relations: A Study of the ERM Crisis of September 1992." *German Politics* 3 (1) 75–90.

Gleske, Leonhard. 1964. "Währungs- und budgetpolitische Aspekte der Integration." In Deutsche Bundesbank, *BAP* 74, 11 November: 1–8.

———. 1968. "Zur Frage der Währungsunion im Gemeinsamen Markt." Reprinted in Deutsche Bundesbank, *BAP* 21, 15 March: 3–6.

———. 1970. "Währungspolitik und Agrarmarkt in der Europäischen Wirtschaftsgemeinschaft." *Europa-Archiv* 25(1): 15–23.

Goodman, John. 1992. *Monetary Sovereignty: The Politics of Central Banking in Western Europe*. Ithaca: Cornell University Press.

Gowa, Joanne. 1989. "Rational Hegemons, Excludable Goods, and Small Groups: An Epitaph for Hegemonic Stability Theory?" *World Politics* 41 (3): 307–24.

Gros, Daniel, and Niels Thygesen. 1992. *European Monetary Integration*. London: Longman.

Hafer, R. W., and A. M. Kutan. 1994. "A Long-Run View of German Dominance and the Degree of Policy Convergence in the EMS." *Economic Inquiry* 32 (4): 684–95.

Hall, Peter A. 1986. *Governing the Economy: The Politics of State Intervention in Britain and France*. Cambridge: Polity Press.

Hallstein, Walter. 1973. *Die Europäische Gemeinschaft*. Düsseldorf: Econ Verlag.

Harden, Ian. 1993. "The European Central Bank and the Role of National Central Banks in Economic and Monetary Union." In *Economic and Monetary Union: Implications for National Policy-Makers*. Ed. Klaus Gretschmann. Dordrecht: Martinus Nijhoff Publishers: 149–67.

Healey, Denis. 1989. *The Time of My Life*. London: Michael Joseph.

Hefeker, Carsten. 1996. *Interest Groups and Monetary Integration: The Political Economy of Exchange Regime Choice*. Boulder: Westview.

Heisenberg, Dorothee. 1994. "German Financial Hegemony or Simply Smaller Win-Sets? An Examination of the Bundesbank's Role in EMS and EMU Negotiations." Paper prepared for presentation at the Annual Meeting of the American Political Science Association, New York, 1–4 September.

———. 1999. *The Mark of the Bundesbank: Germany's Role in European Monetary Cooperation*. Boulder: Lynne Rienner.

Hellmann, Rainer. 1979. *Gold, the Dollar, and the European Currency Systems: The Seven Year Monetary War*. New York: Praeger.

————. 1983. "Mit neuen Leitkursen ins fünfte EWS-Jahr." *VWD Finanz- und Wirtschaftsspiegel.* 22 March. Reprinted in *BAP* 30, 23 March: 12–13.

Hendricks, Gisela. 1988. "Germany and the CAP: National Interests and the European Community." *International Affairs* 65 (1): 75–87.

Henning, C. Randall. 1993. "European Monetary Integration in Its Global Context." Paper presented to the American Political Science Association Annual Meeting, Washington, D.C., 2–5 September.

————. 1994. *Currencies and Politics in the United States, Germany, and Japan.* Washington, D.C.: Institute for International Economics.

————. 1998. "Systemic Conflict and Monetary Integration in Europe." *International Organization* 52 (3): 537–73.

Hueglin, Thomas O. 1992. "Gross-Deutschland in Europe: Planned or Unplanned Effects of the German *Anschluss* on Hegemonic Leadership in the European Community." In *The Internationalization of the German Political Economy: Evolution of a Hegemonic Project.* Ed. William D. Graf. New York: St. Martin's Press: 285–306.

Huffschmid, Jörg. 1998. "Hoist with its Own Petard: Consequences of the Single Currency for Germany." In *The Single European Currency in National Perspective: A Community in Crisis?* Ed. Bernhard H. Moss and Jonathan Michie. London: Macmillan: 87–104.

Hrbek, Rudolf, and Wolfgang Wessels, eds. 1984. *EG-Mitgliedschaft: Ein vitales Interesse der Bundesrepublik Deutschland?* Bonn: Europa Union Verlag.

Ifo-Institut für Wirtschaftsforschung. *Ifo-Schnelldienst.*

International Monetary Fund. *Balance of Payments Yearbook.* Various years.

————. *International Financial Statistics.* Various years.

————. *International Financial Statistics Yearbook.* Various years.

Ishiyama, Yoshihide. 1975. "The Theory of Optimum Currency Areas: A Survey." International Monetary Fund, *Staff Papers* 22 (2): 344–83.

Italianer, Alexander. 1993. "Mastering Maastricht: EMU Issues and How They Were Settled." In *Economic and Monetary Union: Implications for National Policy-Makers*. Ed. Klaus Gretschmann. Dordrecht: Martinus Nijhoff: 51–113.

Jenkins, Roy. 1989. *European Diary: 1977–1981*. London: Collins.

———. 1991. *A Life at the Centre*. London: Macmillan.

Jochimsen, Reimut. 1993. "Economic and Monetary Union: A German Central Banker's Perspective." In *Economic and Monetary Union: Implications for National Policy-Makers*. Ed. Klaus Gretschmann. Dordrecht: Martinus Nijhoff Publishers: 195–213.

Kaelberer, Matthias. 1996. "Germany's Incentives for European Monetary Cooperation." *German Politics and Society* 14 (3): 31–53.

Kaltenthaler, Karl. 1997. "The Sources of Policy Dynamics: Variations in German and French Policy towards European Monetary Co-operation." *West European Politics* 20 (3): 91–110.

———. 1998. *Germany and the Politics of Europe's Money*. Durham and London: Duke University Press.

Katzenstein, Peter J. 1987. *Policy and Politics in West Germany: The Growth of a Semi-Sovereign State*. Philadelphia: Temple University Press.

———, ed. 1997. *Tamed Power: Germany in Europe*. Ithaca: Cornell University Press.

Kaufmann, Hugo M. 1985. *Germany's International Monetary Policy and the European Monetary System*. New York: Brooklyn College Press.

Kawai, Masahiro. 1992. "Optimum Currency Areas." *The Palgrave Dictionary of Money and Finance*. New York: The Stockton Press: 78–81.

Kenen, Peter B. 1995. *Economic and Monetary Union in Europe: Moving beyond Maastricht*. Cambridge: Cambridge University Press.

Kennedy, Ellen. 1991. *The Bundesbank: Germany's Central Bank in the International Monetary System*. London: Royal Institute for International Affairs.

Keohane, Robert O. 1980. "The Theory of Hegemonic Stability and Changes in International Regimes, 1967–1977." In *Change in the International System*. Ed. Ole R. Holsti, Randolph M. Siverson, and Alexander L. George. Boulder: Westview Press: 131–62.

———. 1984. *After Hegemony: Cooperation and Discord in the World Political Economy*. Princeton: Princeton University Press.

———, and Joseph S. Nye. 1977. *Power and Interdependence: World Politics in Transition*. Boston: Little, Brown and Company.

Kindleberger, Charles P. 1973. *The World in Depression, 1929–1939*. Berkeley: University of California Press.

———. 1981. "Dominance and Leadership in the International Economy: Exploitation, Public Goods, and Free Rides." *International Studies Quarterly* 25 (2): 242–54.

Kloten, Norbert. 1981. "Zur 'Endphase' des Europäischen Währungssystems." *Europa-Archiv* 36(1): 21–30.

Kohler, Beate, and Gert Schlaeger. 1971. *Wirtschafts- und Währungsunion für Europa*. 2nd ed. Bonn: Europa Union Verlag.

Kolodziej, Edward A. 1974. *French International Policy under de Gaulle and Pompidou: The Politics of Grandeur*. Ithaca: Cornell University Press.

Krämer, Hans R. 1970. *Die Bemühungen der EWG um die Errichtung einer Währungsunion*. Kieler Diskussionsbeiträge zu aktuellen wirtschaftspolitischen Fragen 6, Institut für Weltwirtschaft Kiel.

Krasner, Stephen D. 1976. "State Power and the Structure of International Trade." *World Politics* 28 (3): 317–47.

———. 1991. "Global Communications and National Power: Life on the Pareto Frontier." *World Politics* 43 (3): 336–66.

Kruse, D. C. 1980. *Monetary Integration in Western Europe: EMU, EMS and Beyond*. London: Butterworths.

Lahnstein, Manfred. 1978. "Über die Währungsunion zur Wirtschaftsunion?" In *Europa-Archiv* (9): 263–70.

Lambsdorff, Otto Graf. 1978. "Rede des Bundesministers für Wirtschaft, Dr. Otto Graf Lambsdorff, in der Sitzung des Deutschen Bundestages am 6. Dezember 1978." *Bulletin des Presse- und Informationsamtes der Bundesregierung.* 8 December.

Lankowski, Carl S., ed. 1993. *Germany and the European Community: Beyond Hegemony and Containment.* New York: St. Martin's Press.

Loedel, Peter Henning. 1994. "Regional Bargaining Strategies and Multiple Games: German Monetary Policy and the Franco-German Axis." Paper prepared for presentation at the Annual Meeting of the American Political Science Association, New York, 1–4 September.

———. 1999. *Deutsche Mark Politics: Germany in the European Monetary System.* Boulder: Lynne Rienner.

Loth, Wilfried, William Wallace, and Wolfgang Wessels. 1995. *Walter Hallstein—Der vergessene Europäer?* Bonn: Europa Union Verlag.

Loriaux, Michael. 1991. *France after Hegemony: International Change and Financial Reform.* Ithaca: Cornell University Press.

Ludlow, Peter. 1982. *The Making of the European Monetary System.* London: Butterworths.

Markovits, Andrei S., and Simon Reich. 1991a. "Should Europe Fear the Germans?" *German Politics and Society* 23 (2): 1–20.

———. 1991b. *"Modell Deutschland* and the New Europe." *Telos* 89 (Fall): 45–64.

———. 1997. *The German Predicament: Memory and Power in the New Europe.* Ithaca: Cornell University Press.

Marsh, David. 1992. *The Bundesbank: The Bank That Rules Europe.* London: Heinemann.

Martin, Lisa L. 1993. "International and Domestic Institutions in the EMU Process." *Economics and Politics* 5 (2): 125–44.

Mastropasqua, Cristina, Stefano Micossi, and Roberto Rinaldi. 1988. "Interventions, Sterilisation and Monetary Policy in

European Monetary System Countries, 1979–1987." In *The European Monetary System*. Eds. Francesco Giavazzi, Stefano Micossi, and Marcus Miller. Cambridge: Cambridge University Press: 252–91.

Matthes, Heinrich. 1983. "The European Monetary System and International Currency Questions." *Intereconomics*. March/April: 60–64.

————. 1988. "Die Entwicklung des EWS mit Blick auf 1992— Thesen zum gegenwärtigen Stand der Debatte um das EWS." In *Europa-Banking: Bankpolitik im europäischen Finanzraum und währungspolitische Integration*. Ed. Dieter Duwendag. Baden-Baden: Nomos Verlagsgesellschaft: 85–109.

McCarthy, Patrick. 1993. "France Looks at Germany, or How to Become German (and European) while Remaining French." In *France-Germany, 1983–1993: The Struggle to Cooperate*. Ed. Patrick McCarthy. New York: St. Martin's Press: 51–72.

McCormick, John. 1996. *The European Union: Politics and Policies*. Boulder: Westview.

McKeown, Timothy J. 1983. "Hegemonic Stability Theory and 19th Century Tariff Levels in Europe." *International Organization* 37 (1): 73–91.

McNamara, Kathleen R. 1993. "Common Markets, Uncommon Currencies: Systems Effects and the European Community." In *Coping with Complexity in the International System*. Ed. Jack Snyder and Robert Jervis, Boulder: Westview Press: 303–27.

————. 1998. *The Currency of Ideas: Monetary Politics in the European Union*. Ithaca: Cornell University Press.

Methfessel, Klaus. 1996. *Wenn die D-Mark geht: Wie Sie nicht zum Verlierer durch die europäische Währungsunion werden*. Düsseldorf: Econ.

Meyer-Horn, Klaus. 1963. "Langer Weg zur Währungsunion der EWG." *Sparkasse* 11 (1 June 1963). Reprinted in *BAP* 44, 10 June: 8–10.

Mitterrand, Francois. 1992. "Declarations de Monsieur Francois Mitterrand, President de la République, à "occasion de l'émission de TF 1 'Aujourd'hui l'Europe,' La Sorbonne, Paris, 3 septembre 1992." Reprinted in *BAP* 61, 9 September: 1–2.

Moravcsik, Andrew. 1991. "Negotiating the Single European Act: National Interests and Conventional Statecraft in the European Community." *International Organization* 45 (1): 19–56.

———. 1998. *The Choice for Europe: Social Purpose and State Power from Messina to Maastricht*. Ithaca: Cornell University Press.

Münchmeyer, Alwin. 1968. "EEC in Need of a Currency Union." *Intereconomics* 3(9): 264–66.

Mundell, Robert A. 1968. *International Economics*. New York: Macmillan.

Nölling, Wilhelm. 1993. *Monetary Policy in Europe after Maastricht*. New York: St. Martin's Press.

Oatley, Thomas H. 1997. *Monetary Politics: Exchange Rate Cooperation in the European Community*. Ann Arbor: University of Michigan Press.

Obstfeld, Maurice. 1993. "The Adjustment Mechanism." In *A Retrospective on the Bretton Woods System: Lessons for International Monetary Reform*. Ed. Michael D. Bordo and Barry Eichengreen. Chicago: The University of Chicago Press: 201–56.

———. 1998. *EMU: Ready or Not?* Essays in International Finance 209, Princeton: International Finance Section, Princeton University, July.

Overturf, Stephen Frank. 1997. *Money and European Union*. New York: St. Martin's Press.

Padoa-Schioppa, Tommaso. 1988. "The European Monetary System: A Long-Term View." In *The European Monetary System*. Ed. Francesco Giavazzi, Stefano Micossi, and Marcus Miller, Cambridge: Cambridge University Press: 369–84.

————. 1994. *The Road to Monetary Union in Europe: The Emperor, the Kings, and the Genies*. Oxford: Clarendon Press.

Pauly, Louis. 1997. *Who Elected the Bankers? Surveillance and Control in the World Economy*. Ithaca: Cornell University Press.

Pearce, Joan. 1983. "The Common Agricultural Policy: The Accumulation of Special Interests." In *Policy-Making in the European Community*. 2nd ed. London: John Wiley and Sons: 143–75.

Peeters, Theo. 1982. "EMU: Prospects and Retrospect." In *European Monetary Union: Progress and Prospects*. Ed. by Michael T. Sumner and George Zis. New York: St. Martin's Press: 1–17.

Pöhl, Karl Otto. 1987. "Pressekonferenz vom 14. September 14 1987." In *BAP* 66, 16 September: 1–3.

Putnam, Robert D. 1988. "Diplomacy and Domestic Politics: The Logic of Two-Level Games." *International Organization* 42 (3): 427–60.

Ross, George. 1995. *Jacques Delors and European Integration*. New York: Oxford University Press.

Russo, Massino, and Giuseppe Tullio. 1988. "Monetary Coordination within the European Monetary System: Is There a Rule?" International Monetary Fund, Washington, D.C., *Occasional Paper* 61, September.

Sachs, Jeffrey, and Charles Wyplosz. 1986. "The Economic Consequences of President Mitterrand." *Economic Policy* 2 (April): 262–321.

Sandholtz, Wayne. 1993a. "Choosing Union: Monetary Politics and Maastricht." *International Organization* 47 (1): 1–39.

————. 1993b. "Monetary Bargains: The Treaty on EMU." In *The State of the European Community, Vol. 2: The Maastricht Debates and Beyond*. Ed. Alan W. Cafruny and Glenda G. Rosenthal. Boulder: Lynne Rienner: 125–42.

————, and John Zysman. 1989. "1992: Recasting the European Bargain." *World Politics* 42 (1): 95–128.

Scharrer, Hans-Eckart. 1973. "Europäische Wirtschafts- und Währungsunion—Pragmatismus ohne politisches Konzept." In *Europäische Wirtschaftspolitik: Programm und Realität*. Bonn: Europa Union Verlag: 81–158.

Schiller, Karl. 1971. "Ausführungen von Bundeswirtschaftsminister Professor Schiller über die Sitzung des Ministerrates der Europäischen Gemeinschaften am 8. und 9. Februar in Brüssel, Bonn, 10. Februar 1971." Reprinted in *BAP* 13, 16 February: 5–7.

Schlüter, Peter-W. 1982. "Die ECU und der Europäische Währungsfonds." *Integration* 5(2): 54–73.

Schmidt, Helmut. 1978. "Erklärung der Bundesregierung über die Ergebnisse des Europäischen Rates in Brüssel." *Bulletin des Presse- und Informationsamtes der Bundesregierung*, 8 December.

———. 1987. *Menschen und Mächte*. Berlin: Siedler.

———. 1990. *Die Deutschen und ihre Nachbarn*. Berlin: Goldmann.

———. 1993. *Handeln für Deutschland: Wege aus der Krise*. Berlin: Rowohlt.

Schönfelder, Wilhelm, and Elke Thiel. 1994. *Ein Markt - Eine Währung: Die Verhandlungen zur Europäischen Wirtschafts- und Währungsunion*. Baden-Baden: Nomos.

Smeets, Heinz-Dieter. 1990. "Does Germany Dominate the EMS?" *Journal of Common Market Studies* 29 (1): 37–52.

Smith, Michael E., and Wayne Sandholtz. 1995. "Institutions and Leadership: Germany, Maastricht, and the ERM Crisis." In *The State of the European Union, Vol. 3: Building a European Polity?* Ed. Carolyn Rhodes and Sonia Mazey. Boulder: Lynne Rienner: 245–65.

Snidal, Duncan. 1985. "The Limits of Hegemonic Stability Theory." *International Organization* 39 (4): 579–614.

Spaventa, Luigi. 1980. "Italy Joins the EMS: A Political History." The Johns Hopkins University. Bologna Center. *Occasional Paper* No. 32, June.

Sperling, James. 1994. "German Foreign Policy after Unification: The End of Cheque Book Diplomacy?" *West European Politics* 17 (1): 73–97.

Spero, Joan E., and Jeffrey A. Hart. 1997. *The Politics of International Economic Relations*. 5th ed. New York: St. Martin's Press.

Statler, Jocelyn. 1979. "The European Monetary System: From Conception to Birth." *International Affairs* 55 (2): 206–25.

Strange, Susan. 1976. *International Monetary Relations*. Vol. 2 of *International Economic Relations of the Western World, 1959–1971*. Ed. Andrew Shonfield. London: Oxford University Press.

Svensson, Lars E. O. 1994. "Fixed Exchange Rates as a Means to Price Stability: What Have We Learned?" *NBER Working Paper* No. 4504.

Taylor, Paul. 1983. *The Limits of European Integration*. New York: Columbia University Press.

Teivainen, Teivo. 1997. "The Independence of the European Central Bank: Implications for Democratic Governance." In *The Politics of Economic and Monetary Union*. Ed. Petri Minkkinen and Heikki Patomäki. Boston: Kluwer Academic Publishers: 55–75.

Teltschik, Horst. 1991. *329 Tage: Innenansichten der Einigung*. Berlin: Siedler.

Tew, Brian. 1988. *The Evolution of the International Monetary System, 1945–88*. London: Hutchinson.

Thatcher, Margaret. 1993. *The Downing Street Years*. New York: HarperCollins.

Theurl, Theresia. 1992. *Eine gemeinsame Währung für Europa: 12 Lehren aus der Geschichte*. Innsbruck: Österreichischer Studien Verlag.

Thygesen, Niels. 1993. "Towards Monetary Union in Europe: Reforms of the EMS in the Perspective of Monetary Union." *Journal of Common Market Studies* 31 (4): 447–72.

Tietmeyer, Hans. 1969. "Europa-Währung eine Fata morgana?" In Deutsche Bundesbank. *BAP* 68, 17 September: 11–13.

———. 1994. "On the Architecture of EMU." In *30 Years of European Monetary Integration: From the Werner Plan to EMU.* Ed. Alfred Steinherr. London: Longman: 31–37.

Troeger, Heinrich. 1963. "Europäische Währungs- und Finanzpolitik." *Die Neue Gesellschaft* 3. Reprinted in Deutsche Bundesbank, *BAP* 39, 17 May: 1–6.

Tsoukalis, Loukas. 1977. *The Politics and Economics of European Monetary Integration.* London: George Allen & Unwin.

Ungerer, Horst, Jouko J. Hauvonen, Augusto Lopez-Claros, and Thomas Mayer. 1990. "The European Monetary System: Developments and Perspectives," International Monetary Fund, Washington, D.C., *Occasional Paper* 73, November.

van Ypersele, Jacques, and Jean-Claude Koeune. 1984. *The European Monetary System: Origins, Operation and Outlook.* Luxembourg: Office for Official Publications of the European Communities.

Vereinigte Wirtschaftsdienste. 1970. "Auf dem Wege zur EWG-Währungsunion: Einig über Ziel, uneinig über Etappen - Sonderausschuß soll Stufenpläne koordinieren." Reprinted in *BAP* 15, 27 February: 14.

———. 1972a. "Divergenzen im EWG-Währungsausschuß über Fond für wirtschaftliche Zusammenarbeit." Reprinted in *BAP* 63, 7 September: 8–9.

———. 1972b. "EG-Kommission schlägt Bandbreiteneinengung von 4.5% auf 2% und Intervention in Gemeinschaftswährungen vor." Reprinted in *BAP* 6, 18 January: 6–7.

———. 1972c. "EWG hält an Währungssolidarität fest." Reprinted in *BAP* 45, 28 June: 5–6.

———. 1973. "EWG-Interventionssystem soll elastischer und wirksamer angewendet werden." Reprinted in *BAP* 1, 2 January: 15–16.

Vereinigte Witschaftsdienste, Devisen und Finanzen. 1963. "Abs: Europäische Währungsunion wäre verfrüht." Reprinted in *BAP* 3, 9 January: 6–7.

Vereinigte Witschaftsdienste, Finanzen. 1978. "Bonner Grundsätze für das europäische Währungssystem." Reprinted in *BAP* 65, 25 August 1978.

Vereinsbank in Hamburg. 1963. "Dorniger Weg zur Währungsunion." *Wirtschaftsbericht.* Juli/August. Reprinted in *BAP* 65, 28 August 1963: 6–7.

Vocke, Wilhelm. 1966. "Voraussetzungen und Grundzüge einer Europäischen Währungs-Union." In *BAP* 78, 21 October: 1–4.

von Falkenhausen, Gotthard Freiherr. 1963. "Probleme einer Europäischen Wirtschaftspolitik." In *BAP* 2, 8 January: 3–4.

von Hagen, Jürgen, and Michele Fratianni. 1990. "German Dominance in the EMS: Evidence from Interest Rates." *Journal of International Money and Finance* 9: 358–75.

Wadbrook, William Pollard. 1972. *West German Balance-of-Payments Policy: The Prelude to European Monetary Integration.* New York: Praeger.

Walsh, James I. 1994. "International Constraints and Domestic Choices: Economic Convergence and Exchange Rate Policy in France and Italy." *Political Studies* 42 (2): 243–58.

Webb, Michael C. 1991. "International Economic Structures, Government Interests, and International Coordination of Macroeconomic Adjustment Policies." *International Organization* 45 (3): 309–42.

———. 1995. *The Political Economy of Policy Coordination: International Adjustment since 1945.* Ithaca: Cornell University Press.

Weber, Axel A. 1990. "EMU and Asymmetries and Adjustment Problems in the EMS: Some Empirical Evidence." *CEPR Discussion Paper* 448. London: Centre for European Policy Research.

Wilking, Susanne. 1992. "Abstieg in die 'zweite Liga'? Die Debatte über die italienische Europapolitik." *Integration* 15 (3): 141–53.

Willgerodt, Hans, Alexander Domsch, Rolf Hasse, and Volker Merx. 1972. *Wege und Irrwege zur europäischen Währungsunion.* Freiburg: Rombach.

Wolf, Dieter, and Bernhard Zangl. 1996. "The European Economic and Monetary Union: 'Two-level Games' and the Formation of International Institutions." *European Journal of International Relations* 2 (3): 355–93.

Woolley, John T. 1992. "Policy Credibility and European Monetary Institutions." In *Europolitics: Institutions and Policymaking in the "New" European Community.* Ed. Alberta M. Sbragia, Washington: Brookings: 157–90.

Wyplosz, Charles. 1989. "Asymmetry in the EMS: Intentional or Systemic?" *European Economic Review* 33 (2/3): 310–20.

Newspapers and Periodicals

Börsen-Zeitung

The Economist

Financial Times

Frankfurter Allgemeine Zeitung

Frankfurter Rundschau

General-Anzeiger

Handelsblatt

Ifo-Schnelldienst

The Independent

Neue Zürcher Zeitung

Schweizer Finanz-Zeitung

Der Spiegel

Stuttgarter Zeitung

Süddeutsche Zeitung

Der Tagesspiegel

Die Tageszeitung

The Times

Wall Street Journal

Die Welt

Wirtschaftswoche

Die Zeit

SUNY series in Global Politics

James N. Rosenau, Editor

List of Titles

247

After Authority: War, Peace, and Global Politics in the 21st Century—Ronnie D. Lipschutz

Pondering Postinternationalism: A Paradigm for the Twenty-First Century?—Heidi H. Hobbs (ed.)

Beyond Boundaries?: Disciplines, Paradigms, and Theoretical Integration in International Studies—Rudra Sil and Eileen M. Doherty (eds.)

Why Movements Matter: The West German Peace Movement and U.S. Arms Control Policy—Steve Breyman

International Relations—Still an American Social Science?: Toward Diversity in International Thought—Robert M.A. Crawford and Darryl S.L. Jarvis (eds.)

Which Lessons Matter?: American Foreign Policy Decision Making in the Middle East, 1979–1987—Christopher Hemmer (ed.)

Hierarchy Amidst Anarchy: Transaction Costs and Institutional Choice—Katja Weber

Counter-Hegemony and Foreign Policy: The Dialectics of Marginalized and Global Forces in Jamaica—Randolph B. Persaud

Global Limits: Immanuel Kant, International Relations, and Critique of World Politics—Mark F. N. Franke

Index

249